The

Giggly

Guide

to

Grammar

The Giggly Guide to Grammar

Written and Illustrated by
Cathy Campbell

Discover Writing Press

Shoreham, Vermont

Discover Writing Press
www.discoverwriting.com
P. O. Box 264
Shoreham, VT 05770
800-613-8055

Printed and bound in Canada

ISBN: 978-1-931492-22-5
Library of Congress Control Number: 2007941201

16   8

Ann Dumaresq, Senior Editor
Michael Burke, Editor
Cover and text design by Bookwrights

For information about Discover Writing workshops and in-services for Professional Development in teaching writing, summer writing retreats and other offerings, call 800-613-8055 ext. 3# or visit our web site at www.discoverwriting.com.

Dedication

Every beetle is a gazelle in the eyes of its mother.

—Moorish proverb

To Mother, with all of my love.

Contents

Mechanics

Preface

I learned my best lesson about teaching from a ninth grader. Not long out of college, I was hired to teach freshman English, and, armed with an education degree, I was ignorant enough to think that I knew everything about the job.

When my very first open house rolled around, I was ready. I greeted every parent at my classroom door with confidence; and in front of the packed classroom, I wowed them and zowed them with my firm grasp of the curriculum. I was perky. I bounced around the room, waved my arms for emphasis, and used stirring voice inflections as I described the works of Homer and Shakespeare and Dickens, works that were soon going to electrify the lives of their teenagers. In short, I was spectacular.

Or so I thought.

The next day, my shoulder still a little sore from patting myself on the back for a job well done, I told my first class of barely awake students how much I had enjoyed meeting their parents (and, it went without saying, how much they had enjoyed meeting me.) Then, still beaming, I asked, "So, what did your parents say about me?"

Yes, there is such a thing as a stupid question. The class sat lifeless and droopy-eyed until one girl, Samantha, finally raised her hand.

"My Dad said that you reminded him of ...." Her forehead wrinkled. She was experiencing a temporary memory lapse and seemed to be searching for the words.

Of course, I completed her thought to myself: *Margaret Thatcher? Madame Curie? Oprah?*

Samantha's eyes looked upward. She was waiting, waiting for the words to pop into her head.... "He said you reminded him of...uhmm...."

My thoughts were coming ever faster. *Mother Teresa? Meryl Streep? the woman in the anti-wrinkle cream commercial (after use)?*

Suddenly, Samantha's eyes widened. A tiny firework had just exploded in her head. She had retrieved the thought.

"I remember, I remember," she said. "My dad said you reminded him of a gerbil."

The truth dropped out of thin air like an anvil. My ego was flattened faster than a slow toad on a busy Texas road.

A gerbil. Leave it to a freshman to teach me a little humility.

It's that spirit of humility that I bring to this book. I don't consider myself an expert on grammar, but I'm smart enough to consult the works of the people who are. Sometimes, though, even the experts disagree. Take for instance the question of how to show the plurals of numbers and letters. This daunting problem pits the pro-apostrophe camp (R's, 5's 1930's) against the anti-apostrophe camp (*Rs, 5s, 1930s*), and some people prefer to have a toe in both camps (R's, 5s, 1930s)

In cases like these, I resorted to one of three solutions: (1) I cite the simplest answer (2) I cite the way I was taught in the good ol' days by the strictest grammarians, the nuns at St. Anne's Catholic School or (3) I just get frustrated, twirl my finger, and see where it lands. Solution number three is by far the most entertaining.

Speaking of humility, I realize that *illustrated by* is printed on the cover, but as my students often remind me, I'm not what you'd call an artist. However, the publisher nixed my suggestion to replace these words with "doodled by," thinking that the statement lacked a certain gravitas. Just for the record, I'm painfully aware that all of my characters look very much alike with their goofy smiles and desperate need of orthotics, but for good reason: I can only draw people with goofy smiles who are in desperate need of orthotics and orthodontics. Let's just say, my range is slightly limited.

Finally, I have to admit that I'm a hypocrite...sort of. In this book I break many of the rules I tell my students to follow: I speak in second person, begin sentences with "and," and even include sentence fragments. I cover myself, though, with a golden rule of writing that I believe trumps all others: consider the audience and the purpose. I hope my readers include everyone from students who detest the word *grammar* (go figure), to warped people like me who read grammar books for fun. (My family thinks I need to get a dog.) I consider the reader my friend, and my goal is not only to inform, but also to entertain.

I hope I've succeeded.

Cathy

Grammar

1
Nouns, Pronouns, and Adjectives

Nouns

Nouns are easy varmints to get to know. Simply put, a noun is the name of a person, place, thing, or idea.

people: *James Dean, doctor, singer, Tarzan, Bart Simpson*
places: *New Guinea, city, Transylvania, Bedrock*
things: *nostril, tuba, dentures, uvula, monkey*
ideas or qualities: *peace, love, honor, anger*

Common and Proper Nouns

Nouns are usually divided into two main classes: common and proper. A common noun is just a general person, place, or thing; but a proper noun refers to a *particular* person, place, or thing. Unlike common nouns, proper nouns are capitalized.

common	proper
frog	*Kermit*
team	*Mighty Ducks*
city	*Whoville*
artist	*Salvador Dalí*
band	*The Convulsing Turnips*
ape	*King Kong*

lizard

Godzilla

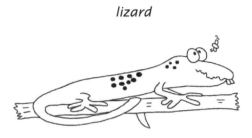

Some nouns are called compound because they're made up of two or more words. Sometimes the two words are written as one, sometimes they're written separately, and sometimes they're hyphenated.

Compound nouns: *armpit, tapeworm, jack-in-the-box, toenail, earlobe, slime ball*

A collective noun refers to a group made up of several elements.

Collective nouns: *committee, flock, jury, family, herd*

Just for fun, here's a list of other collective nouns that might come in handy sometime. Some of these sound like I made them up, but I couldn't be so creative.

a murder of crows
a bloat of hippos
a charm of hummingbirds
a rabble of butterflies
a quiver of cobras
a nuisance of house cats
a parliament of owls
a wake of buzzards

a mob of emus
a business of ferrets
a scurry of squirrels
a crash of rhinos

FYI Three little words—*a*, *an*, and *the*—are called <u>articles</u>, or <u>determiners</u>. When you see one of these words, you know that a noun is about to pop up before your very eyes.

a *thirsty* **tick**   **an aardvark**   **the** *large facial* **wart**

note: drawings not to scale

Exercise 1

For grins and giggles, make a list of twenty nouns. Without looking at the sentence, fill in the blanks in the following sentences with nouns chosen at random from the list. See what kind of bizarre tale you can create.

"I really wanted to do my homework yesterday," Swineburn explained to his English teacher, "but you'll never believe what happened to me. I was walking down the street just minding my own business. As I passed the _____, I was shocked to see a _____ dressed in a _____ arguing with a _____ wearing a _____. They began to wrestle, so in a panic I went to get help. Not watching where I was going, I tripped over a _____ in the middle of the street. I heard an object hit the pavement, so I felt in my pocket and discovered that I had lost the _____ my _____ had given me. While I desperately searched the ground on my hands and knees, thousands of tiny _____

began swarming up my legs. Then, to my horror, I saw a _____ coming my way. I
scurried to the side of the road and accidentally tripped over a _____ and broke my
_____. As I lay helpless on the sidewalk, the biggest _____ I have ever seen
started running toward me. I cried for help and was rescued by a _____ riding a
_____.

"After I said 'thank you,' I made my way home and grabbed a huge serving of _____
from the fridge to calm my nerves. I took my snack up to my room and finally began
working on my homework. I had just finished writing my last sentence when I heard a
deafening noise. The sound grew louder and louder until a huge _____ crashed
through the ceiling and landed right on top of my homework. Upon hearing the noise, my
whole family rushed upstairs, and we all stood gaping at the monstrosity hulking on top
of my paper. Since none of us could budge the obstruction, we decided to leave it there
and decorate it with _____.

"And, oh, by the way, the _____ that you're wearing today looks lovely on you,
Miss Veiny. Uh, what did you say? No credit? Yes, ma'am, I understand your position. And,
oh, by the way, you have a piece of _____ in your teeth."

The End

Forming Plurals of Nouns

The word *singular*, of course, means only one, and *plural* means more than one. It's
pretty simple to form the plural of most nouns; you just add *s* or *es*. However,
the English language is full of oddballs, and many nouns don't follow this
simple rule. Here are some rules to help you spell the plural of those
ornery nouns that don't fit the mold:

1. The plural of a noun ending in *y* preceded by a consonant is
   formed by changing the *y* to *i* and adding *es*.

baby—babies
buggy—buggies

2. The plural of a noun ending in *y* preceded by a vowel is formed by adding *s*.

   guy—guys
   ray—rays

3. The plurals of *some* nouns ending in *f* or *fe* are formed by changing the *f* to *v* and adding *s* or *es*.

   leaf—leaves
   calf—calves
   wife—wives
   knife—knives
   roof—roofs (Surprise! *Rooves* is not a word, but some folks pronounce the plural of *roof* as though it were! Go figure.)
   scarf—scarves (*Scarfs* is also correct, although *scarves* is the more common form.)

4. The plural of a noun ending in *o* preceded by a vowel is formed by adding *s*.

   radio—radios
   rodeo—rodeos

5. The plural of a noun ending in *o* preceded by a consonant is formed by adding *es*.

   hero—heroes
   torpedo—torpedoes
   tomato—tomatoes
   potato—potatoes

   This rule has a weird exception, though. In many cases, if a noun ends in *o* preceded by a consonant *and refers to music*, you form the plural by adding just *s*.

   solo—solos
   piano—pianos
   alto—altos
   soprano—sopranos
   piccolo—piccolos

6. Some nouns are the same in the singular and plural.

   deer (The preferred plural of *reindeer* is *reindeer*, but *reindeers can be a second choice*.)

fish (Fishes is also correct.)
trout
Japanese
sheep

7. Form the plural of a compound noun that is written as a hyphenated word by making plural the most important word, which is usually a noun.

brothers-*in-law*
sergeants-*at-arms*
runners-*up*

FYI If it's difficult to tell which is the most important word, add *s* to the last word.

merry-go-rounds   *drive-ins*

8. If a compound noun is written as one word, add *s* or *es* to form the plural.

footballs
spoonfuls
grandmothers
classrooms
passerby—An exception!!—*passersby*

9. Occasionally a noun is just plain strange; its plural is formed in an irregular way.

mouse—mice (not *meeses*)
ox—oxen
die—dice
foot—feet
tooth—teeth
louse—lice
octopus—octopi (*Octopuses* is also correct.)
hippopotamus—hippopotami (*Hippopotamuses* is also correct.)

10. Add *'s* to form the plural of capital letters, numbers, and symbols. It's also acceptable in these cases to just add *s* (without the apostrophe) if doing so presents no confusion.

*Zzuzzuzzanna's last name has seven **Z's** (or Zs) in it.*
*My zip code has five **9s** (or 9's) in it.*

Yolanda typed too many 's in the e-mail address, so Theodore never received her message that his ventriloquist lesson had been cancelled.

Always add *'s* to form the plural of lowercase letters, and of words and expressions used to represent themselves.

*Dana thinks her name has too many **a's**, so she changed it to Dn.*
*When some people, like, talk and stuff, they, like, use too many **like's** and **stuff's**.*

For some strange reason, most people don't use an apostrophe to form the plural of centuries and decades.

*In the **1960s**, many vegetarians snacked on corn chips and catnip.*

Exercise 2

Now see if you can form the plurals of the following nouns:

1. shelf
2. freshman
3. elf
4. Chinese
5. ox
6. hero
7. trio
8. knife
9. sister-in-law
10. baby
11. calf
12. potato
13. rodeo
14. piano
15. editor in chief
16. commander in chief
17. A
18. spoonful
19. soprano
20. deer
21. fish
22. library
23. passerby
24. 1980
25. octopus

Exercise 3

Once again, change these singular nouns to plurals.

1. lady
2. salmon
3. tomato
4. duo
5. oboe
6. louse
7. 13
8. journey
9. leaf
10. wolf
11. patio
12. self
13. American
14. Japanese
15. tooth
16. half
17. country
18. father-in-law
19. delegate-at-large
20. sheep

Exercise 4

Another challenge! Find the misspelled nouns in the following sentences, and spell each correctly.

1. Do sheeps count people to fall asleep?

2. Many of the looker-ons were surprised to see thirty moose dancing in the street.

3. Otis found two lices in his strawberries and pancakes, so he used one of his knifes to pick off the pests.

4. In green valleys in Vermont, many mouses wear scarfs and dance playfully to the music blaring from distant radioes.

5. Figaro made all *A*'s on his art projects, which included his two papier-mâché monkies.

6. The Joneses are raising three foxes, two oxes, and a toad.

7. The Americans, the Chineses, and the Japaneses won gold medals in the underwater hula-hoop competition.

8. The reindeer tiptoed on the roofs of many houses while Santa dropped donuts, duct tape, and dumplings down the chimnies.

9. Little Winfred enjoys eating fried green tomatoes while he listens to sopranos singing songs about trouts.

10. The two runner-ups in the Miss Pesky Insect Beauty Pageant received jumbo helium-filled mosquitoes for prizes.

Writing Pointer

When you write, it's a good idea to try to make the reader see pictures in his or her head, and to try to make the pictures (or even better, the video) as in-focus as you possibly can. One way to help make the picture as precise as possible is to use specific nouns instead of vague, wishy-washy, general nouns or pronouns. Which of the following sentences gives you a better mental picture?

The girl fed her pet its dinner.

or

Yoko fed her unicorn yams and yogurt.

Personally, I believe the second sentence telegraphs a clearer mental picture to the reader. The first picture is . . . well . . . blurry.

Exercise 5

See if you can make more interesting sentences by replacing the vague nouns with more specific nouns and descriptive words. Find at least two fuzzy nouns or pronouns to change that you believe will make a more interesting and vivid sentence.

Example: *Are you going to lug all of those things with you on the trip?*
New and improved example: *Are you going to lug your microwave, refrigerator, television, electric guitar, and poodle with you on your hike into the rain forest?*

1. Gasp! Are you going to wear those clothes to the event?

2. When I found a pest in my meal at the restaurant, my stomach felt like something was tumbling around inside.

3. My weird neighbor has a house full of strange stuff.

4. My crazy relative talks to inanimate objects.

5. Aunt Eglantin always cooks an atrocious meal for the holiday.

6. The man wearing an outfit climbed the building and waved to everyone below.

7. The athlete demonstrated his strength by tossing a huge object.

8. Marjorie won a prize for her act in the school talent show.

9. Kippy was not allowed to watch his favorite TV show because he didn't do his chores.

10. Zena likes to sing karaoke songs and to pretend she's a big star.

Pretty simple stuff, huh? So now it's time to move on to those crazy old pronouns.

Pronouns

A pronoun is a word that takes the place of one or more nouns. While there are a billion gazillion nouns, there are far fewer pronouns. (As a matter of fact, you'll find almost all the little critters on a few short lists that just happen to be in this chapter.) Take a look at the following sentences and see if you notice anything unusual about the way they're written (duh).

Semore is an unusual child. Yesterday, Semore shaved his head with Semore's father's electric razor. Then Semore carefully braided the hairs on Semore's legs and arms. On Semore's face, Semore applied a rub-on tattoo of a small warthog. Semore's parents hope that Semore is simply going through a phase.

It doesn't take a neurosurgeon to figure out that this paragraph contains waaaaaaaaay too many *Semore*'s. Why? No pronouns! Let's face it. Language would be pretty boring if we had to use the same words over and over. Pronouns help to alleviate some of the monotony. The sentences sound much better written with pronouns:

*Semore is an unusual child. Yesterday, **he** shaved **his** head with **his** father's electric razor. Then **he** carefully braided the hairs on **his** legs and arms. On **his** face, **he** applied a rub-on tattoo of a small warthog. Semore's parents hope that **he** is simply going through a phase.*

Whew. That's better. The second paragraph replaces names with personal pronouns. You're probably familiar with personal pronouns. Here's the list.

Personal Pronouns:

	singular	plural
First Person:	*I, me,*	*we, us*
Second Person:	*you*	*you*
Third Person:	*he, him,*	*they, them*
	she, her	
	it	

it ↥

Did you know that there are all kinds of pronouns? Here are some other common pronouns.

Possessive Pronouns:

	singular	plural
First Person:	*my, mine*	*our, ours*
Second Person:	*your, yours*	*your, yours*
Third Person:	*his, her, hers, its*	*their, theirs*

Reflexive Pronouns:

Singular: *myself, herself, himself, itself*
Plural: *ourselves, yourselves, themselves*

FYI There is no such word as *hisself* or *theirselves*. The correct forms are *himself* and *themselves*.

Wrong: *Chuck chuckled to **hisself** because Huck swallowed a hockey puck.*
Right: *Chuck chuckled to **himself** because Huck swallowed a hockey puck.*

Wrong: *Instead of receiving party favors, all of the children at little Benji's birthday celebration were allowed to help* **theirselves** *to any of the moles burrowing in the backyard.*

Right: *Instead of receiving party favors, all of the children at little Benji's birthday celebration were allowed to help* **themselves** *to any of the moles burrowing in the backyard.*

Demonstrative Pronouns:

this   that   these   those

Interrogative Pronouns

(used to ask questions: *Who sneezed?*)

what   which   who   whom   whose

Common Indefinite Pronouns:

all	*both*	*few*	*nobody*	*several*
another	*each*	*many*	*none*	*some*
any	*either*	*more*	*no one*	*somebody*
anybody	*everybody*	*most*	*nothing*	*someone*
anyone	*everyone*	*much*	*one*	*something*
anything	*everything*	*neither*	*other*	

FYI Oftentimes indefinite and interrogative pronouns don't have antecedents. An *antecedent* simply means the word (or words) to which the pronoun refers. Look at the following sentence:

Domenica raises earthworms, and she teaches them amazing tricks.

In this sentence, *Domenica* is the antecedent to the pronoun *she*, and *earthworms* is the antecedent to the pronoun *them*.

Roll over.

However, you will often run across a sentence like the following, which has a mysterious indefinite pronoun that chooses to remain anonymous or an interrogative pronoun whose identity is unknown:

Someone raises earthworms.

Someone is an indefinite pronoun, and, in this sentence, it doesn't have an antecedent to identify it.

Who let the ferret out?

Who is an interrogative pronoun, and its identity is unknown.

Exercise 6

List all of the pronouns in the following sentences, followed by their antecedents. (Some indefinite pronouns might not have antecedents.)

1. Aunt Zippy, whose hair is always frizzed and frazzled, believes that she is a human lightning rod.

2. Cousin Cuthbert doesn't smoke or drink alcohol because he wants to preserve his brain cell.

3. Because Marvin has a twisted sense of humor, he named his three-legged dog *Skip.*

4. According to a government survey, 85 percent of chronic liars, who deny lying on government surveys, lie on government surveys.

5. While doing her deep-breathing exercises, Jane sprained a lung.

6. After dining on a scrumptious meal of frog legs and chips, the beautiful princess was distraught to learn that she had just eaten her Prince Charming.

7. Who saw Aunt Britt act like a nitwit in her chicken outfit?

8. Because Sarah shuns sharks, she only surfs in the Sahara.

9. Howie was astounded because before he introduced himself to the psychic, she immediately knew his name contained a vowel.

10. Nine out of ten doctors agree that children who are afraid of large grinning mice should not visit Disneyland or family pizza parlors.

Exercise 7

The following paragraph is mighty monotonous. Substitute pronouns for overused words to add a little variety.

Sally sells socks on the seashore. For each sock, Sally charges seven cents. As a bonus gift, Sally gives each customer a free sack of sand with every sock sold. One Saturday, Sally sold seventy thousand socks, and Sally retired. Now Sally lives with Sally's sister, Sarah, in Seattle, and Sally and Sally's sister sew socks for sumo wrestlers in Samoa. Sometimes the sisters still saunter by the sea, and Sally and Sarah sing songs about seals, simians. and celery.

That's enough engrossing information about pronouns. Now it's time to embark upon those scintillating adjectives.

Adjectives

Adjectives are words that modify nouns or pronouns. *To modify* simply means to describe or add detail in some way. Some adjectives help add sparkle to the language by helping to create pictures in the reader's mind.

Take a look at this sentence:

The rat devoured the cheese.

Yawn. Pretty dull. You probably get a fuzzy mental picture. However, add a few adjectives, and suddenly the blurry mental picture sharpens:

The rat, gigantic, crazy-eyed and straggly, bared its sharp, pointed fangs and devoured the cheese.

Now that's better.

Adjectives answer four questions about nouns or pronouns:

What kind?

Hungry, *hairy* trolls lie quietly under **toll** bridges waiting for **tasty roly-poly** elves and gnomes.

How many?

Samantha practiced the Heimlich maneuver on her little brother and dislodged **three** *army men,* **two** *bottle caps, and* **one** *secret decoder ring.* (Heimlich, little, army, bottle, and secret are also adjectives, but they answer the question *what kind?*)

Which one?

Waiter, there's a sea monkey in **this** *soup.*

Margie, **those** *new lip implants certainly accent your eyes.* (New and lip are also adjectives. They answer the question *what kind?*)

How much?

Though **much** *time has passed, Delbert has lost* **little** *weight on his parsley and donut diet.* (Parsley and donut are also adjectives. They answer the question *what kind?*)

Beware Sometimes English is just plain confusing because some words lead double lives. A word, for example, might be a noun in one case and an adjective in another.

Not-so-smart little Ripley traded his bicycle for a **pickle***.*

Pickle is a noun.

To impress his friends, he put a pig's kidney in his empty **pickle** *jar.*

Pickle is an adjective that tells what kind of jar.

Adjective or Pronoun?

Sometimes a word might be an adjective in one case and a pronoun in another:

Wait, Alastair! Don't feed **that***!* (pronoun)
Wait, Alastair! Don't feed **that** *bear!* (adjective)

In the first sentence, *that* is a pronoun—a demonstrative pronoun to be exact—because it takes

the place of a noun (*bear*, to be exact). In the second sentence, however, *that* is an adjective that tells *which* bear.

The moral of this story is that you need to look at how a word is used in a sentence to determine whether it's a noun, pronoun, adjective, etc. A word might be one part of speech in one situation, and, presto change-o, it might act as something else in another situation. Life can be so complicated.

FYI You already know that some nouns are called proper because they refer to specific persons, places, or things. Some adjectives are formed from proper nouns, and guess what they're called? Proper adjectives, did you say? Ding ding ding! You're right. Proper adjectives, like proper nouns, are capitalized:

> *Except for the **African** killer bees and **South American** ants, Thadeus enjoyed his camping trip.*

So . . . since you capitalize the proper noun *Germany*, you also capitalize the adjective *German*. You capitalize *Shakespeare*, so you also capitalize *Shakespearean*. You capitalize *Texas*, so you also capitalize *Texan*. Need I go further? (snooozzzzzzzzee) I think you get the picture.

So, you see, carefully selected adjectives can add pizzzzzzzzazzzzzzz to your language!

FYI Technically speaking the words *a*, *an*, and *the*, also known as *articles* or *determiners*, are adjectives because each answers the question *which one?* about a noun or pronoun. However, just to keep things simple, instead of calling them adjectives, we'll set them off in a class by themselves and call them . . . hmm . . . let's see . . . *articles* or *determiners*! (How's that for creativity?)

Exercise 8

In the following sentences, write every adjective you see and, next to it, write the word it describes.

1. For the talent competition, the Miss America contestant balanced four ferrets on her head, hopped on one leg, and sang "We Are the World."

2. The irate shop teacher refused to dismiss the restless class until the students helped him find his missing finger.

3. To increase business at her new electrolysis boutique, Mabel advertised a reduced price on the removal of extra-thick back and nose hair.

4. For Thanksgiving dessert, Aunt Erma served her tasty bologna pudding topped with M & M's and chocolate sprinkles.

5. During the day, Barney flips burgers, and every night he earns extra cash as a speed bump.

6. In a tragic, freak baking accident, Cousin Ditsy shut the oven door and crushed the Pillsbury Dough Boy.

7. To project a friendlier image, the police department now sprays criminals with floral-scented Mace and detains them with Velcro handcuffs.

8. Dr. Steinfranken, a dentist who clearly has many issues, calls his young patients *little, evil, spittle people.*

9. Wacky Uncle Wilbur believes that empty pods discarded by alien podpeople make attractive, sturdy storage bins for the tool shed and garage.

10. Young werewolves irritate and embarrass their parents when they braid their coarse hair into dreadlocks.

Writing Pointer

Remember that when you write, you always want to try *showing* your reader what's happening, instead of just *telling* them. Therefore, try to avoid blah adjectives, which I like to call *blahjectives*, at all cost! A blahjective is just . . . well . . . blah. It's vague and gives the reader a fuzzy mental picture.

Here's a list of a few blahjectives:

awesome	awful	gorgeous	super
bad	enormous	happy	terrible
cute	excellent	sad	ugly
good	outstanding	large	fabulous
great	big	small	
gross	little	amazing	
horrible	lovely	mad	
mean	beautiful	scary	
nice	nasty	exciting	
pretty	terrific	wonderful	

Take a look at this description:

My Fourth Grade Teacher

I remember my fourth grade teacher. She was extremely ugly, and she wore gross clothes that no one would be caught dead in. The sound of her awful voice caused the class to cringe. Just watching her was difficult because she had some very peculiar habits that drove the class crazy. Her cruel teaching methods stand out most in my mind, though. This woman has left mental and emotional scars on me that will last a lifetime.

Do you have a clear picture? Probably not. The paragraph is teeming with *blahjectives* like *ugly, gross, awful, peculiar.* So, how do you make the writing more exciting? One way is to replace, or follow, blahjectives with description that creates a mental picture.

My Fourth Grade Teacher

Chills run down my spine when I think of Miss Prickleberry, my fourth grade teacher. She could have played a mutant on an old episode of Star Trek. *Her curly gray hair stuck out like a chopped-up Brillo pad, and her white scalp showed through in splotchy bald spots like slices of scalloped onions. Her bifocals would slide down her nose, and she peered over them with bulging frog eyes, while each eyebrow danced up and down to a different beat. Beneath her snout, the prickly hairs of a mustache grew like weeds. She must have lived on a diet of water and sprouts because through her reptilian skin, the bones in her knees and elbows jutted out like sharp instruments ready to inflict pain.*

The woman was a walking fashion faux pas. She wore dresses covered with colorful floral prints so that she looked like a mobile sofa. She never wore stockings, so her pale legs, covered with purple webs of varicose veins, looked like road maps of state highways. When she walked around the room, the squeak of her orthopedic shoes and the squawk of her voice caused the students to cringe in their desks as though they were waiting for an enormous predatory bird to attack.

Miss P's actions were as loony as her looks. While we were working, she would clip her toenails, and sometimes she dusted the jumbo flakes of dandruff from her shoulders onto our papers as she walked by. When she spied incorrect answers, she would pounce on her victims, calling them names like "mush mind" and "beetle brain." Merciless Miss Prickleberry has scarred me mentally and emotionally for a lifetime. To this very day, I cannot look at a bowl of mushy mashed potatoes or squash a bug without sobbing uncontrollably.

The End

What a difference description makes!

Writing Pointer

One way to really appeal to your reader's imagination is to use creative comparisons that either follow or replace blahjectives.

An unusual comparison that uses *like* or *as* is called a *simile*. Similes are extremely helpful when you want to flash mental pictures at your readers.

In the second Miss Prickleberry paragraph, you probably noticed these similes:

Her curly gray hair stuck out like a chopped up Brillo pad, and her white scalp showed through in splotchy bald spots like slices of scalloped onions.

. . . the bones in her knees and elbows jutted out like sharp instruments ready to inflict pain.

. . . her pale legs, covered with purple webs of varicose veins, looked like road maps of state highways.

Another nifty descriptive tool is the *metaphor*. A metaphor is also a comparison, but instead of stating right out that something is like something else, the comparison is implied. Metaphors, like similes, compare two things that are normally *not* considered alike:

. . . she peered over them [bifocals] with bulging frog eyes, . . . (Instead of saying directly that the woman is like a frog, the sentence implies it.)

The key is to appeal to your reader's imagination. Be an artist. Paint a word picture.

Exercise 9

Now, see if you can revise the following paragraph. Replace general nouns with specific ones, and replace blahjectives with vivid descriptions. Also, be sure to include some creative similes and metaphors.

The Haunted House

At the end of the street sits the really old, ugly house. It used to belong to a very eccentric person a long time ago. No one has lived in it for many years, though, because of the frightening stories the townspeople tell about the place.

After nightfall, we approached the house together and slowly opened the unlocked front door. With a flashlight we saw that the room we had entered was completely dilapidated. Then, seemingly out of nowhere, a huge creature swooped from the rafters. We were all terrified and hid behind some stuff, not knowing if we would make it out alive.

Now here's a little poem before we move on to verbs, adverbs, and prepositions:

Writing can be lots of fun
For you and me and everyone.
Avoid blahjectives such as *good* and *fine*
And you can make your writing shine.
Add some imaginative similes
And your happy readers will buzz like bees.

Uh . . . poetry isn't exactly my forte.

2
Verbs and Adverbs

Verbs

Verbs are awfully important. As a matter of fact, a verb is an absolutely essential part of a sentence. Without a verb (and a subject) you have no sentence. Well-chosen verbs can add power to your sentences, and punch to your paragraphs. They can make your ideas dance, razzle, and dazzle. Basically, verbs fall into two categories: action and linking.

Action Verbs

Action verbs, you guessed it, show action: *waddle, burp, chortle, slither, snort* . . .

Sometimes you can't actually see the action of action verbs. For example, *think, know, love, desire,* and *understand* are all action verbs, even though the action isn't usually visible. Maybe I should say these are non-action, action verbs.

Transitive and Intransitive Verbs

Action verbs can be divided into two types: transitive and intransitive. A verb is transitive if something in the sentence, either a noun or a pronoun, receives the verb's action. That something is called *the object.* An easy way to figure out if a verb is transitive is to ask *whom?* or *what?* directly after the verb. If you can answer one of these questions, then the verb has an object, and therefore . . . tadaaaahhh . . . it's transitive.

Mindy juggles small mammals for her friends.

In this sentence, *juggles* is a *transitive* verb because it's followed by an object, *mammals*, that receives the action of the verb. *Mammals* answers the question *what?* after the verb. (Mindy juggles *what? mammals*)

A verb is intransitive if it doesn't have an object. The verb expresses action, but nothing in the sentence receives the action.

Mindy juggles for her friends.

In this sentence, *juggles* is *intransitive* because you can't answer the question *whom?* or *what?* directly after it. Therefore, it has no object that receives its action. Instead, the verb is followed by a prepositional phrase (*for her friends*).

Can you tell which of the following sentences contains a transitive verb and which contains an intransitive verb?

Zuni sings like a dying baboon.
Zuni sings zippy show tunes.

You (probably) guessed it. In the first sentence, *sings* is intransitive. No noun or pronoun directly after the verb answers *whom?* or *what?* In other words, the verb has no object that receives its action. Instead, *like a dying baboon* is a prepositional phrase that tells *how* Zuni sings. In the second sentence, however, *sings* is transitive. It's followed by an object, *tunes*, that answers the question *what?* after the verb. Zuni sings *what? Tunes. Tunes* receives the action of the verb.

Exercise 1

Ready for a challenge? Find the verbs in the following sentences, and label each verb either transitive or intransitive. (Hint: Some sentences have more than one verb.)

1. Balfour walked to first base and tripped on his shoelace.
2. Stillman hates exercise and loves mayonnaise pies.
3. Stockwell unpacks boxes of flip flops on the midnight shift at the toe-wear shop.
4. Tod buried his toad when it croaked yesterday.
5. Terry's terrier always tarries behind her.
6. Penn writes smudgy love notes with his soft lead pencils.
7. Harry made an appointment for electrolysis.
8. Rayburn forgot his sunscreen, so he covered himself in whipped cream.
9. Pickford bought a new car one part at a time.
10. Boo hates bad puns.

Linking Verbs

Linking verbs are, well . . . let's just say . . . a little boring because they show no action. The most commonly used linking verbs are forms of *to be*:

be	*shall be*	*should be*
being	*will be*	*would be*
am	*has been*	*can be*
is/are	*have been*	*could be*
was	*shall have been*	*would have been*
were	*will have been*	*could have been*

A linking verb connects (or links) the subject of a sentence to a word that follows it and refers back to the subject. This other word will either be a noun or pronoun that renames the subject, or an adjective that describes the subject. A few examples might help:

People *with stubby toes are actually space* **aliens**.

In this case the linking verb, *are*, connects the subject, *people*, to the noun that renames it, *aliens*. The linking verb here acts like a kind of equals sign (*people* = *aliens*). Here's another example:

Fluffy's **hair ball** *is* **hefty**.

In this sentence, the linking verb, *is*, connects the subject, *hair ball*, to the adjective, *hefty*. *Hefty* describes *hairball* (*hefty hair ball*). Remember, a linking verb is followed by a word that refers back to the subject. This word will be either a noun or pronoun renaming the subject, or an adjective describing the subject. Look at the difference in this sentence:

Fluffy gagged on a hair ball.

Notice that the verb, *gagged*, is not followed by a word that describes or renames the subject, *Fluffy*. Instead, the verb is followed by a prepositional phrase, *on a hairball*. As you have probably guessed, *gagged* is an action verb, not a linking. It's intransitive because it has no object that receives the action of the verb.

FYI Not all *to be* verbs are linking verbs. A waiter at a fancy-schmancy restaurant might tell you this:

Your fried cow's lips are here.

In this sentence, the verb, *are*, is a form of *to be*. However, *are* is not followed by a word that renames or describes the subject, *lips*. Instead, *are* is followed by an adverb, *here*. Therefore, in this case, *are* shows state of being, but it isn't technically a linking verb. I know, it's a picky point. Suppose, however, your waiter says this:

*Your fried cow's **lips** are **crispy**.*

Now *are* acts as a linking verb because it connects the subject, *lips*, with an adjective, *crispy*, that describes the subject (*crispy lips*).

Beware Some verbs might look like they convey action, but in some instances, they actually function as linking verbs. Here's a list of tricky verbs that are *action* in some cases, and *linking* in others:

appear	*grow*	*seem*	*stay*
become	*look*	*smell*	*taste*
feel	*remain*	*sound*	*turn*

*Opal **grows** jumbo okra.*

In this case, *grows* is an action verb. It's transitive because you can answer the question *what?* immediately after the verb. *Okra* is the object that receives the action of the verb. (Opal grows *what? Okra.*)

*Rumford's **gerbil** grows **plump**.*

Here the verb, *grows*, links the subject, *gerbil*, to a main word, *plump*, after the verb. Because *plump* is an adjective that refers back to and describes the subject (*plump gerbil*), *grows* is, by gosh, a linking verb.

*Arnie's **armpits** look **hairy**.*

Look, in this example, is a linking verb because it connects the subject, *armpits*, with the adjective, *hairy*, that describes the armpits *(hairy armpits).*

*Arnie **looks** at his (hairy) armpits.*

Looks, in this case, is an action verb. It tells what Arnie, the subject, does. *Looks* is intransitive because it's not followed by a noun or pronoun that receives the action of the verb. In other words, you can't answer the question *whom?* or *what?* after the verb. Instead it's followed by a prepositional phrase (*at his hairy armpits*).

Exercise 2

Each of the following sentences contains a linking verb. Write the linking verb, along with the two words that it links together (the subject and the word after the verb that either describes or renames the subject).

Example: Bugsy is a pest control engineer.   Answer: is, Bugsy-engineer

1. Harry is very bald.

2. Ripley's pants are torn.

3. Flip-flops look sloppy on teenyboppers.

4. Tonee's toenails look pointy.

5. Henrietta's pet chicken smells foul.

6. Old gum on a hot day is gooey on your shoe.

7. With a little salt, crispy crickets taste delicious.

8. *Snoologaloopy* sounds strange for a first name.

9. That hairless cat is really a chunky rat.

10. The tiny eels between my toes feel really slimy.

Exercise 3

In the following sentences, find the verbs, and label each as either *A* (for *action*) or *L* (for *linking*). (Hint: Some sentences have more than one verb.)

1. Brent tripped on a piece of lint.

2. Bland's dog's name is *Dog*.

3. Cecil traded his sedan for some lovely second-hand rubber bands.

4. Kit, please change the cat litter.

5. In humid climates, the early bird catches feather fungus.

6. Darby always garbles his words when his mouth is full of marbles.

7. Stubs stubbed his toe on a grub worm.

8. At midnight, Thortonberry looks hairy because he is really a werewolf.

9. Ogden is the precocious child who always draws pictures of complex blobs.

10. Some walruses are wimps in warm weather.

11. Hot, stringy melted cheese from a fresh pizza causes painful lip burns.

12. Bunny ears look ridiculous on most people.

13. Felicia flicked a fly off of her face and knocked herself unconscious.

14. Kippy performed a backflip and landed in the bean dip.

15. Aunt Gabby blabs so much that in the summer her tongue is always sunburned.

Verb Phrases

A *phrase* is merely a group of related words without a subject and verb. A verb phrase consists of one or more helping verbs followed by a main verb. The verb phrase acts as one verb. (Yes, I'm happy to say that the helping verb and main verb bond.) *To be* verbs are often used as helping verbs.

Here's a list of common helping verbs:

has	*can*	*might*
have	*may*	*must*
had	*should*	*do*
shall	*would*	*did*
will	*could*	*does*

Let's look at some sentences that contain verb phrases:

*Bozo **is making** balloon marsupials for the children.*
   Is functions as a helping verb (not a linking verb), and *making* is the main verb. The whole verb phrase, *is making*, is an action verb.

*Mallory **was yodeling** in the shower.*

Was functions as a helping verb (not a linking verb), and *yodeling* is the main verb. The whole phrase, *was yodeling*, is an action verb.

*Mickey **will perform** the part of a tap dancing tick in his school play.*

Will is a helping verb, *perform* is the main verb, and the entire verb phrase, *will perform*, is an action verb.

*Mimi's macaroni **is growing** mossy.*

This one is a little tricky. *Is growing* is the verb phrase, and although it sounds like an action verb, here it's actually linking. It connects the subject, *macaroni*, with an adjective that describes it, *mossy*.

FYI Sometimes an adverb might interrupt a verb phrase. Don't let this situation throw you:

*For a dazzling aquatic display, Jerome **is** cleverly **plopping** Alka Seltzer into his fish tank.*

The adverb, *cleverly*, interrupts the verb phrase, *is plopping*.

*Grandpa Clodhopper **has** always **been** a nonstop knuckle popper.*

The adverb, *always*, interrupts the verb phrase, *has been*.

Beware In questions, parts of the verb phrase are sometimes separated:
***Does** your parrot **speak** Swahili?*

Rewording the question into a statement makes finding the complete verb phrase easier.

*Your parrot **does speak** Swahili.*

The entire verb phrase is *does speak*. *Does* is the helping verb and *speak* is the main verb.

***Can** Fulbright really **converse** with spider mites?*

Once again, if you reword this question into a statement, you can more easily recognize the entire verb phrase.

*Fulbright really **can converse** with spider mites.*

The entire verb phrase is *can converse*. *Can* is the helping verb and *converse* is the main verb. Simple!

Exercise 4

Now it's really showtime! Pick out all of the verbs and verb phrases in the following sentences. If a verb or verb phrase is action, write *A* after it. If it's linking, write *L* after it.

1. Zits give lots of people fits.

2. People who live in glass houses should buy squeegees.

3. Cousin Ludwig decorated his yard with large statues of figs.

4. Podgy hogs never should jog in hot weather.

5. You should not cry over spilled milk, especially if you are lactose intolerant.

6. Tomella's long toes become tangled when she does the fandango.

7. Buffy rushed to the emergency room when she suffered a paper cut.

8. Some teachers seem harmless, but they are actually interplanetary pod people.

9. Except on the top, front, back, and sides of his head, Lester's hair transplant was a success.

10. Lazy Lynette never lifts a finger, so her piano performances are very monotonous.

11. Dudley lost his fudge in a muddy puddle.

12. Connie passed her course in advanced rabbit and duck shadow puppetry.

13. For his art project, Wilbur is drawing a picture of a giant, inflamed pancreas.

14. At parties, Samantha dresses her pet gerbils in tiny tights and dangles them from strings down the backs of her friends.

15. Unexpectedly, Martha's eyebrows grew long and bushy overnight, and they covered her face by morning.

16. Sid's friends think he is crazy because he is raising squids in his swimming pool.

17. Muffy is a sensitive environmentalist who collects money and provides thousands of largemouth bass with lip balm.

18. For National Tooth Decay Day, Skippy's third-grade class dressed like giant toothbrushes and jumbo rolls of dental floss.

19. In his neighbor's satellite dish, Norman mixes super-sized servings of stir-fried vegetables.

20. Knowledgeable outdoorsmen always perform thorough tick checks after they spend several hours in the woods.

21. For a new fashion trend, Madge shaved her eyebrows and replaced them with tiny tattoos of turquoise parrots.

22. Gerhard can't hear because he sticks pickles in his ears.

23. Because she is compassionate, Darma supplies all of her roach motels with fire alarms.

24. After Marvin left a tuna sandwich beneath his bed for two months, his room smelled slightly fishy.

25. Zippy, a very dexterous chimpanzee, roller skates in figure eights, juggles bowling balls with his toes, and twirls toothpicks on his nose.

Writing Pointer

Sometimes you can strengthen your writing by replacing wimpy linking verbs with strong, specific action verbs. Trying to eliminate linking verbs often forces you to be more creative. Take a look:

My little brother is a slob. His face is always dirty and his hair is greasy.

Yawn. Boring. However, by replacing the linking verbs with strong action verbs and interesting description, you can add some pow, punch, and flare to your writing.

Flea-covered dogs follow my little brother, the slob, wherever he shuffles. Gutter mud and strawberry jam clog his every facial pore. Upon his head, his hair clumps in tangled, oily strings that writhe and wriggle on breezy days like shiny worms twisting on a hot sidewalk.

Voila! No linking verbs! A few strong verbs and adjectives and a spiffy comparison (otherwise known as a *simile*) can go a long way in creating mental images for your reader.

Exercise 5

Let your imagination run wild and rewrite the following very boring sentences. Replace the humdrum adjectives (like *gross* and *sickening* and *awful*) and lackluster linking verbs (like *is* and *are*)—zzzzzzzzzzzzz. Instead, create vivid mental pictures with some specific nouns, vivacious action verbs, dazzling descriptive words, and compelling comparisons.

My sister's (or brother's or mother's or father's or uncle's or ferret's) cooking is gross. Last night she (or he or it) made a really horrible dinner. The roast beef was charred and the salad was sickening. The baked potatoes were so overcooked that I could barely eat one. The dessert was awful, too. She (or he or it) really needs some cooking lessons.

That's enough about verbs. It's time to mosey on to adverbs.

Adverbs

You already know that adjectives modify nouns and pronouns. Well, an adverb is a single word that modifies a *verb*, an *adjective*, or another *adverb*.

Adverbs modify *verbs* by answering these questions:

Where: *Don't put your retainer **there**.*
         *I have a little bump **here** on my lip.*
When: ***Tomorrow** Marvin will complete his brain surgery correspondence course.*
         *Aliens visit Earth **daily** to procure foot powder and clam chowder.*
         *In his garage, Ashlinn is **still** building the world's largest fiberglass bass.*
How: *Norman is certain that little men are **secretly** hiding in his microwave.*
         *Samantha **proudly** displays her collection of ceramic slugs to friends and relatives.*
To What Extent: *Studies **convincingly** demonstrate that electric rollers **greatly** stimulate brain cells and **dramatically** increase IQ's.*

FYI Sometimes adverbs begin questions:

Where did Samantha Sue buy her attractive salamander skin boots?

The adverb *where* modifies the verb *did buy*.

When did Sylvester decide to become a bungee cord tester?

The adverb *when* modifies the verb *did decide*.

Adverbs also modify *adjectives*:

*Doing **extremely** high kicks in her geriatric aerobics class, Mrs. Whipple lost her **very** expensive diamond ring and a glass eye.*

The adverb *extremely* modifies the adjective *high* by telling *how high*. The adverb *very* modifies the adjective *expensive* by telling *how expensive*.

*Cubby's parents agree that at age three he is **too** young to operate a forklift.*

Too is a very common adverb. It modifies the adjective *young*, which, in turn, describes the pronoun *he*.

*Thorton received an F on his **very** creative art project because the teacher didn't understand that he had drawn a blank.*

The adverb *very* modifies *creative*, an adjective that describes *project*.

FYI Like *too* and *very*, the following adverbs frequently modify adjectives:

extremely	*entirely*	*unusually*
dangerously	*especially*	*rather*
definitely	*quite*	*completely*
surprisingly	*terribly*	*dreadfully*

Just to make things a little more confusing, besides modifying *verbs* and *adjectives*, adverbs also modify *other adverbs*:

*Kippy the chiropractor works **extremely hard** at his backbreaking job.*

Extremely is an adverb that modifies another adverb, *hard*; and *hard* modifies (by answering *to what extent?*) the verb, *works*.

Only yesterday, Horatio **very proudly** graduated as valedictorian of his muffler and brake repair class.

Only is an adverb that modifies the adverb *yesterday*, and *very* is an adverb modifying the adverb *proudly*.

Instead of paying for a personalized license plate, recently Mrs. CBJ456 **quite cleverly** *changed her name.*

Quite is an adverb that modifies the adverb *cleverly*. *Cleverly* answers *how?* about the verb, *changed*. *Recently* is also an adverb. It answers *when?* about the verb.

Exercise 6

Write every adverb, along with the word it modifies, in each of the following sentences.

Example: Aunt Gerdy drove carefully down the median of the very busy road to avoid all of the crazy drivers.

Answer: carefully—drove (The adverb *carefully* answers *how?* about the verb *drove*.) very—busy (The adverb *very* answers *to what extent?* about the adjective *busy*.)

1. Most people think Mona is slightly loony because she frequently catches tuna that swim lazily in a rather deep lagoon.

2. At Camp Happy Tick, the counselors showed the very attentive children an unbelievably simple method of making extremely tasty squirrel jerky.

3. When she jumps high hurdles, Aunt Myrtle never wears a girdle.

4. After Skippy deeply searched his soul, he eventually decided to quit his job as a door-to-door toothbrush salesman and to become a mime.

5. Dunmore has invented an incredibly useful hat that effectively detects meteors and other potentially dangerous objects falling from the sky.

6. Sometimes Heloise hopes that she someday will become famous for her folk songs about dandruff, rashes, and skin diseases.

7. Today Lolita sold twelve, do-it-yourself liposuction attachments for home vacuum cleaners to slightly pudgy aerobics instructors with too much cellulite.

8. Recently Boris angrily called the Home Shopping Network and loudly demanded a refund for his defective chigger farm.

9. Moose was extremely alarmed to discover that his tattoo artist had misspelled *Mom*.

10. Melvin spends too much money on mousse and gel for his lengthy chest hair.

Writing Pointer

Sometimes you can make your writing more concise and more entertaining by eliminating some adverbs in favor of strong, specific verbs. For instance, instead of writing that he *walked slowly*, you could say he *sauntered*. Instead of writing that she talked *softly* and *unintelligibly*, you could say that she *mumbled*.

A story like this is a real yawner:

*Late at night, Newton **bravely** walked through the forest. His heart pounded **quickly** because he did not know what he would see. He had heard tales that a vicious monster lived **secretly** in the treetops, and he wanted to see for himself.*

Writing doesn't have to be boring. You can perk up a yawner paragraph by making a few simple adjustments. Just add some strong verbs in place of lame adverbs and wimpy linking verbs, and provide some interesting description. Those nifty similes and metaphors always add a little sparkle—or gloom and doom. The next paragraph is a little more interesting than the last.

The moon, a golden quarter in the sky, cast a feeble light below. Six-year-old Newton crept through the woods. In his hand he gripped his flashlight, and, with wide eyes, he followed its beam through the leaves of the still trees. He tried to will himself into bravery, but his knees, trembling as though he were walking through an arctic cold instead of the sweltering Georgian summer heat, gave him away. His heart felt like a gong bonging in his chest, and the blood in his temples was throbbing to the beat. He had heard that a six-headed baboon with fangs like butcher knives lived hidden in the treetops. He had heard that it waited to pounce on its next victim like a giant, bloodthirsty tick. He had heard that it craved the flesh of young prey, and it left only bones behind. He had heard all of these stories, and part of him knew such tales were foolish—but were they?

Exercise 7

See if you can add some pizzazz to the following story. These simple steps will help you:

1. Avoid wimpy linking verbs (like *was* and *were*), and use strong action verbs instead.

2. Replace vague, boring adjectives (like *big* and *messy*) with vivid description.

3. Replace fuzzy adverbs (like *gladly, wildly, gleefully*) with strong action verbs and/or description.

4. Add some interesting comparisons, ones that tickle your reader's imagination.

In other words, be an artist and paint word pictures for your reader. Remember, details are your friends. Let me clarify. *Interesting* details are your friends.

Paint away!

Eudora gladly accepted the job to babysit for the neighbors. She knocked confidently on the door of the Morgans' big house, where she was met by three messy brats. After the parents quickly and happily said good-bye, Eudora tried to amuse the tots with all sorts of goofy games, but the children weren't interested. For the next three hours, they acted horribly. When the Morgans finally arrived home, the house was a disaster, and the tots played gleefully as Eudora tried frantically to free herself from the trap that the brats had constructed.

Now onward to the final three parts of speech: prepositions, conjunctions, and interjections.

3

Prepositions, Conjunctions, and Interjections

Prepositions

How about this for a definition: a preposition is a word that shows the relationship between a noun or pronoun and another word in a sentence. I know—the meaning is about as clear as a Milk Dud in mud. To simplify things, try thinking of a squirrel and a log (or a roach and a pudding, or the unicorn and the garden, or a wrestler and a vat of Jell-O).

The squirrel can be *in* the log, *on* the log, *by* the log, *over* the log, *under* the log, *near* the log, *behind* the log, *in front of* the log, *around* the log, *above* the log, *below* the log. . . . All of the words beginning these phrases are, yep, you guessed it, prepositions. Why? All of these words show the relationship of a noun (*squirrel*) or pronoun to another word in the sentence (*log*).

However, the squirrel-log example doesn't generate *all* of the prepositions. Here's a more comprehensive list:

Common Prepositions

aboard	before	down	off	till
about	behind	during	on	to
above	below	except	onto	toward
across	beneath	for	opposite	under
after	beside	from	out	underneath
against	besides	in	outside	until
along	between	inside	over	up
among	beyond	into	past	upon
around	but (except)	like	since	with
as	by	near	through	within
at	despite	of	throughout	without

Some prepositions are made up of two or more words. These are called compound prepositions:

Common Compound Prepositions

according to	by means of	instead of	prior to
ahead of	in addition to	in view of	
apart from	in back of	next to	
as of	in front of	on account of	
aside from	in place of	on top of	
because of	in spite of	out of	

Prepositions are temperamental little critters that insist on beginning phrases. (A phrase is simply a group of words that does not contain a subject and a verb.) As a matter of fact, a preposition must always, always, always start a phrase; you'll never find a preposition just standing by itself. (Not only are they temperamental, but they're also insecure.) These phrases are called *prepositional phrases* (makes sense).

A prepositional phrase always, always, always begins with a preposition and ends with a noun or pronoun. The noun or pronoun ending the phrase is called the object of the preposition.

prep   o.p.
under the pachyderm

In this phrase, *under* is the preposition, and *pachyderm* is the object of the preposition. You might have gobs of modifiers in between:

under the leathery, large, yet amiable pachyderm

Even with loads of added adjectives, *under* is still the preposition beginning the phrase, and *pachyderm* is still the object of the preposition.

FYI You can have a compound (more than one) object ending a prepositional phrase:

*Because Mookie is planning a trip to **Maryland**, **Michigan**, and **Mars**, he needs ninety-two new pairs of **underwear**.*

Maryland, Michigan, and *Mars* are the objects of the preposition *to*; *underwear* is the object of the preposition *of*.

A sentence can contain any number of prepositional phrases, and these phrases can pop up anywhere in the sentence. (They can function as adverbs or adjectives, but more about that later.) Can you find the prep phrases in this sentence?

During a session of hypnosis with his psychiatrist, Mortimer discovered that in his previous life he was actually a zucchini.

Right-o: *during a session, of hypnosis, with his psychiatrist, in his previous life*

Beware *To* is not always a preposition. *To* together with a verb (*to giggle, to wiggle, to chitter, to chatter, to wobble, to gobble . . .*) is known as an infinitive, not a prepositional phrase.

*It's hard **to play** the fiddle while you twiddle your thumbs.*

To play is an infinitive, not a prepositional phrase.

Exercise 1

Each of the following sentences is just chock-full of prepositional phrases. See if you can find them all. Be sure to write the complete phrase, not just the preposition. Remember, a prepositional phrase must begin with a preposition and end with a noun or pronoun. Each sentence contains several phrases.

1. Witches and warlocks with tooth decay make appointments at midnight with skilled dentists who practice near graveyards on the full moon of each month.

2. In dark and dirty kitchens, some spoiled roaches pick at their food and refuse to eat stale lunchmeat or old shredded wheat.

3. Hundreds of three-headed eels slithered from the bottom of a polluted lagoon and sank their teeth into the tires of a stalled bus carrying European tourists traveling to the International Florists' Convention.

4. Because of the large tattoo of a rodent beneath her left eye, Moonbeam cannot get a job as a receptionist in a law office, in spite of the fact that she can type 14,002 words a minute.

5. Three hundred Slinkys went berserk inside of a giant toy store and almost strangled twelve shoppers looking for Etch-A-Sketches.

6. People who cover their bodies with maple syrup and roll in the dirt need several bars of bath soap, in addition to psychiatric treatment.

7. According to the evening news, many children who live around tropical regions suffer from hearing loss because, for some unknown reason, large balls of wax accumulate inside of their ear canals.

8. Furry Daddy Longlegs that live beneath baseboards escape at night and play kickball with small potatoes.

9. On Tuesdays and Thursdays, talented Agnetta attends her beginners' baton twirling lessons, and then she rushes to her advanced underwater opera singing class.

10. To the amazement of passersby, some spunky groundhogs parachute into crowds of people during rush hour and land on their feet.

Beware Sometimes a word can be a preposition in one sentence and an adverb in another. (A quick review: An adverb is a word that tells *when, where, why,* or to *what extent* about a verb, adjective or other adverb.) Remember, a preposition always, always, always (need I go on?) begins a phrase that ends in a noun or pronoun (the object of the preposition). An adverb, on the other hand, just sort of dangles by itself in a sentence. Take a look at these sentences:

*The bee buzzed **inside**.*

In this sentence, *inside* does not begin a phrase. It stands alone and tells where the bee buzzed. Since it modifies the verb, it's, by geebees, an adverb.

*The bee buzzed **inside** Vladimir's ear.*

In this case, *inside* is a preposition, and *inside Vladimir's ear* is the prepositional phrase. *Ear* is the object of the preposition.

Can you tell which of the following sentences contains a prepositional phrase and which contains an adverb?

Ronald fell off.
Ronald just fell off the turnip truck.

If you say that the first sentence contains an adverb, you're the grand prize winner. The word *off* modifies the verb *fell,* by telling *where* Ronald fell, so *off* is an adverb. In the second sentence, however, *off* begins a prepositional phrase, *off the turnip truck,* and *truck* is the object of the preposition. The entire phrase acts as an adverb telling where Ronald fell, but more about types of phrases in Chapter 5.

Exercise 2

See if you can identify the underlined words as either prepositions or adverbs.

1. During rainstorms, Binky moves his sheep <u>inside</u> so that they won't shrink.

2. Newton keeps his newts <u>inside</u> a fruit jar.

3. Zoey hopped <u>around</u> the supermarket in a rubber chicken suit and gave samples of deviled eggs to customers who walked <u>by</u>.

4. Lizards without tongues can't catch flies that buzz <u>around</u> or lick Popsicles that melt and trickle <u>to</u> the ground.

5. Ripley likes chocolate chips sprinkled <u>on</u> his bean dip.

6. When large ducks hiccup, the sound is heard all <u>around</u>.

7. To protect himself from radioactive waves generated by dwarf poodles, Cousin Filmore wraps himself <u>in</u> oodles of aluminum foil before he goes <u>out</u>.

8. Tiny munchkins jump and tumble <u>inside of</u> plastic ping-pong balls.

9. Timmy bought a portable ladder so that he could talk <u>over</u> people's heads.

10. <u>After</u> a busy day, Santa enjoys winding <u>down</u> with a relaxing game of elf toss.

FYI Strict grammarians say not to leave a preposition hanging at the end of a sentence or question. Why? A preposition always, always, always starts a phrase that ends in a noun or pronoun. A poor prep can't be left alone dangling by itself. Therefore, you would never say this:

*I wonder where my head is **at**.*

Instead of ending the sentence with the preposition *at*, just leave it off:

I wonder where my head is.

That's better. Likewise, if you're trying to speak formally, you should never ask a question like this:

Who did you get that onion-flavored gum from?

Instead, you should rephrase the question so that the preposition isn't just stuck alone at the end. In a grammatically correct world, you should say something like this:

From whom did you get that onion-flavored gum? Or *Who gave you that onion-flavored gum?*
Or, better yet: Who gave you that foul-smelling stuff?

Exercise 3

Reword each sentence or question to eliminate the pesky preposition at the end.

Example: *What should Aunt Meara clip her ear hairs with?*

Answer: *With what should Aunt Meara clip her ear hairs?*

1. Where did you leave your muskrat at?

2. Why did you pluck all of the ducks for?

3. I wonder whom I should give this stray cockatoo to.

4. Where is my imaginary friend sitting at?

5. What do you sharpen your toenails with?

6. Where do vampire bats live at?

7. What should Biff eat his sliver of liver with?

8. Where have all of the emus gone to?

9. Grandpa never remembers where his Harley is at.

10. What time do we get out of this class at?

Writing Pointer

Sometimes writing can get a little boring if all the sentences follow the same pattern. Take a look at these sentences:

Aunt Daisy was hungry on Sunday, so she drove her new van to the market to buy a can of Spam. She noticed at the door of the store a man holding a large canned ham. This flimflammer stammered, with a smirk on his face, that he would trade her his ham for her shiny new van. She fell for his balderdash in a flash, gave him her shiny new van, and walked home and ate her jumbo baked ham. She can't drive to the store anymore when she wants a can of Spam because she has no van. She rides her pet camel to market instead, but she never knows where to park it.

Do you see a problem (other than the fact that Aunt Daisy is a loon)? The story is interesting, but the sentences all begin in the same way. They all start immediately with the subject, which is almost always *she*. Moving different things like phrases and clauses to the beginning of sentences can help break up what I like to call the *Spot* pattern. (You know . . . *Spot is a dog. Spot runs fast.*)

On Sunday *Aunt Daisy was hungry, so she drove her new van to the market to buy a can of Spam.* **At the door of the store**, *she noticed a man holding a large canned ham.* **With a smirk on his face**, *this flimflammer stammered that he would trade her his ham for her shiny new van.* **In a flash**, *she fell for his balderdash, gave him her shiny new van, and walked home and ate her jumbo canned ham. Because she has no van, she can't drive to the store anymore when she wants a can of Spam. Instead, she rides her pet camel to market, but she never knows where to park it.*

Voila! By moving some prepositional phrases (*On Sunday, At the door of the store, With a smirk on his face, In a flash*), we've eliminated the *Spot* pattern. In other words, changing sentence beginnings is a type of Spot remover.

Punctuation Pointer

If you begin a sentence with a long prepositional phrase (four words or more), follow the phrase with a comma.

> *After many long and comprehensive tests, doctors discovered that Buzzy is allergic to tennis ball fuzz.*

If a sentence begins with two or more prepositional phrases, follow only the last phrase in the series with a comma.

> Wrong: *On rainy days, in July and August, flies hide beneath the wings of magpies to stay dry.*
>
> Right: *On rainy days in July and August, flies hide beneath the wings of magpies to stay dry.*

Sometimes you might choose, simply for clarity, to put a comma after a short prepositional phrase that begins a sentence:

In the dark, Parker's shark-shaped birthmark sparkles.
In 1992, 743 cows simultaneously refused to moo.
Better: *Exactly 743 cows refused to moo in 1992.*

Exercise 4

Try changing each of the following sentences by moving a prepositional phrase to the beginning. Don't forget to add commas where necessary.

Example: *Gertrude always carries a sprig of parsley and a smoked perch in her purse.*

Answer: *In her purse, Gertrude always carries a sprig of parsley and a smoked perch.*

1. Lizzy's hissing lizard hides in her frizzy hair on drizzly days.

2. Cherrie won the big hair contest at the county fair in February.

3. Uncle Flake was flattened by a giant falling finch in a freak accident.

4. Little Whitney keeps the whale that she ordered through the mail in a large vat of ginger ale.

5. Tasha always wears her favorite squash-flavored lip gloss at posh parties.

6. Brice finally finished a jigsaw puzzle of a piece of rice in an ice storm after years of trying.

7. Dobs hopes to make gobs of money with his mail order bobby pin business.

8. Moe accidentally sucked up the skinny mailman with his jumbo leaf blower.

9. Pinocchio knows he needs a nose job before his next movie role.

10. Thirty flouncing fleas flourish in Cousin Gomer's goatee.

Now that you're a semi-prep-pro, let's move onward to conjunctions, the penultimate part of speech that we'll examine.

Conjunctions

Conjunctions are connecting words that join words or groups of words. There are three types of conjunctions: *coordinating*, *correlative*, and *subordinating*.

Coordinating Conjunctions

A *coordinating conjunction* is a single word that joins words or groups of words. These are the most common coordinating conjunctions:

for   and   nor   but   or   yet   so

The acronym FANBOYS might help you remember them (or if you're a little weird, you could use BANYOFS or YANOFBS or NOFABYS). Coordinating conjunctions always join items of the same type:

*Because it was raining <u>cats</u> **and** <u>dogs</u>, Cassy received several scratches.*
(two nouns)
*Wilbur <u>wheezes</u> **and** <u>sneezes</u> when he approaches dusty zebras.*
(two verbs)
*Ranger Bob warned the little scouts to never set up camp <u>next to downed electrical wires</u> **or** <u>near a raging forest fire</u>.* (two prepositional phrases)
*<u>Donald skillfully caught the baseball with his teeth</u>, **and** <u>in only three years, his dental work will be complete</u>.*
(two independent clauses—see Chapter 6)

Correlative Conjunctions

Correlative conjunctions are almost the same as coordinating conjunctions, except that they come in pairs. These are the most common correlative conjunctions:

both/and   either/or   neither/nor   not only/but also   whether/or

*A comprehensive insurance policy **not only** protects against damage from hurricanes, **but** it **also** covers injuries from attacks by wild woodchucks.*

*Monique hopes to open **either** a roller rink **or** a bulldozer boutique.*

Beware Certain words might act as prepositions in some sentences and conjunctions in others. Take a look:

> *Reginald was once a tree surgeon, **but** he was too emotional when he had to give a patient the axe.*

But is a conjunction because it connects two sentences.

> *Ramona ate everything on her plate **but** the barbecued bat.*

But is a preposition. The entire prepositional phrase is *but the barbecued bat. Bat* is the object of the preposition. (A tip: When *but* means *except*, it's a preposition.)

> *Ronald whistles when he breathes, **for** he has three nostrils.*

For is a conjunction connecting two sentences. (Another tip: When *for* means *because*, it's a conjunction.)

> *To his parents' dismay, Milton traded the family's computer, car, and cat **for** a lava lamp.*

For is a preposition beginning the phrase *for a lava lamp. Lamp* is the object of the preposition.

We'll save subordinating conjunctions for Chapter 6 when we look at clauses.

Exercise 5

It's time for another scavenger hunt. See if you can find all of the conjunctions (coordinating and correlative) in the following sentences.

1. When he grows up, Timmy doesn't know whether to study to become a brain surgeon or a human cannonball.

2. Gertrude, a bacteriologist, plans to name her children either *Staphylococcus aureus* or *Leptospirilla ichterohemorrhagia*.

3. Trudy has oodles of poodles and gobs of frogs, but she wants lots of potbellied pigs.

4. Skeeter read that most accidents happen at home, so now he lives on the street.

5. During the movie, Petey was glued to his seat, for he sat on a slobbery wad of gum.

6. Not only is Lulu a hula-hoop champ, but she's also a butcher, a baker, and a cuckoo clock maker.

7. Either bobbing for lobsters or pinning the tail on the giant snail are Amos's favorite party games.

8. Neither an aardvark nor a shark feeds on tree bark.

9. Billy had his fill of dill pickles and Popsicles, but he threw a fit, for he wanted more pitted olives.

10. Norman had cold feet before the track meet, so he ran in fuzzy wool socks and furry sneakers.

11. Both Dye and Elvira like anchovies and pepperoni on their ice cream.

12. Blinky always wins at tiddlywinks, yet at other games he stinks.

13. Audrey loves polka dots, but she hates circles and spots.

14. Neither Ebenezer nor his brother Geezer left the cat in the freezer.

15. Uncle Buddy's slugs nibble on too much fudge, so they're growing pudgy.

Writing Pointer

You can use conjunctions occasionally for effect to give your writing some power and vigor and smack and punch. Instead of using commas, sometimes for emphasis you can string together words in a series with conjunctions. You can also link together a series of phrases or independent clauses with conjunctions.

FYI If you link a items in a list together with conjunctions, you don't need to separate the items with commas.

For breakfast I like to eat eggs and toast and muffins and cereal and pizza and tofu and a heaping bowl of spicy gruel.

Stringing items together with conjunctions instead of separating them with commas can add emphasis and give a kind of rhythm to a passage. In Charles Dickens' novel *Great Expectations*, for example, the main character and narrator, Pip, describes his encounter as a young boy with a scary escaped convict in a graveyard. To make the man seem really rough and tough and scruffy, Dickens strings bunches of words and phrases together with *and*'s.

(Disclaimer: In the following passage, Dickens' use of commas illustrates one punctuation rule that's omitted from most grammar books: famous writers will punctuate pretty much any way they darn well please.)

. . . a man started up from among the graves . . . A fearful man, all in coarse gray, with a great iron on his leg. A man with no hat, and with broken shoes, and with an old rag tied round his head. A man who had been soaked in water, and smothered in mud, and lamed by stones, and cut by flints, and stung by nettles, and torn by briars; who limped, and shivered, and glared and growled; and whose teeth chattered in his head as he seized me by the chin.

Not only do you find this technique of stringing words together with conjunctions in works by famous authors, but you also find this little trick in a children's story. . . .

*"I'll huff **and** I'll puff **and** I'll blow your house down!*

. . . and in poems like this one by one of my favorite wordsmiths of all time, Shel Silverstein. These lines are from the poem "Jimmy Jet and His TV Set" (see above disclaimer):

He watched till his eyes were frozen wide,
***And** his bottom grew into his chair.*
***And** his chin turned into a tuning dial,*
***And** antennae grew out of his hair.*
***And** his brains turned into TV tubes,*
***And** his face to a TV screen.*
***And** two knobs saying "vert" and "horiz"*
Grew where his ears had been . . .

Exercise 6

See if you can write some punchy sentences about the following topics by stringing items together with conjunctions.

Example: the actions of an annoying mutt

*Fido jumped on my leg **and** chewed on my bed **and** growled at the cat **and** fell asleep in my lap **and** licked my nose **and** played with my toes **and** nuzzled my chin, **and** I think I'll keep him.*

Be sure that you write complete sentences, not just lists.

1. the actions of a child with poor table manners

2. the actions of a fidgety student before a big test

3. all the things a spoiled child might ask for on his or her birthday

4. the actions of a first time driver

5. the actions of a clumsy waiter

Wow! Gosh! Gee! It's time for the final part of speech . . . (Drum roll) . . . Interjections!

Interjections

Golly! Interjections are simply words that express emotion.

Generally these words are set off from the rest of the sentence by an exclamation mark.

Oops! Your toupee just blew away!

Sometimes a milder interjection is not set off with an exclamation mark. Instead, it's part of the sentence, followed by a comma.

My, I believe your lovely potted plant is trying to dance.

Ta daaaaaaaaaaaaaaaaaaahhhhhhhhhhhhhhhh! Now you know a little about the eight, count 'em, eight parts of speech. These little guys are the building blocks that combine to form larger parts of the sentence. Language is merely a giant Lego set. If you put all of the words together correctly and imaginatively, you can create a masterpiece!

4

Parts of the Sentence:
Subject, Predicate, and Complement

Not just any ol' clump of words can be a sentence. No-ooooooooo. A group of words must express a complete idea before it can earn the lofty title of *sentence*. Otherwise, these words are just wannabes called *fragments*. A *fragment* is a group of words that does not express a complete thought.

Fragment: *hanging from the chandelier*
Sentence: *Grandma is hanging from the chandelier by her toes again.*

Fragment: *while dining out*
Sentence: *While dining out, Thadeus was surprised to find a bushy, fake sideburn in his soup.*

Fragments aren't all bad. We use them all the time when we talk. However, you should use complete sentences when you write formally. English teachers just fall to pieces when they read fragments. (Get it? Pieces? Fragments?) In some cases, fragments are okay to use for effect even in formal writing, but you have to be aware of what you're doing.

To express a complete thought, a sentence must have a subject and a predicate. Let's take a look at the subject.

The Subject

The subject is the person, place, thing, or idea that's the main focus of the sentence.

Buddy *blows up rubber gloves to make fake udders.* (*Buddy* is the subject.)
Dotty *writes touching tales about friendly head lice.* (*Dotty* is the subject.)

Sometimes the subject is made up of more than one word. The *complete subject* is the main word in the subject *and* all of the words that go along with it. The *simple subject* is simply the main word of the subject.

Plump, lazy gerbils *should not snooze in front of moving steamrollers.* (The complete subject is *plump, lazy gerbils*. The simple subject is *gerbils*.)
On bad hair days, **Matilda, a fashionable young lady**, *wears colorful, eye-catching shower caps to hide her trussed-up tresses.*

The complete subject is *Matilda, a fashionable young lady*. The simple subject is just plain ol' *Matilda*.

FYI You will never, ever, ever, ever, ever find the simple subject in a prepositional phrase. Therefore, if you're trying to determine the simple subject of a sentence, just cross prepositional phrases out in your mind. The little critters just get in the way.

Last week Dweezle was attacked by a flock of crazy sheep.

To find the simple subject in this sentence, just be rude and ignore the prepositional phrases *by a flock* and *of crazy sheep*. Thus, the simple subject can't be *flock* or *sheep*. The simple subject is, you guessed it, *Dweezle*.

Exercise 1

Find the complete subject in each of the following sentences.

1. On his lunch break, Jake developed a bellyache after eating twelve beefsteaks, a cheese-cake, a pancake, and two pitted dates.

2. Drakleberry's overweight snake developed a serious backache.

3. During the holiday shopping season, Bucky, an alert security guard, nabbed a perpetrator shoplifting a refrigerator.

4. Ludwick, the unlucky leprechaun, found a pot of stew at the end of the rainbow.

5. To get rid of unwanted houseguests, after a day or two Wilameena pretends to be a screeching tree monkey.

6. According to the author of a best-selling book of helpful hints, sequin-covered fish sticks make lovely party gifts.

7. At a press conference, the company president announced a recall of thousands of defective thimbles.

8. In Washington, Derwood lobbies for lobsters' rights.

9. To make a living, Manfred manufactures manhole covers in assorted colors.

10. After a strenuous audition, Perketta landed a job as a professional smiler, waver, and look-amazed in television infomercials.

Sometimes subjects can come in pretty weird places. Questions, sentences that begin with *here* or *there*, and commands can all be tricky when it comes to determining the subject.

Finding Subjects of Questions

To find the subject in a question, the best thing to do is to rephrase the question into a statement:

How can you tell if a hippo is bloated?

In this case, rephrase the question into a sentence: *You can tell a hippo is bloated (how)*.

Now it's easy to see that the subject is *you*.

Why is Ulrick chewing on that rubber chicken?

Reword this question into a statement: *Ulrick is chewing on that rubber chicken (why)*. Voila! The subject is *Ulrick*.

Finding Subjects in Sentences Beginning with *Here*

Here is never a subject. Remember, only nouns (or noun phrases) and pronouns can be subjects, and *here* is an adverb. When sentences begin with *here*, the subject comes after the verb.

Here is a portly platypus.

To find the subject, just rephrase the sentence: *A portly platypus is here*. Easy schmeasy. *Platypus* is the subject and *is* is the verb.

Finding Subjects in Sentences Beginning with *There*

There, like *here*, can never be the subject of a sentence because it, too, is an adverb. Sometimes *there*, like *here*, begins a sentence and comes before the subject. To find the subject of a sentence beginning with *there*, rephrase the sentence. When doing so, oftentimes you can omit the word *there*:

There are little green bumps on your face.
Little green bumps are on your face.

Now it's as clear to see as a crow in snow: The subject is *bumps* and the verb is *are*.

FYI When *there* comes before the verb in the place you would normally expect to find the subject (generally at the beginning of a sentence), it's called an *expletive*. An *expletive* functions as nothing more than a sentence starter or a space filler, but it doesn't add anything to the meaning. With a little rewording, an expletive can generally be eliminated.

There are dust bunnies hiding under the bed.
Dust bunnies are hiding under the bed.

Writing Pointer

Sometimes the expletive *there* signals (warning! warning!) weak writing. If you just indicate that something is *there*, something just exists, you haven't said much. Writing that contains too many expletives often lacks substance, and it's just plain dull. Take a look at this paragraph.

Gum Chewers

There are many types of gum chewers that make my life miserable. For instance, **there are** the "smackers." They chew their gum with their mouths open and make disgusting noises. Also, they usually cram several packs into their mouths. **There are** also the "airhead" chewers. They try to make the biggest bubbles they possibly can. When one of their bubbles pops, gook goes everywhere. Then **there are** the grossest chewers, the "sit on it" chewers. They stick their used gum anywhere but in the trash. Some unsuspecting student eventually falls victim to one of these sticky wads. All of these types of rude people need to learn some manners.

This pitiful little paragraph has no personality. One reason is that the expletive *there* is everywhere (*There are many types of gum chewers; For instance, there are the "smackers"; There are also the "airhead" chewers ...*). They invade the poor paragraph like alien beings attacking a host body and zapping it of energy and individuality. In other words, the paragraph lacks voice.

By getting rid of the *there* sentences, and by focusing on action verbs instead of state of being verbs, you can transform bland writing into writing that has character (voice!).

Down with Tacky Smackers!

I'm generally a pretty easygoing person, but I have to admit, that some people I absolutely cannot tolerate. Who are these beings, you ask? Gross-me-out gum chewers, of course.

Many types of gross-out chewers, GOCs for short, make life miserable for the rest of us polite chewers (PCs). One group of GOCs, the "smackers," chew with their mouths open while large, gooey wads move up and down and up and down to the sounds of "smack, squish, smack, squish." A single stick of gum isn't enough for one of these GOCs. Like crazed chipmunks hoarding nuts for the winter, these GOCs cram their mouths with several pieces (or, in some cases, packs) at a time. Then they can't understand why others are unable to decipher their garbled words: "mmmmfff anmmmphph esammmphph ugmmmphph" (Translation: "Got another piece of gum?")

A member of another closely related species of chewer, the "airhead," tries to blow the biggest bubble possible. When the bubble pops, and it always does, a thin mucus-like film covers the chewer's face and neck. These chompers think that they're amusing their friends, but the unfortunate people sitting by them are splattered with large drops of slobber.

These pathetic chewers, however, pale next to the most obnoxious of all offenders: the "sit on it" chewers. After a good chew, these Neanderthals deposit their slimy wads beneath furniture or simply drop them on the floor. Heaven forbid that one of these chewers should have to walk an entire three feet to the trash can. In the classroom, the poor person who takes a seat after a GOC has marked the territory is likely to end up with a kneecap glued to the underside of the desk or a foot stuck firmly to the floor. In the meantime, the GOC goes merrily off to bum the next fix—peppermint, spearmint, cinnamon, or fruity—oblivious to the misery he or she has left behind.

So what are the timid PCs of the world to do in the face of such blatant, gauche behavior? PCs of the world, unite! It's time that we stomp out the chompers that are driving us bonkers. These people need to shape up, or spit out.

Exercise 2

See if you can take an expletive-filled piece of writing and perform a little magic. Reword sentences to get rid of unnecessary *there*'s and boring state-of-being verbs. Let your personality shine through.

Some strange people think that camping in the woods is fun. Boy, are they wrong. Based on my last (and only) family camping "vacation," there are many reasons I avoid communing with nature. First of all, in the woods, there are vicious insects—ants, ticks, and mosquitoes to name just a few. I had to drench myself in gallons of bug spray for protection; mosquitoes would stick to me and drown. Also, there was nothing for us (Mom, Dad, Sis, and me) to do during the day but to look at trees and squirrels. At night there was nothing to do but to sit around the campfire. (Actually, this was the highpoint of the trip. I told my little sister the story about how there is a guy with a hook who terrorizes kids when they're home alone. It made her cry).

Most importantly, though, there are dangers in the woods. There are snakes and bears and even crazy squirrels, just waiting to attack. Take my advice: There are safer and more exciting ways to spend your time—counting floor tiles, for example. At least it beats being the main course in a mosquito buffet.

Finding Subjects of a Command

Did you know one word could be a sentence?

Sit.   Run.   Smile.

These are all sentences. How can this be? Aha! These sentences have invisible subjects. More precisely, the subject for each sentence is the understood *you*: *you* sit, *you* run, and *you* smile.

Tie your shoelaces.
Take out the trash.
Pluck your eyebrows.
Wipe the gravy off your chin.

Since each of these sentences is also a command, the subject of each is the understood *you*. Even if a command includes a name, the subject is still *you*.

Mortimer, don't feed bologna to the bears.
Watch out for those vicious sea monkeys, Bethany!

Neither *Mortimer* nor *Bethany* is the subject of its sentence. The subject of each of these commands is still that sneaky little understood *you*.

Compound Subjects

Sometimes a sentence has two or more subjects. These subjects, called compound subjects, are joined by a conjunction and have the same verb:

Ernie and Prudence chew bubble gum.

Ernie and *Prudence* make up the compound subject and *chew* is the verb.

Ernie, Prudence and their goldfish chew bubblegum.

Ernie, Prudence and goldfish make up the compound subject, and *blew* is the verb.

I could go on (*Ernie, Prudence, their goldfish, and their dog Spot chew bubblegum*), but I think you get the idea. Now it's time for some *action*!

Exercise 3

Simply find the simple subjects in the following questions, statements, and commands.

1. Don't swallow that egg, Fred!

2. Are some Cyclopes sensitive about their unibrows?

3. Herby and Howie write clever jingles about foot powder and clam chowder.

4. Uncle Arnie, an avid fisherman, has a lead role in a heartbreaking opera about carp.

5. Is jelly made out of jellyfish?

6. Why don't cats ever land on their heads?

7. Does Cousin Elmo really have an extra toe?

8. Is this your toupee in the soufflé, Ray?

9. Why don't people call *butterflies flutterbies*?

10. There are many good reasons not to operate small kitchen appliances while bathing.

11. Barking sharks and wailing snails are rare in some parts of Arkansas.

12. Here is the blueprint for the very first automatic navel lint remover.

13. There is a pushy papaya salesman at the door.

14. Do mosquitoes have tiny teeth?

15. Is that a unicorn crooning in the cornfield?

The Predicate

In addition to a subject, every sentence needs a predicate. *Predicate* is actually just a fancy-schmancy name for a verb (a word that shows action or state of being). The *complete predicate* is the verb and all of the words and phrases that go along with it. To find the complete predicate, first find the subject, and then ask what it's doing, or what's being said about it. The *simple predicate* is simply the verb by its lonesome. (Don't forget that the verb can be a phrase, such as *is burping* or *has been wiggling*, which is made up of more than one word.)

Ramona reads mystery stories by the light of her ponderous firefly.

In this sentence, the complete (and simple, for that matter) subject is *Ramona*, and the complete predicate is *reads mystery stories by the light of her ponderous firefly.* The simple predicate is *reads.* Easy stuff.

At the dinner table, Reginald cleans his toenails with his steak knife.

In this case, the complete (and simple) subject is *Reginald.* Can you guess the complete predicate? Easy! Everything that isn't part of the complete subject is the complete predicate (in other words, all of the leftovers): *At the dinner table, cleans his toenails with his steak knife.* Even though the phrase *At the dinner table* is at the beginning of the sentence, it's part of the complete predicate because it tells *where* about the verb *cleans. Cleans,* you guessed it, is the simple predicate.

Compound Verbs

A compound verb is made up of two or more verbs that have the same subject.

For exercise, Cousin Moe curls and wiggles his toes.

Cousin Moe is the subject, and *curls* and *wiggles* make up the compound verb.

Cicero often walks and sometimes bowls in his sleep.

Cicero is the subject; *walks* and *bowls* make up the compound verb.

For her science presentation, Wilma will sing a song and recite a poem about parasites.

Wilma is the subject and *will sing* and *recite* form the compound verb. In this sentence, the helping verb, *will*, is not repeated before the verb, *recite*, even though it's understood (*will recite*). In a compound sentence with a verb phrase, you don't have to repeat the helping verb with the second verb if the helping verb is the same.

Exercise 4

It's time for the big challenge. Find both the simple subject and the simple predicate in each of the following sentences or questions.

1. Contact lenses are in the eyes of the beholder.

2. Tilly and Liv shiver and quiver when they eat liver.

3. The Venus flytrap swallowed the cat and then spat it at the yappy lap dog.

4. Against his parents will, Newton watches his b's and u's instead of his p's and q's.

5. In a strange turn of events, Tye found a tiny fish eye in his French fries.

6. Mrs. Granberry delighted the winners of the spelling bee with prizes of large stalks of broccoli.

7. Where did you buy that lovely, invisible tie? (Don't forget to reword the question into a statement.)

8. People with fuzzy eyebrows should pluck them or dye them mauve.

9. Why does Skippy keep his toenail clippings in an empty corn chip bag?

10. At half time in the crowded stadium, Kippy played an original version of "Over the Rainbow" with his armpit.

The Complement

As you already know, every sentence not only must have a subject and a verb, but must also be a complete thought. Sometimes a subject and verb need a word to fully complete the meaning of the sentence.

Boris owns   Broomhilda misplaced   Fido found

A word that completes the meaning of the subject and verb is called a complement. (Get it? complement? completes?)

sub.   verb   complement
<u>Boris</u> <u>owns</u> a <u>Tasmanian devil</u>.

sub.   verb   complement
Broomhilda misplaced her refrigerator.
sub.   verb complement
Fido found a bone.

FYI The complement will always, always be a noun, pronoun, or adjective. Also, a complement will never, ever, ever, ever, ever be in a prepositional phrase.

Take a look at these sentences. Can you tell which one has a complement?

Morris bathes his chimpanzee.
Morris swings from trees with his chimpanzee.

In the first sentence, *chimpanzee* is the complement. In the second sentence, however, the prepositional phrases *from trees* and *with his chimpanzee* follow the verb. Since a complement will never, ever, ever, ever be in a prepositional phrase, chimpanzee *can't* be the complement in the second sentence. In other words, the second sentence doesn't contain a complement. It's *complementless* (made-up word).

Complements come in three types: *direct objects*, *indirect objects*, and *subject complements*.

Direct Objects

A direct object will always be a noun or pronoun, and it will always come after an action verb. That's because it receives the action of the verb. Here's a spiffy way to find the direct object: just ask *whom?* or *what?* after the action verb. Don't forget to just snub those prepositional phrases. Pretend they don't exist if you're trying to find a direct object (because complements are never, ever, ever, ever in prepositional phrases).

Goodness, Egbert, you certainly have an unusual growth on your head.

In this sentence, *you* is the subject and *have* is the verb. Now just ask *have what?* and you can find the direct object—*growth*. Ignore *on your head* because it's a prep phrase.

Freda painted an extraordinary picture of a plump, pitted olive.

Here *Freda* is the subject, and *painted* is the verb. Just ask *painted what?* and it's easy to see that the direct object is *picture*. Of course, (I know this is getting really annoyingly redundant), ignore the prepositional phrase *of a plump, pitted olive.*

> *Thadeus complimented Nadine on her new Tyrannosaurus earrings.*

If you think *Thadeus* is the subject and *complimented* is the verb, you're precisely correct (sorry, no big prize). Ask *whom?* (or *what?*) after the verb, and, voila! you find the direct object, *Nadine. On her new Tyrannosaurus earrings* is . . . all together now . . . a prepositional phrase, so just ignore it.

Beware Remember that a direct object must always be a noun or pronoun and will never be in a prep phrase. Don't be confused by a sentence like this:

> *At midnight, some disturbed lobsters howl loudly at the moon.*

The subject is *lobsters,* and the action verb is *howl.* However, the verb is followed by an adverb, *loudly,* which tells how the lobsters howl, and a prep phrase, *at the moon.* A direct object must be either a noun or pronoun after the action verb, and it can't be in a prep phrase. Therefore, this poor deprived sentence has no direct object.

Sometimes you might have a compound direct object:

> sub.　　verb　　　　d.o.　　　　　　d.o.
> *Horace polishes his furniture and silverware with luncheon meat.*

You might also have a compound verb with a direct object after each verb:

> 　　　　　　　sub.　 verb　　　d.o.　　　　　　　　　verb
> *Tiny space aliens landed their ship on Kirby's head and explored*
> 　　d.o.
> *his toupee.*

Now here's a test. Can you find the complement (or complements) in this sentence?

> *Fire eaters suffer from severe heatburn and take extra-strength antacids after their performances.*

If you said that the sentence has only one direct object, you're correcto. The subject of the sentence is *fire eaters*, and the sentence contains a compound verb. The first action verb, *suffer*, is followed by a prepositional phrase, *not* by a direct object. However, the second action verb, *take*, is followed by *antacids*, a noun that answers the question *what?* after the verb (*take what? antacids*). Therefore, taa daaah . . . the sentence only contains one direct object: *antacids*.

Now let's mosey on to another type of complement, indirect objects.

Indirect Objects

An indirect object, if a sentence has one at all, will come before the direct object. Like the direct object, it will always be a noun or pronoun. So how do you find the varmints? First determine direct object, and then ask *to whom?* or *for whom?* or *to what?* or *for what?* about the direct object.

Static electricity gives Lizzy's hair the frizzies.

Electricity is the subject of the sentence, and *gives* is the verb. Now ask *what?* (or *whom?*) after the verb, and you find the direct object, *frizzies.* (*Electricity gives what? frizzies.*) Now ask *to whom?* or *to what?* about the direct object *frizzies*, and you find the answer is *hair* (*Electricity gives frizzies to what? hair*). Thus, *hair* is the indirect object.

Can you find the direct and indirect objects in this sentence?

Ms. McDougal read her class a story about Toodles, the dysfunctional doodlebug.

If you said that *story* is the direct object (it answers the question *what?* after the verb *read*) and *class* is the indirect object (it answers the question *to whom?* about the direct object), you're correct! If you said that *Toodles* or *doodlebug* is a direct or indirect object, boo hiss, you were fooled by one of those tricky prep phrases. Remember, ignore them.

FYI You might occasionally have a sentence with a compound indirect object:

               subject   verb   i.o.   i.o.

For special occasions, <u>Stevey</u> <u>sends</u> his <u>friends</u> and <u>relatives</u> attractive plaster

  d.o.

<u>statues</u> of feet.

You could even have a compound direct *and* indirect object.

subject	verb		i.o.		i.o.	d.o.		d.o.

Wynonna taught her hamster and garden snake a song and a tap dance from a hit Broadway show.

Beware You might think that a word in a prepositional phrase is an indirect object because it answers the question *to whom? for whom? to what?* or *for what?* about the direct object. Always remember and never forget that an indirect object must come *before* a direct object, and it can't be in a prep phrase. The following poor sentence has no indirect object.

subject verb d.o.
Norma taught the jig to her piglets.

Piglets answers *to whom?* or *to what?* However, it *can't* be an indirect object. Why? It's in a prep phrase, and it doesn't come *before* the direct object, *jig.* The following sentence contains an indirect object.

subject verb i.o. d.o.
Norma taught her piglets the jig.

Piglets is the indirect object. It comes *before* the direct object. Also, it's *not*, repeat, *not*, in a prep phrase, and it answers the question *to whom?* about the direct object, *jig.*

Now that you're an object whiz, it's time for a third type of complement, the subject complement.

Subject Complements

Unlike direct and indirect objects, which only follow *action verbs*, subject complements only come after *linking verbs*. This is an important point.

There are two types of subject complements: *predicate nominatives* and *predicate adjectives.*

A predicate nominative is a noun or pronoun that follows a linking verb. A predicate nominative explains or identifies the subject of the sentence.

Gomer's best friend is his pet eggplant.

In this sentence, *eggplant* is the predicate nominative. Why? you might ask. It's a noun that follows the linking verb *is*, and it renames the subject *friend.* In case you're wondering, *Gomer's* is a possessive adjective describing *friend.* It's *not* the subject of the sentence.

Can you find the predicate nominative in this sentence?

Reckless low-flying ducks are dangerous creatures.

Creatures is the predicate nominative. It's a noun that follows the linking verb *are*, and it renames the subject, *ducks*.

Try one more:

The large thing on my head is an overfed hedgehog.

Here you have a linking verb, *is*. The predicate nominative is *hedgehog*. It renames the subject, *thing*. (*On my head* is a prepositional phrase, so just ignore it.)

A predicate adjective is alllllllllmost the same as a predicate nominative. The only difference is that a predicate adjective is an adjective, instead of a noun or pronoun, following a linking verb. (That's why some brilliant person named it predicate *adjective*. Don't ask me why that brilliant person didn't name predicate nominative *predicate noun*.)

The food in your refrigerator is slightly furry.

In this sentence, *food* is the subject and *is* is the linking verb. *Furry* is an adjective that follows the linking verb and completes the meaning of the sentence. Therefore, *furry* earns the honored title of predicate adjective. Notice that furry *describes* the subject, *food (furry food)*. A predicate adjective *describes* the subject. A predicate nominative *renames* the subject.

Do you see the predicate adjective in this sentence?

Gee, your pet manatee is lovely.

Of course, you know that *lovely* is the predicate adjective because it's the adjective following the linking verb. *Lovely* describes the subject, *manatees (lovely manatees)*, and completes the meaning of the sentence.

Beware Don't forget that some linking verbs like to go incognito. Words like *look, seem, taste, feel, appear,* and *smell,* to name a few, can be linking verbs depending on how they're used in a sentence.

The hair on Paddington's three-headed cat is straggly.
The hair on Paddington's three-headed cat seems straggly.
The hair on Paddington's three-headed cat feels straggly.

The hair on Paddington's three-headed cat looks straggly.

In each of these sentences, *straggly* is the predicate adjective that follows the linking verb *is*, *seems*, *feels*, or *looks*. Why are all of these verbs linking verbs? Simple. Each of these verbs links the subject to a word (or words) that describes the subject. In each sentence, *straggly* describes the subject, *hair*. By the way, *Paddington's* is a possessive adjective describing *cat*. It's not the subject—but you knew that.)

Can you find the predicate adjective in this sentence?

Paddington's three-headed cat is a flea trap.

Trick question! This sentence has no predicate adjective. The subject is *cat*, the linking verb is *is*, and *trap* is the complement. However, *trap* can't be a predicate adjective because it's a *noun*, not an adjective. Instead, *trap* is a predicate *nominative*, a noun following a linking verb that completes the meaning of the sentence.

Beware One final little ol' word of warning. Predicate nominatives and predicate adjectives (like other types of complements) will never be in prepositional phrases. (Did I detect a yawn? Does this sound vaguely familiar?) Don't be fooled by a sentence like this:

Paddington's three-headed cat is out of the bag.

No complement in this sentence. Just one of those phrases, *out of the bag*, that you're sick of hearing about, so I won't even say its name. (a prepositional phrase—Sorry! I couldn't help myself).

Exercise 5

Now it's time (drum roll) to test yourself. See if you can find all of the most important parts of the sentence. Write the subject, verb, and complement. Label each word using the following code: subject (S), verb (V), direct object (DO), indirect object (IO), predicate nominative (PN), predicate adjective (PA). A sentence might have only a subject and verb—no complement.

1. Bertha bought her boyfriend a bug zapper for his birthday.

2. According to crime statistics, stalkers eat large quantities of celery.

3. People under large boulders are generally flat.

4. Professor Englebert gives fascinating lectures on Monet, ballet, and tooth decay.

5. Some vegetarians are slightly green, and they lean toward the sun.

6. Every morning Mr. Potato Head picks his nose.

7. The art teacher praised Billy for his squiggly lines.

8. During his two-hour bath, Calhoun turned slightly pruny.

9. Ms. Perkinsky showed her class a touching movie about Arnie, the antisocial aardvark.

10. Harpo told his mother an imaginative story about Peter, the puny potted plant with potential.

11. Fillmore invented a solar-powered ketchup and jelly packet opener and became a billionaire.

12. Through meditation, Mr. Potato Head finds his inner tuber.

13. At restaurants, you should always check catfish for fleas.

14. Tod taught his toad the game of leap frog.

15. For the Homecoming Dance, Carlos gave Darcia a lovely parsley corsage.

16. There's a hair in your hair, Claire!

17. After his camping trip, little Ripley gave his mother a bulging bag of bugs.

18. After a cloning experiment, Beatrice was beside herself.

19. Why do roaches always die on their backs instead of their stomachs?

20. With glue and paste, Marwood molded his hair into the shape of a large parrot.

21. The cow jumped over the moon and into the lagoon.

22. The obese man with poor eyesight mistook the skinny child for a toothpick.

23. Fuzzy, adventurous squirrels sometimes annoy their parents and hang dangerously from the ledges of very tall office buildings.

24. For an inexpensive decorative touch, Fruitsy sticks Gummy Bears on her sweaters and pets.

25. Nearsighted cooks sometimes mistake wrinkled roly-poly bugs for prunes.

26. Large, tubby babies drool and spit in the faces of gleeful grandmothers.

27. In some wealthy neighborhoods, jumbo rats feed on the fresh scraps of broiled ostrich leg and baked lobster.

28. To the surprise of the family, Uncle Hermie came out of his hernia operation with a tail.

29. Please tiptoe.

30. Matilda and Manfred have become millionaires with their washateria-fast-food mortuary.

31. There's something hanging from your nose, Rose.

32. For your birthday, here is an origami possum.

33. Walk like a duck.

34. Don't make volcanoes with your mashed potatoes and gravy.

35. Unger gave himself a pat on the back and injured a lung.

5

Dazed by Phrases?

Now that you know the components of the sentence—subject, predicate (verb), and sometimes complement—let's look at some groups of words called *phrases* that you find in sentences.

A phrase is simply a group of words that cannot stand alone as a sentence because it lacks a subject and verb. A phrase, depending on the type, acts as a noun, adjective, or adverb. Just to make life complicated, there are several types of phrases.

Prepositional Phrases

Prepositions, as you probably recall from Chapter 3, are words such as *at, in, around, near,* and *on* that show the relationship of a noun to the rest of the sentence. You probably also recall that a preposition always, always, always begins a phrase that ends with a noun or pronoun (the object of the preposition).

The flea is sitting on the beagle.

Prepositional phrases act either as adjectives to describe nouns, or as adverbs to tell *when, where, how, or to what extent about verbs, adjectives,* and other *adverbs.*

Adverb Phrases

Just like a one-word adverb, an *adverb phrase* is a prepositional phrase that modifies (or tells about) a verb, adjective, or another adverb.

An adverb phrase that modifies a verb answers the question *when? where? how? how much?* or *how far?* about that verb.

Over the summer, Buckly developed a taste for tofu-based products.

Over the summer tells **when** about the verb *developed*.

The moth flew **around my nostrils**.

Around my nostrils tells **where** about the verb *flew*.

Ralph suffers **from uncontrollable gum growth**.

From uncontrollable gum growth explains **how** or **in what way** about the verb *suffers*.

The millipede won the race **by a centimeter.**

By a centimeter tells **by how far** about the verb *won*.

In addition to verbs, adverb phrases also modify adjectives.

Melanie was very melancholy **about her mushy melons**.

About her mushy melons modifies the adjective, *melancholy*.

Norton was happy **with his recent neck transplant**.

With his recent neck transplant modifies the adjective *happy*.

Last but not least, adverb phrases modify other adverbs.

Vernon won the eel-eating contest, and later **in the day** he felt his stomach squirming.

In the day is an adverbial phrase that modifies the adverb *later*.

FYI More than one phrase might modify the same word.

At noon, several woozy baboons swim **in the lagoon**.

The phrase *at noon* tells when the baboons swim, and the phrase *in the lagoon* tells where they swim.

Also, adverb phrases are versatile varmints because you can move them around in a sentence. This little trick comes in handy if you find yourself starting sentences in the same old way.

*Woolly sheep stink **in storms**.*
***In storms**, woolly sheep stink.*
*Haddie straps tiny saddles **onto her seahorses**.*
***Onto her seahorses**, Haddie straps tiny saddles.*

Adjective Phrases

Just like a single word adjective, an adjective phrase modifies a noun or pronoun, and it answers the question *which one?* or *what kind?* Unlike an adverb phrase that you can move around in a sentence, an adjective phrase must follow the word it modifies.

*Because of their outstanding underarm hygiene, the students in Miss Higgleby's class won trophies **of tiny armpits**.*

Of tiny armpits is an adverb phrase modifying the noun *trophies*. The phrase tells what kind of trophies.

*All **of the customers** ordered the tofu and toadstool gruel.*

Of the customers is an adjective phrase modifying the pronoun *all*.

*Those long, hairy things **on the ends of your feet** are toes.*

On the ends is an adjective phrase modifying *things*, and *of your feet* is another adjective phrase modifying *ends*.

Beware Make sure that adjective phrases are close to the words they modify. Otherwise, horror of horrors, you create a grammatical monster known as the *misplaced modifier*. Sometimes sentences with misplaced modifiers present some mighty bizarre mental images.

Wrong: *Trapped in a jar, Beatrice keeps her beetles.*
Right: *Beatrice keeps her beetles trapped in a jar.*

Wrong: *The dog bit the girl with the large fangs.*
Right: *The dog with the large fangs bit the girl.*

Wrong: *With skinny limbs and termites, Boomer cut down the tree.*
Right: *Boomer cut down the tree with skinny limbs and termites.*

Wrong: *With a tattoo of Frankenstein on his face, Grandpa scolded the rude teenager.*
Right: *Grandpa scolded the rude teenager with a tattoo of Frankenstein on his face.*

Exercise 1

Now see if you can find all of the prepositional phrases in these sentences. Identify each phrase as either adjective (adj) or adverb (adv). Be sure to write the whole phrase and not just the preposition.

1. Gork, the boorish caveman, always looks like a dork at dinner when he eats his wild boar with his fingers, not a fork.

2. Because of some unknown cause, on Monday at midnight Morley morphed into a mole and dug a ten-foot-deep hole.

3. Some medical specialists assert that spit from spiders in Spain and Japan will relieve the common cold faster than aspirin can.

4. After only two months in business, the assertiveness training school for wimps and wannabe winners doubled its tuition because it knew the pupils wouldn't object.

5. Because of the windy weather, Heather decided that she shouldn't wear her dress that is made with feathers.

6. Every year at midnight on December 31, vampires in colorful party hats dance around a campfire, and they don't return to their comfy coffins until dawn.

7. In a terrible freak accident during a normal day at the office, Frodo stapled his lip to a document containing a comprehensive survey about the number of careless workplace mishaps.

8. After his birthday party, Biffy cried into the night because, instead of a beautiful white mare, his parents gave him six packages of underwear.

9. People never sit by Bork during funny movies because he snorts like a porker when he chortles.

10. Dr. Decayder, a dexterous dentist, melts and molds used retainers into lovely holiday ornaments, places them inside of boxes that are decorated with pictures of tiny teeth, and gives them to his patients with braces.

So much for prepositional phrases. It's time to shuffle on to another type of phrase, the appositive.

Appositive Phrases

An *appositive* is a noun or pronoun that directly follows and renames another noun or pronoun in the sentence.

*My dog **Spot** is covered in stripes.*

Spot is an appositive that renames the noun *dog*.

An *appositive phrase* contains an appositive and all the words that modify the appositive.

*Melba uses a special ingredient, **a chunky kitty litter**, in her banana bran muffins.*

A chunky kitty litter is an appositive phrase that renames the noun *ingredient*.

*Broderick's girlfriend, **an attractive mermaid**, has a swimming pool in her backyard.*

An attractive mermaid is an appositive phrase that renames the noun *girlfriend*.

*Suellen, **Sally's sister**, hides sausages under the sofa.*

Sally's sister is the appositive that renames the noun *Suellen*.

Punctuation Pointer Most of the time appositive phrases are set off by commas—but sometimes they're not. Set an appositive phrase off with commas if it is *not essential* to the meaning of a sentence. In other words, you could leave the phrase out, and the reader would understand clearly to whom or to what you are referring. *Don't* put commas around an *essential* appositive phrase. It provides necessary information to identify the person, place, or thing it renames.

Essential: *Hilda's English class was assigned the book **War and Peace** to read over the weekend.*

The appositive, *War and Peace*, is necessary. Otherwise you wouldn't know what book the class was assigned.

Nonessential: *War and Peace, **the class's assigned book**, weighs sixteen pounds.*

The appositive, *the class's assigned book*, provides nonessential information that could be dropped from the sentence. Without the appositive, you would still know exactly what book weighs sixteen pounds.

FYI If an appositive follows a *proper* name, always set the appositive off with commas.

Gordon, a goofball, stuffed his mouth with gum balls.

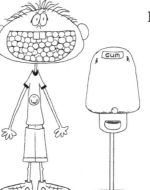

Here's a picky point. Remember that an appositive phrase always has a noun as the main word. Not all groups of words set off by commas are appositives.

Elves, short and plump, have difficulty finding footwear that fits.

Notice that, though the words *short and plump* are set off by commas, these words don't form an appositive phrase because an appositive must contain a noun or pronoun as the main word, and *short* and *plump* are adjectives. However, by adding a noun, you can magically create an appositive.

*Elves, short and plump **creatures**, have difficulty finding footwear.*

Ta dahhhh! Now the main word of the phrase is the noun *creatures*, and, therefore, the phrase *short and plump creatures* is an appositive.

Verbals

A *verbal* (which, by the way, almost rhymes with *gerbil*) is a word that will try to fool you. The name is appropriate because a verbal is a form of the verb; however, it functions as a different part of speech. There are three types of verbals: *participles*, *gerunds*, and *infinitives*.

Participles and Participial Phrases

A *participle* is a form of the *verb*, but it functions as an *adjective*. A participle, like your basic adjective, answers the question *which one?* or *what kind?* about a noun or pronoun.

*Why aren't **squirming** tapeworms digested in the intestines?*

Even though *squirming* is a verb form, it actually answers the question *what kind?* about the noun *tapeworms*. Since *squirming* is a verb form that functions as an adjective, it's a participle.

There are two types of participles, present and past. A present participle always ends in *ing*. A past participle *generally* ends in *ed*, but, wouldn't you know it, many are irregular (*shaken, broken, paid*), so you can't always tell a past participle by its ending.

*Jane complained, "My **misguided** accountant advised me to invest in socks; but, darn it, the sock sector unraveled, and my **stinking** stock flopped."*

Misguided has an *ed* ending, but don't be fooled. Although it's a verb form, it's not acting like a verb. It actually describes the noun *accountant*. Because it's a verb form that acts as an adjective, it's a participle. Likewise, *stinking* is a verb form that describes the noun *stock*. Since it's a verb form that acts as an adjective, it, too, is a participle.

*The badly **shaken** spiders scurried from the **worn** shoe when they saw five humongous, **wiggling** toes descending upon them.*

Both *shaken* and *worn* are irregular past participles. Each is a form of a verb (*shake, wear*), but neither has the typical *ed* ending. *Wiggling* is a present participle that describes *toes*. (A present participle is always regular; it always ends in *ing*.)

Beware Sometimes it's easy to confuse a participle with an actual verb.

*In the **snorting** contest at the County Fair's Annual Porcine Day Celebration, Howie won first prize, a bronze nose.*

Snorting is a participle because it describes the noun *contest*.

A participle by itself can't be the verb of a sentence. To function as a verb, a participle must be accompanied by a helping verb.

*Howie **is snorting** like a chortling pig.*

Snorting is part of the verb, *is snorting*. *Is snorting* is the main verb of the sentence. *Chortling* is a participle that describes *pig*.

A *participial phrase* consists of a participle and the complements and modifiers that go along with it. Like a one-word participle, a participial phrase acts as an adjective to modify a noun or pronoun.

***Wearing a sheet with eyeholes**, little Manfred went trick-or-treating as a mattress.*

Wearing a sheet with eyeholes is a participial phrase modifying *Manfred*.

*Hungry, desperate vegetarians **marching in front of the capitol** declared that cows are plants.*

Marching in front of the capitol is a participial phrase modifying *vegetarians*.

***Wearing a long veil and a thong bikini**, the bride shocked the wedding guests.*

Wearing a long veil and a thong bikini is a participial phrase that modifies *bride*.

Beware Notice that a participial phrase can come at the beginning, middle, or end of a sentence, but the phrase should be close to the word or words it modifies. Otherwise, you create a *dangling participle*.

Just like other types of misplaced modifiers, dangling participles can cause you to conjure up some pretty silly images.

Wrong: ***Dressed in high heels and a tight black dress**, Bubba escorted Edna into the theater.*

Right: *Bubba escorted Edna, **dressed in high heels and a tight black dress**, into the theater.*

Wrong: ***Covered with fleas**, my neighbor owns that stray cat.*

Right: *My neighbor owns that stray cat **covered with fleas**.*

Wrong: **Swimming in the aquarium**, *Peabody observed the octopus.*
Right: *Peabody observed the octopus* **swimming in the aquarium**.

Punctuation Pointer

If a participial phrase is *essential*—in other words, if it's *necessary* in order to identify the noun or pronoun to which it refers—then *don't* use commas to separate it from the rest of the sentence. If the phrase is *nonessential*—in other words, it's *not necessary* in order to identify the noun or pronoun to which it refers—then *do* set it off with commas. Sometimes this is a tough decision to make.

Essential: *The man clipping his toenails in the theater disturbed the audience.*

Clipping his toenails is necessary to identify which man.

Nonessential: *Izzy's igloo, located in Antarctica, comes complete with shag carpet and ceiling fans.*

Located in Antarctica is nonessential information because Izzy probably has only one igloo, and it's not necessary to specify its location. However, you would write this sentence *without* commas if Izzy owns *more* than one igloo (maybe one in the Bahamas as well), and you were trying to specify the igloo to which you were referring.

One type of verbal down, just two more to go!

Gerunds and Gerund Phrases

Like a participle, a gerund is a form of a verb. Don't be fooled, though. It actually functions as a *noun* in the sentence.

Gerunds, like some participles, end in *-ing*. The difference between a gerund and a participle is simply the way each is used in a sentence. A participle functions as an *adjective*, and a gerund functions as a *noun*. As a matter of fact, the same word could act as a gerund in one sentence, a participle in another, and part of the verb in still another.

Gerund: ***Drooling*** *is rude.*

Drooling is a gerund because it's used as a noun, the subject of the sentence.

Participle: ***Drooling*** *and spitting, the baby reached for the fuzzy stuffed guppy.*

Drooling is used as an adjective to describe the noun *baby*. *Spitting*, likewise, is used as an adjective to describe *baby*. Therefore, both *drooling* and *spitting* are participles.

Verb phrase: *The baby* ***is drooling*** *into the mashed carrots.*

In this case, *drooling* is not a gerund or participle. It's part of the verb phrase *is drooling*. *Is drooling* is the main verb of the sentence.

A *gerund phrase* consists of a gerund and all of its complements and modifiers.

Gerund: ***Walking*** *is good for the health.*
Gerund phrase: ***Walking across a busy freeway*** *can be harmful to the health.*

A gerund or a gerund phrase is used in the same position that a noun is used in a sentence. Like a noun, a gerund or gerund phrase might function as a *subject, direct object, indirect object, object of the preposition*, or *predicate nominative*.

Subject: ***Sitting on burning ashes*** *causes rashes and hot flashes.*
Direct object: *The judge forbids* ***snoozing, sneezing, and snoring in his courtroom***.
Indirect object: *Ramona has given underwater* ***dancing*** *her best effort.*
Object of the preposition: *Rhonda won first place in the rodeo for* ***riding a rodent***.
Predicate nominative: *Wakefield's favorite hobby is* ***photographing fruitcakes***.

Infinitives and Infinitive Phrases

An infinitive generally consists of the word *to* followed by a verb: *to giggle, to wiggle, to hobble, to gobble*, etc.

Beware It's easy to mistake a prepositional phrase beginning with *to* for an infinitive. Here's a valuable piece of information: *to* followed by a noun or pronoun is a prepositional phrase, and *to* followed by a verb form is an infinitive.

Infinitive: *The muscular mice threw dice **to scare** away the advancing lice.*

Prepositional Phrase: *The unusually fit lice tossed the dice back **to the surprised mice**.* (*To* is a preposition and *mice* is the object of the preposition.)

An infinitive can function as a noun, adjective, or adverb within a sentence:

Noun: ***To belch*** *is rude.* (subject)

*Truman tried **to belch**.* (direct object)

*Figaro's favorite activity is **to belch**.* (predicate nominative)

Adjective: *Molly made the decision **to belch**.* (*To belch* modifies the noun *decision*.)

Adverb: *Hogs are happy **to belch**.* (*To belch* modifies the adjective, *happy*.)

*Patsy politely left the party **to belch**.* (*To belch* answers the question *why?* about the verb *left*.)

An *infinitive phrase* consists of an infinitive plus all of its modifiers and complements. The entire phrase acts like a noun, adjective, or adverb.

To ride a roller coaster with a rhinoceros *is risky.*

The infinitive phrase is acting as a noun. It's the subject of the sentence. Notice that the entire phrase includes the infinitive *to ride*, its complement, *a roller coaster*, and a prepositional phrase, *with a rhinoceros*.

*Jack and Jill went up the hill **to fetch a feisty ferret**.*

The infinitive phrase, *to fetch a feisty ferret*, acts as an adverb that answers the question *why?* about the verb *went*.

*Lakeesha was surprised **to see a bumblebee with knees**.*

The infinitive phrase, *to see a bumblebee with knees*, functions as an adverb modifying the adjective *surprised*. The entire phrase includes the infinitive *to see*, the complement *a bumblebee*, and the prepositional phrase *with knees*.

*The dentist gave Orland an order **to stop chewing on doorknobs**.*

The infinitive phrase, *to stop chewing on doorknobs*, functions as an adjective describing the noun *order*.

***To consume his daily iron requirement**, Hayden swallows nails.*

The infinitive phrase, *to consume his daily iron requirement*, functions as an adverb that answers the question *why?* about the verb *swallows*.

Beware Sometimes the word *to* is omitted in an infinitive. It's simply understood.

Jade did not dare wade in the water swarming with worms and germs.

The word *to* before *wade* is understood. You probably notice also that this sentence happens to include a participial phrase—*swarming with worms and germs*—that modifies the noun *water*.

Exercise 2

Now test your phrexpertise (phrase expertise). See if you can identify each underlined phrase in the following sentences as one of the following: *prepositional* (prep), *appositive* (a), *participial* (p), *gerund* (g), or *infinitive* (i).

1. Petunia was nervous <u>about her first sword swallowing lesson</u>.

2. Pigs <u>wearing high heels</u> trot with zeal.

3. Doctors were amazed <u>to see the ghost of Elvis in the X-ray of Mr. Bittleman's pelvis</u>.

4. At summer camp, Arnie sighted a large animal, <u>a water buffalo</u>, <u>grazing in the woods</u>.

5. <u>To appear popular</u>, Cuthbert drives with three mannequins in the front seat <u>of his pickup</u>.

6. When he backs up the car, Iggy annoys his friends <u>by making beeping noises</u>.

7. Frogger uses a remote control <u>to operate his remote control</u>.

8. Holden was scolded for <u>sucking his mashed potatoes through a straw</u>.

9. An officer ticketed Grandpa <u>for driving without tires</u>.

10. <u>Pretending he was a walrus</u>, Elroy stuck French fries up his nose.

11. <u>To avoid calling attention to himself</u>, Rutherford sometimes wears a paper sack over his head.

12. <u>Performing plastic surgery on yourself</u> can be hazardous to your health.

13. In the cryogenics lab, Edward developed a head cold from <u>working around all of the cold heads</u>.

14. Mr. Fibbleberry, <u>a paranoid man</u>, believes that the Joneses are trying <u>to keep up with him</u>.

15. Bartlet, <u>an avid fisherman</u>, has written his first opera about carp.

16. Only heartless jerks feed beef jerky <u>to poor tooth-less turkeys</u>.

17. Grumpy, <u>one of the seven dwarves</u>, has many issues because people always judge him <u>by his name</u>.

18. The scout received his merit badge <u>for grooming squirrels and woodchucks</u>.

19. People with tiny teeth have problems <u>eating tough cookies</u>.

20. After Kyra dotted her eyes, she couldn't see <u>to cross her *t*'s</u>.

21. <u>To get the attention of overly aggressive players</u>, the referees at the local high school use tubas, not whistles.

22. After she gave up caffeine, Priscilla tried <u>to channel her nervous energy</u> into <u>knitting blankets for beached whales</u>.

23. <u>Bobbing for lobsters</u> is a fun, but painful, party game.

24. Dotty was alarmed <u>to find a whisker</u> on her hot dog.

25. Heinrich annoys people behind him in line <u>by continually clearing his sinuses</u>.

Exercise 3

In this passage from *James and the Giant Peach*, see if you can identify the underlined phrases: *prepositional* (prep), *participial* (p), *appositive* (a), *gerund* (g), or *infinitive* (i).

The Centipede, who had begun <u>dancing wildly around the deck during the song</u>,[1] had suddenly gone too close <u>to the downward curving edge</u>[2] of the peach, and <u>for three awful seconds</u>[3] he had stood <u>teetering on the brink</u>,[4] <u>swinging his legs frantically in circles</u>[5] in an effort <u>to stop himself from *falling over backward into space*</u>.[6] But before anyone could reach him—down he went! He gave a shriek <u>of terror</u>[7] as he fell, and the others, <u>rushing to the side and peering over</u>,[8] saw his poor long body <u>tumbling over and over through the air</u>,[9] getting smaller and smaller until it was out of sight. . . .

"I'm going down after him!" cried James, <u>grabbing the silk string</u>[10] as it started coming out of the Silkworm and <u>tying the end of it around his waist</u>.[11] "The rest of you hold on <u>to Silkworm</u>[12] so I don't pull her over with me, and later on, if you feel three tugs <u>on the string</u>,[13] start hauling me up again!"

He jumped, and he went tumbling down <u>after the Centipede</u>,[14] down, down, down, toward the sea below, and you can imagine how quickly the Silkworm had <u>to spin to keep up with the speed of his fall</u>.[15]

6

Eliminating Clause-trophobia

Now that you're a phrase master, let's pause and look at clauses. Clauses are a step higher on the grammar ladder than phrases. You've probably noticed that the grammatical units (parts of speech, parts of sentence, phrases, clauses) become progressively more complex. A clause contains two important elements that phrases don't have: a subject and a verb. Clauses fall into two basic categories: independent and dependent.

FYI Just to clutter your mind a little more, *independent clauses* are also called *main clauses*, and *dependent clauses* are also referred to as *subordinate clauses*. (The word *subordinate* means "in a lesser position," so this name makes sense. A subordinate clause is less than a sentence.)

Independent Clause vs Dependent Clause

What's the difference between an independent clause and a dependent clause? An independent clause can be a sentence all by itself, and a dependent clause can't. For all you visual learners out there, think of an independent clause as an adult who can stand on his or her own two feet, and think of a dependent clause as a child who needs some help to stand.

In other words, a dependent clause is a sentence fragment, a sentence wannabe. Take a look:

When Myrtle bowls

You can probably tell that, although this group of words contains a subject (*Myrtle*), and a verb (*bowls*), it's not a complete idea. Because it can't stand alone as a sentence, it's a *dependent clause*. You can sometimes (but not always) transform a dependent clause into an independent clause by taking away the first word that makes the idea subordinate (less than a sentence):

Myrtle bowls.

In addition, you can always (not just sometimes) add an independent clause to a dependent clause to create a sentence:

When Myrtle bowls, her teammates are required to wear helmets. Every sentence has to have at least one independent clause, and some sentences have two:

Nate was going to stop procrastinating, but *he's decided to wait.* (Two independent clauses are joined by the conjunction *but*.)

Some sentences even have more than two independent clauses:

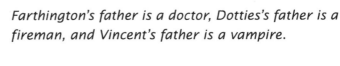

Farthington's father is a doctor, Dotties's father is a fireman, and Vincent's father is a vampire.

Exercise 1

In the following sentences, see if you can identify each underlined word group as an *independent clause* (I), a *dependent clause* (D), or just a measly little *phrase* (P). (Remember, a phrase does not contain a subject and verb.)

1. <u>Little Wilbur threw a tantrum on his birthday</u> because he wanted creamed corn instead of cake.

2. When he styles his chest hair, <u>Stanley uses volume-increasing mousse to achieve a manly look.</u>

3. In a romantic twist of fate, Quigley and Kaitlyn fell in love on a crowded elevator <u>when their dental headgears intertwined.</u>

4. "Is it true <u>that baboons eat ticks</u>?" asked Rick.

5. Tootsie answered an employment ad <u>for a mall elf</u>, but she was under-qualified.

6. <u>Eunice stopped wearing eucalyptus lotion</u> after she was attacked by a group of hungry sloths.

7. Norman wore his best jacket to the dance, but <u>he forgot his pants</u>.

8. <u>For some reason</u>, porcupines often have bonding issues.

9. Because Rockefeller dropped his clock, <u>it never ticks and only tocks</u>.

10. Fabio bought a commemorative stamp <u>that commemorates the first commemorative stamp</u>.

The Adjective Clause

An adjective clause (surprise!) acts like an adjective, and it's one of three types of dependent clauses (*adjective*, *adverb*, and *noun*).

that   which   who   whom   whose

These words are called *relative* pronouns because each *relates* (get it?) a clause to the noun it modifies:

> *Hamsters that injure their hamstrings are hampered from doing handsprings.*

The relative pronoun, *that*, relates the adjective clause, *that injure their hamstrings*, to *hamsters*, the noun the adjective clause modifies.

> *He who loses his head needs no hat.* —ancient proverb. (Okay, I admit it. It's not ancient. I just made it up).

The relative pronoun, *who*, relates the adjective clause, *who loses his head*, to *he*, the pronoun the adjective clause modifies.

Sometimes adjective clauses also begin with adverbs like *where*, *when*, and *why*.

> *Cousin Henrietta always tells the story about the time when she was on an elevator with someone who looked a little like someone who might be famous.*

When she was on an elevator with someone modifies the noun *time*.

Relative pronouns are actually multitalented. Not only do they relate clauses to nouns, but often they also act as either subjects or objects in their own clauses:

> *Aphrodite recently joined a self-help group for people who are addicted to self-help groups.*

Who is the subject of the clause *who are addicted to self-help groups.*

> *For some reason, the children's book that Opal wrote about head lice, an invisible terror, was not a best seller.*

That is the direct object of the clause *that Opal wrote*. (Remember, to find a direct object, ask *what*? or *whom*? after an action verb. Opal wrote *what*? that.)

Essential and Nonessential (a.k.a. Restrictive and Nonrestrictive) Adjective Clauses

An adjective clause is *essential* or *restrictive* if it's truly necessary to identify the noun or pronoun it modifies in a sentence. On the other hand, a *nonessential* (also known as *nonrestrictive*) adjective clause simply adds information that isn't necessary to identify the noun or pronoun it modifies.

*Tadpoles **that swallow marbles** sink when they try to swim.*

The adjective clause, *that swallow marbles*, modifies the noun *tadpoles*. The clause is necessary because it identifies which tadpoles sink when they swim. Without it, the sentence reads as though all tadpoles sink when they swim. Therefore, the clause is *essential* or *restrictive*.

*Tadpoles, **which are smaller than rhinos**, become bloated when they swallow cantaloupes.*

The adjective clause, *which are smaller than rhinos*, modifies the noun *tadpoles*. The clause is *nonessential* or *nonrestrictive* because it adds information that isn't critical to the meaning of the sentence. As a matter of fact, you could lift the clause out of the sentence, and the main idea of the sentence remains intact.

Punctuation Pointer

When a clause is nonessential (not necessary), it's set off from the rest of the sentence with commas.

*With his new braces, **which have pieces of taco salad caught in them**, Erkle can receive messages from alien life forces.*

The fact that Erkle's dental hygiene needs improvement has nothing to do with his ability to receive alien messages. Since the clause isn't necessary to identify Erkle's braces, the clause is set off with commas.

On the other hand, if a clause is essential (necessary), don't isolate the poor critter with commas:

*The messages **that Erkle receives through his braces** are prank calls from bratty, little space aliens.*

Not *all* messages are prank calls by irksome little space aliens. The clause *that Erkle receives through his braces* is necessary to identify the *type* of messages that are from the bratty little extraterrestrial tricksters. The clause isn't set off by commas because it's essential to the meaning of the sentence.

How would you punctuate these sentences? Hint hint hint: one contains an essential clause, and one contains a nonessential clause.

Chucky who has a degree in psychology counsels angst-ridden teenage monkeys.
Everyone who counsels angst-ridden teenage monkeys must have a degree in psychology.

In the first sentence, the clause *who counsels angst-ridden teenage monkeys* is nonessential. If you leave the clause out, the sentence makes sense because the clause isn't necessary to identify the word it modifies (*Chucky*). Therefore, the clause is set off by commas: *Chucky, who has a degree in psychology, counsels angst-ridden teenage monkeys.*

In the second sentence, the clause *who counsels angst-ridden teenage monkeys* is essential. If you leave the clause out (or set it off with commas), the main idea of the sentence is that *everyone* must have a degree in psychology. Since the clause is necessary to clarify who must have a degree in psychology, the clause isn't set off by commas.

The basic rule goes like this: When a clause is essential, commas are not essential, and when a clause is nonessential, commas are essential. Go figure.

Now here's a really picky English teacher point. Can you tell the difference in the meaning of these two sentences?

Jed's brother who sheds is named Harry.
Jed's brother, who sheds, is named Harry.

In the first sentence, *who sheds* is an essential clause because it's not set off by commas. Therefore, you can assume Jed has more than one brother because the clause is necessary to identify which brother is named Harry. In the second sentence, *who sheds* is nonessential because it's set off by commas. Therefore, you can figure that Jed has only one (apparently quite hirsute) brother, so the clause *who sheds* isn't necessary to identify which brother is named Harry. The clause simply adds a superfluous, furry fact.

FYI Clauses that begin with *that* are generally essential, so they're usually not set off by commas. Clauses that begin with *which*, on the other hand, are nonessential and should be set off by commas. Take a gander:

Geese that feast on greasy gravy are generally obese.
Obese geese, which are common in the East, feast on greasy gravy.

In the first sentence, *that feast on greasy gravy* is an essential clause. It begins with the relative pronoun *that* and is not set off by commas. It's needed to identify exactly which geese are obese. In the second sentence, *which are common in the East* is a nonessential clause. It begins with the relative pronoun *which* and is set off by commas. The clause isn't necessary to identify the type of geese (*obese geese*) that gorge on grease.

FYI (again) The relative pronouns *that* and *which* generally refer to things, and *who* refers to people:

The children who *sold the most candy bars for the Thespian Club had to act as though they won a prize.*
Mr. Squawkleman, a slightly myopic but considerate driver, always replaces the neighborhood **pets that** *he runs over.*
Novack has **a birthmark, which** *is shaped like a hunchbacked yak, on his back.*

FYI (one more time) Sometimes the relative pronoun *that* is invisible when it begins a clause. You can't see it, but it's understood:

Where's the picture of the squiggly line you painted in your art class, Lynard?

The subordinate clause is actually **that** *you painted in your art class*, but the relative pronoun *that* is omitted. Don't ask me why. I guess it saves time talking. Every .00000000000009 of a nano-second counts.

Exercise 2

In each of the following sentences, write the *adjective* clause and the word it modifies. If the clause is nonessential, place commas where you would find them in the sentence. Some sentences have more than one subordinate clause, but be careful; not all of the clauses in the exercise function as adjectives. Remember, an adjective only modifies a noun or pronoun.

Example 1: *Bedbugs that sweat too much should sleep without sheets.*
Answer: *that sweat too much—bedbugs*

Example 2: *Bedbugs which are little-bitty critters are difficult to hug.*
Answer: *,which are little bitty critters,—bedbugs*

1. Archeologists in Australia have found remnants of an ancient people who had no cavities in their teeth, but they had several holes in their heads.

2. The apple that Adam swallowed whole is stuck below his Adam's apple.

3. Hazel whose lung capacity is quite amazing can play the tuba while she scubas.

4. Fleas which have no knees need no knee socks.

5. Every holiday Xavier sends her relatives Styrofoam that's wrapped in bubble wrap.

6. Fleet fleas flee from the fleece of sheep that prance around too fleetingly.

7. As part of his unconventional teaching strategy, Mr. Egerdy awards A's to students who pay him large amounts of cash in small bills.

8. Otters that get too hot ought not to trot.

9. Armstrong who lifts weights to build strong arms dropkicks lead kegs to develop hefty legs.

10. According to an in-depth study by the Department of Transportation, most traffic accidents that occur in this country result from some form of driving.

11. Aunt Shashon who is in a constant state of denial covers her dashboard with masking tape when a warning light comes on.

12. Is this the spot where Spot dug up Aunt Dot's ashes?

13. Tamina whose face is covered with freckles sometimes is mistaken for a mobile map of Alabama.

14. A guest who sweats on a table setting at a banquet has poor etiquette.

15. To uncover the reason that Congress orders too many costly investigations, Congress ordered a costly investigation.

The Adverb Clause

Okay. Here's a tough question: An adverb clause functions in a sentence as a) a toaster b) a hamster c) an adverb d) a small rock.

If you guessed *c*, by gosh, you're right. If you guessed *a*, *b*, or *d*, don't fret; but, as you can clearly tell, grammar can be tricky at times.

An adverb clause is simply a type of dependent clause that functions as an adverb. Like a one-word adverb, an adverb clause answers the question *how? when? where? why? how much?* or *under what condition?* about a *verb*, an *adjective*, or another *adverb*.

Take a look at a few examples:

After Little Miss Muffet ate too much whey, she weighed way too much to sit on a tuffet.

After Little Miss Muffet ate too much whey answers *when?* about the verb *weighed*.

"*If an octopus only had three legs*, would it be called a *tripus*?" asked little Dreyfus.

If an octopus only had three legs answers *under what condition?* about the verb *would be called*.

Binky's mother was upset because Binky brought home a tarantula for a pet.

Because Binky brought home a tarantula for a pet answers *why?* about the adjective *upset*.

People misunderstand Stan because he always stands on his hands.

Because he always stands on his hands answers *why?* about the verb *misunderstand*.

Aston proudly burped louder than anyone else in his kindergarten class.

Than anyone else in his kindergarten class answers the question *how much?* or *to what degree?* about the adverb *louder*.

Adverb clauses begin with little gizmos called *subordinating conjunctions*. These are some of the most frequently used:

Subordinating Conjunctions

after	*as long as*	*if*	*than*	*when*	*while*
although	*as soon as*	*in order that*	*though*	*whenever*	
as	*because*	*since*	*unless*	*where*	
as if	*before*	*so that*	*until*	*wherever*	

Beware Words like *after, as, since, before,* and *until* are sneaky critters. They look like subordinating conjunctions, but sometimes they function as prepositions that begin phrases, not clauses. Remember, a prepositional phrase always begins with a preposition and ends with a noun or pronoun.

> **After much debate**, *the senators voted to make the daisy the state flower and fonse-caea pedrosoi the state fungus.*

After begins the prepositional phrase *after much debate.*

> **After Hailey quit biting her nails**, *she began chewing on screws.*

After is a subordinating conjunction that begins the adverb clause, *after Hailey quit biting her nails.* The subject of the clause is *Hailey,* and the verb is *quit.* Just in case you're wondering, *biting her nails* is a gerund phrase that functions as the direct object of the clause.

Punctuation Pointer

When an adverb clause begins a sentence, it should be followed by a comma:

After Noah's boa escaped, it swallowed Uncle Opie's bowling trophy.
When Toby probed his nose, he found a dozing two-toed toad.

Exercise 3

Now see if you can find the adverb clauses in these sentences, along with the word each clause modifies:

1. Because Fireman Myron tried to put out a fire with a hair dryer, he was fired.

2. When Tom kept thumping on his tom-toms, his annoyed little brother promptly stomped on them.

3. Mitsy mumbles and mutters because she's always eating peanut butter.

4. Donald ducked as soon as he saw the hockey puck, but it still stuck between his teeth.

5. Phil filled his truck with mud before he made a mountain out of a molehill.

6. Daisy is dazed for days whenever she sees her daisies dancing like crazy.

7. Wynn wins every game of gin because he's a swindler.

8. Because Bob can't swim, he bobs.

9. Rose uses a flexible hose because she grows her roses in circles, not rows.

10. When Stan is actually dancing, people think he's just standing.

11. Whenever Muffy muffs the muffins, they have no fluff.

12. As long as Pen has a penchant for chewing on pens, his dentist will be stupendously rich.

13. Bea's annoying bees are always beeping when they should be buzzing.

14. Because of Cy's size, he often looks people in the shins and not the eyes.

15. While libations were served to the librarians, Libby ad-libbed a speech advocating liberal jail sentences for people with overdue books.

The Noun Clause

The last, but not least, type of clause is the *noun clause*. Noun clauses pop up in places where you would expect to find nouns or pronouns. The noun clause might fill the position of a *subject*, a *direct object*, an *indirect object*, an *object of the preposition*, or a *predicate nominative*. This type of clause usually begins with some of the same pronouns that begin adjective clauses:

> who   whoever   whom   whomever   that   what   whatever

These pronouns often (but not always) function as subjects or objects of the clauses they begin.

Whoever ate that piece of fudge actually swallowed a pudgy bug.

The clause *whoever ate that piece of fudge* is the subject of the sentence. The pronoun *whoever* is also the subject of its own clause.

One finding of the Highway Commission revealed that 67 percent of all roadkill is due to squirrel hazing.

The clause *that 67 percent of all roadkill is due to squirrel hazing* is the direct object of the verb *revealed*. The pronoun *that* functions only to introduce the clause.

The winner is whoever picked the lottery numbers 2, 6, 7, 15, 29, 6, 204, 907, 3, 22, 1, 18, 30, 405, 92, and 508.

The clause *whoever picked the lottery numbers 2, 6, 7, 15, 29, 6, 204, 907, 3, 22, 1, 18, 30, 405, 92, and 508* is the predicate nominative of the sentence, and the pronoun *whoever* is also the subject of its own clause.

Sometimes adverbs start noun clauses:

> when   where   whether   why   how

For the science fair, Eldridge demonstrated how to make furniture polish out of earwax.

The clause *how to make furniture polish out of earwax* is the direct object of the sentence.

Exercise 4

Now try to identify the noun clauses in these sentences. Also, decide the clause's function in the sentence: *subject (S), direct object (DO), indirect object (IO), object of the preposition (OP), predicate nominative (PN), or toad (T). (Just kidding about the last one.)*

1. Oh, dear, I think that Ben has been eating beans again.

2. "I don't know why I got an F on my history report about the 1588 English defeat of the giant Spanish Armadillo," groaned Peabody.

3. Little Broderick gave whoever attended his birthday party a box of rocks.

4. Whoever is competing in the district carp toss should report to the practice field immediately before the equipment spoils.

5. Crazy Uncle Custard always tells stories about what he learned when he worked as a human cannonball.

6. "My philosophy is that people in glass houses should wear at least a twenty-five SPF sunscreen," said Francine.

7. After viewing the police artist's sketch, Toby learned with great embarrassment that his assailant was a tubby dachshund.

8. Whoever walks by will slip and slide where Dillon spilled juice from the pickle jar.

9. Siskel will do whatever it takes to become a licensed phrenologist.

10. Explorers have discovered that cannibals in isolated jungle areas feast on finger food.

11. Fiona has learned that finger puppetry is a very difficult occupation.

12. To her parents' dismay, little Amy announced that she wants to grow up to be a potted plant.

13. Tad saw that his tadpole had grown a tad moldy, so he sold it.

14. Stoey tells whoever will listen stories about trout.

15. To cut calories, Odetta decided that she would quit licking gummy envelopes.

Exercise 5

Now it's time for the clause grand finale! Pick out all of the clauses in the following sentences. (Some sentences have more than one, by the way.) But wait! That's not all. Also, identify each clause as adjective (adj), adverb (adv), noun (n), or (ant) antitranssubstantiative. Just kidding. Antitranssubstantiative isn't a choice. As a matter of fact, it's not even a word.

1. Semore saw more after he found his contact on the floor.

2. Horatio has overprotective parents who cover him in bubble wrap whenever he goes out to play.

3. Mitt faced a terrible dilemma when his mother told him to quit being a quitter.

4. Mrs. Dewir's parrot experienced a close call when it gagged on a feather ball.

5. If dogs could dress their owners up, would they make them wear hair suits?

6. Orlick keeps ticks that he plans to give as gifts in tiny boxes made of sticks.

7. Before you eat, you should always check catfish for fleas, Aretha.

8. Lester was stressed after his stress-ball factory failed.

9. People who sell plastic food containers should periodically burp their bowls.

10. How many trees could a woodchuck chuck if a woodchuck were a duck?

Sentence Structure

Now that your brain is clogged with clauses, it's time for some instruction on structure. *Sentence structure* refers to the number of independent and subordinate clauses in a sentence. There are four types of sentence structure: *simple, compound, complex,* and *compound-complex.*

Simple

A *simple sentence*, simply put, has only one independent clause and no subordinate clauses.

Billy ate.

This sentence is a short, no-frills independent clause. It contains a subject, *Billy*, a verb, *ate*, and it's a complete idea. Don't be fooled, though; a simple sentence can be long and involved if you spiff it up with little extras. For example, you could add:

a compound subject,

Billy and Bartholomew ate.

a compound verb,

Billy and Bartholomew sat and ate.

a complement, such as a direct object,

Billy and Bartholomew sat and ate a bug.

a few one-word adjectives,

Billy and Bartholomew sat and ate a large, squirming, yellow-spotted black bug.

and a phrase (or two or three).

In the backyard, Billy and Bartholomew sat and ate a large, squirming, yellow-spotted black bug for an after-dinner snack.

Even though this sentence is longer than *Billy ate*, it's still, believe it or not, a simple sentence because it still just contains one independent clause and no dependent clauses. It just has a lot of added details. Can you tell which of the following is a simple sentence?

A slug swallowed Billy.

A giant, slithering, slimy slug swallowed Billy and his friend Biff and spit them out like a couple of pieces of flavorless gum.

Okay. Trick question. As you probably know, both are simple sentences. The second one has an extra verb (*spit*) and a couple of extra direct objects (*Biff, them*), along with some adjectives and prepositional phrases. But the longer one still only contains one independent clause. The clause is just gussied up a little.

The moral of this story is that sentence structure has nothing to do with length. It refers to the number and types of clauses.

Compound

A *compound sentence* consists of two independent clauses joined by a coordinating conjunction (*for, and, nor, but, or, yet, so*), or by a semicolon if the clauses are closely related.

> *Little Buford misunderstood his parents' lecture on the birds and the bees, so now he believes he's a larva.*

Two independent clauses are joined by the coordinating conjunction *so*.

> *Binky is known as an original thinker; he convinced his friends to play square around the daisies.*

Two independent clauses are joined by a semicolon instead of a conjunction.

Beware Don't confuse a compound sentence with a compound subject or verb (or both).

> *The dapper Mr. Kopple toppled out of his window and flopped into a pothole.*

This is a simple sentence because it has just one independent clause. It has a compound verb: *toppled, flopped*. To have a compound sentence, though, you must have a sentence (independent clause) on both sides of a conjunction or semicolon. By adding a subject to the last part of the sentence, you can create a compound sentence.

> *The dapper Mr. Kopple toppled out of his window, and **he** flopped into a pothole.*

Punctuation Pointer

A comma is generally necessary before the coordinating conjunction in a compound sentence. If the independent clauses in the sentence are really, really short, though, no comma is necessary.

> *Sally's feet fit her new sandals, but her toenails are too long.*
> *The catfish purred and the shark barked.* (Because the independent clauses are really short, no comma is necessary.)

Complex

A *complex sentence* consists of one independent clause and one or more dependent clauses.

On Halloween, Mrs. Willingham gave every child who knocked at her door a candied yam.

On Halloween, Mrs. Willingham gave every child a candied yam is the independent clause. The dependent clause is *who knocked at his door.* It's an adjective clause modifying the noun *child* to be exact. In this sentence, you actually have a dependent clause smack dab in the middle of an independent clause. Absolutely amazing! It doesn't take much to get an English teacher excited.

Nora worried when her date took her to a seafood restaurant and ordered bait.

The independent clause is *Nora worried.* The dependent clause, *when her date took her to a seafood restaurant and ordered bait*, is an adverb clause modifying the verb *worried.* Notice that the dependent clause actually contains two, count 'em, two verbs: *took* and *ordered.* Absolutely astounding!

When Tammy tampered with the child proof aspirin cap, she twisted so hard that she threw out her back.

This sentence has two adverb clauses: *When Tammy tampered with the child-proof aspirin cap*, which modifies the verb *twisted*, and *that she threw out her back*, which modifies the adverb *hard.*

Compound-Complex

A *compound-complex sentence* contains at least two independent clauses and at least one dependent clause.

Salvador thought that he was becoming a werewolf, but he discovered that he was simply suffering from a glandular disorder.

The two independent clauses are *Salvador thought*, and *he discovered.* These are fancied up with two dependent clauses: *that he was becoming a werewolf* and *that he was simply suffering from a glandular disorder.*

Dee and Leif played on the seesaw, but when Dee stepped off, she saw a falling Leif.

The two independent clauses are *Dee and Leif played on the seesaw* and *she saw a falling Leif.* The dependent clause is *when Dee stepped off.*

Exercise 6

Classify each of the following sentences by structure: simple (s), compound (c), complex (cx), or compound-complex (c-cx).

1. Aunt Harriet carefully crafts her cat's hair balls into lovely cardigans.

2. Everyone knows that Mr. Potato Head knows his noses.

3. Mr. Potato Head has taught Tater, his tot, to be polite whenever he meets an older tuber.

4. Because Tallulah is always on her toes, her arches have fallen.

5. In the bat of an eye, Iris's false eyelash factory failed because the lash-making machine went on the blink, and no one could think how to fix it.

6. Dudley purchased a car without the frills, but he soon decided that it needed a steering wheel.

7. Ironically, Norman can't walk and chew gum, but he can hop and eat lamb chops.

8. Verne was alarmed to discover that his doctor learned brain surgery through a cut-rate correspondence course.

9. A sitting duck has better luck if it learns to duck.

10. Small birds can't chirp when they're burping.

Exercise 7

Now try to identify each sentence's type (use the abbreviations in Exercise 6), and, just for fun, see if you can find the anagram in each sentence. (An anagram is a word that has the same letters as another word, but the letters are arranged differently. Example: ladybug/bald guy or stinker/tinkers)

1. Miles smiles when he eats limes, unless they're covered with slime.

2. Each of the rats that was dying to be a star auditioned for the pest control commercial.

3. For sweet dreams, Shaneika eats a pan of brownies before she takes a nap.

4. When Norma becomes bored on the farm, she dresses her goats in togas, and she pretends that they're Roman.

5. Aunt Sylva believes Elvis lives because she thinks that she saw him on a commercial for Levis.

6. Fritz said that he loves to spit olive pits, but he hates to eat turnip tips.

7. In prehistoric times, dust mites ruled the world and lured dinosaurs to their deaths.

8. When aliens with long capes landed their space ship in a neighborhood in the South, a child gave out a shout because his TV burned out.

9. A busy monkey with no time to dine will sometimes stop at a fast-food restaurant and order ticks on a stick.

10. Aunt Bertha steps on bugs and clobbers pests that swarm around her pot of cobbler as it warms on the top of the stove.

Sentence Variety

So what's the big deal about sentence structure? Why is it important? Well, sometimes you can add a little variety to your writing by varying your sentence types.

Your writing might have too many short sentences. These sound choppy. They can be annoying. They can also be hard to read. The reader always has to stop and start. The writing doesn't flow. The reader's eyes are caught in stop-and-go word traffic. The eyes have to slam on the brakes at every period. The reader gets reading whiplash. All of the sentences might also start the same. They might all begin with the subject. This type of sentence sounds monotonous. This type of sentence suffers from the dreaded Spot Syndrome. (Remember those books for beginning readers? *See Spot run. Spot is a dog. Spot runs fast.*)

On the other hand, some sentences might be too long and complicated because they have too many subordinate clauses, along with an abundance of different kinds of phrases, such as prepositional and participial, that cloud the main idea and make the sentence hard to follow, so that by the time the reader reaches the end of the sentence, he or she, no matter how intelligent, has forgotten the main point of the sentence.

In other words, by varying the structure, beginnings, and lengths of your sentences you can add clarity and eliminate monotony.

Short sentences, and even sentence fragments, at times can be very effective for emphasis.

Zelda plopped on the couch after a relaxing hot shower. Her parents would be out until 1:00 a.m., and she had the house to herself. Nestled into the cushions and munching on popcorn with the intensity of a hyperactive woodchuck, she watched, wide-eyed and mesmerized, as an axe-bearing maniac chased across the TV screen after two terrified teens in a field of tall corn. Minute after terrible minute of gory teen fatalities passed until Zelda could bear the bloodshed no longer and clicked with a frantic finger to an infomercial for an amazing new acne cream.

Her heart and munching rates soon returned to normal as she watched before and after pictures of once pimply people whose pocks had been cured for a mere $19.95 (plus ship-

ping and handling). After fumbling with buttery fingers for a pen, she wrote the toll-free number on the palm of her hand for future reference. Then she heard it. At the window. First a sound. A terrible scratching sound. Then a cry. A terrible tortured cry for help . . .

Long sentences can also be effective for a different kind of emphasis.

Winora wanted to hide behind the stack of canned goods in the corner of the grocery store. Her mother had ordered her to the store to pick up a few things for dinner, and she was stuck with having to take her little brother with her.

"Having a driver's license isn't so great after all," she mumbled, pushing her cart down the cereal aisle while Timmy trailed behind asking for every item that contained a nanogram of sugar. "This is just great. I'll probably see someone I know, and, like always, my spoiled brat I-want-this-I-want-that little brother looks like a walking garbage dump. His nose is runny and his hair is greasy and his sandals are muddy and his toenails are cruddy, and his neck is grimy and his ears are waxy and his pants are torn and his shirt is sweaty and his socks are moldy and he sniffles and snorts and whines and cries, and if he doesn't stop picking his nose, I'll die."

The key is, everybody together now, V-A-R-I-E-T-Y. (I always longed to be a cheerleader back in my high school days. Unfortunately, I have the coordination of a dying June bug.) Variety in your writing makes it more exciting!

In the following story, all of the sentences start in the same way—with a subject. Also, most of the sentences are simple. Only a few sentences contain subordinate clauses. These poor paragraphs are just crying out for help.

Virginia arrived home from school one afternoon. She found on the kitchen table an invitation to a Halloween party. It had come in the mail from her friend Abagail.

"I have to find a costume," she said to her mother. "What should I be?" She and her mother thought and thought. They talked of many possibilities. . . .

Let's leave Virginia behind for just a moment. . . .

The day of the party arrived. Virginia's friend Abagail was the hostess with the most-est. She and her parents had decorated their living room to look just like a haunted house. Cobwebs, weighted down by huge fuzzy spiders, hung from the ceiling. Bats with mechanical wings dangled from the chandelier. In addition, a bloody, limp hand (fake, of course) protruded from behind a plant stand.

Abagail wore a witch's mask. It hid a pimple growing on her nose. She also wore a tattered black dress, a black pointed hat, and black fishnet hose.

Her guests donned all sorts of costumes. Vinnie was dressed like a vampire. He wore fangs and a flowing black cape.

Abagail inquired, "Why did you decide to be a vampire, Vinnie?"

Vinnie replied, "Well, I thought my fangs would hide my tooth. I chipped it last week when I fell on the playground." Then Vinnie tried to eat a tostada covered in bean dip. His fangs were in the way. The dip dribbled down his lip.

Abagail greeted Elanore next. Elanore stumbled through the door wearing huge boots and a way-big hat.

"I like your costume," said Abagail. "Why did you decide to be a cowgirl?"

Elenore picked herself off the floor. She was slightly rankled. She said, "Well, I thought these boots would hide my fat ankles."

The doorbell rang again. This time Abagail greeted Guinivere. She wore pointy ears and pointy shoes. She also wore green velveteen pajamas.

"Your costume is so detailed," admired Abagail. "Why did you decide to be an elf?"

Guinivere replied, "Well, my real ears stick out. These elf ears hide them. I hope you don't mind. It's hard for me to hear. Could you shout?"

Abagail took a sip of punch. Her glass stuck to her long witch's nose and hung down to her chin. Then the doorbell rang again. She opened the door, and Virginia (back in the picture now) stood before her.

"Hi, Virginia," welcomed the hostess, with a glass stuck to her nose. She was shocked to see that Virginia wasn't wearing a costume. She wore just a simple frock. "Oh, dear, didn't you know? Everyone is incognito."

Virginia replied, "Well, I thought and thought, you see. Then I finally decided who I really want to be. I decided I want to be me."

Abagail said, "Oh, but what's that spot on your cheek?"

"This," said Virginia, "is a birthmark. You have to look at it at just the right angle. Then you see that it's shaped like a beautiful spangle. I decided to show it off. I painted it red for everyone to see. I don't want to hide it by wearing a mask or by putting a sheet on my head."

All of the guests that night flocked to talk to Virginia. (She was easy to find because her birthmark glowed in the dark.) She felt good inside. That's because she had nothing to hide.

Moral: Being a witch, a vampire, a cowgirl, or an elf is good. Being yourself is better.

Now take a look at the revised (and, I might add, improved) version. Some sentences now begin in different ways, and some of the sentences have been combined into compound, complex, and compound-complex ones:

When Virginia arrived home from school one afternoon, she found on the kitchen table an invitation to a Halloween party that had come in the mail from her friend Abagail.

"I have to find a costume," she said to her mother. "What should I be?" She and her mother thought and thought of all of the possibilities. . . .

Let's leave Virginia behind for just a moment. . . .

The day of the party arrived, and Virginia's friend Abagail was the hostess with the mostest. She and her parents had decorated their living room to look just like a haunted house. Cobwebs, weighted down by huge fuzzy spiders, hung from the ceiling; bats with mechanical wings dangled from the chandelier; and a bloody limp hand (fake, of course) protruded from behind a plant stand.

Abagail wore a witch's mask that hid a pimple growing on her nose, along with a tattered black dress, a black pointed hat, and black fishnet hose.

Her guests donned all sorts of elaborate costumes. Vinnie was dressed like a vampire with fangs and a flowing black cape.

"Why did you decide to be a vampire, Vinnie?" Abagail inquired.

"Well," replied Vinnie, "I thought my fangs would hide the tooth I chipped last week when I fell on the playground." Then Vinnie tried to eat a tostada covered in bean dip, but his fangs were in the way, and the dip dribbled down his lip.

Next, Abagail greeted Elanore , who wore huge boots and a cowboy hat, as she stumbled through the door.

"I like your costume," said Abagail. "Why did you decide to be a cowgirl?"

"Well," said Elenore, picking herself off the floor, slightly rankled, "I thought these boots would hide my fat ankles."

"I see," replied Abagail, though she didn't really.

Once more the doorbell rang, and Abagail greeted Guinivere, who wore pointy ears, pointy shoes, and green velveteen pajamas.

"Your costume is so detailed," admired Abagail. "Why did you decide to be an elf?"

"Well," said Guinivere, "these elf ears hide my real ears, which stick out. But with these things on, I don't hear well, so could you please shout?"

Just as the doorbell rang again, Abagail took a sip of punch, and her glass stuck to her long witch's nose and hung down to her chin. When she opened the door, little Virginia, back in the picture now, stood before her with a grin.

"Hi, Virginia," welcomed the hostess, with a glass stuck to her nose. She was shocked to see that Virginia wasn't wearing a costume, just a simple frock. "Oh, dear, didn't you know? Everyone is incognito."

"Well," responded Virginia, "I thought and thought, you see, about who I really want to be, and I really want to be—just me."

"Oh," said Abagail, "but what's that spot on your cheek?"

"This," said Virginia, " is a birth-mark. If you look at it at just the right angle, it's shaped like a beauti-ful spangle. To show it off, I painted it red, instead of hiding it by wear-ing a mask or putting a sheet on my head."

That night all of the guests flocked to talk to Virginia (who was easy to find because her birthmark glowed in the dark), and she felt good inside because she had nothing to hide.

Moral: Sometimes, it's better to be yourself than to be a witch, a vampire, or an elf . . . even if it is Halloween.

Exercise 8

See if you can turn the following story, which definitely has some major sentence structure and sentence beginning problems, into one that flows more smoothly. Try combining short choppy sentences into compound, complex, and compound-complex ones. Also, try to get rid of the Spot Syndrome (See Spot run. Spot is a dog. . . .) by beginning some sentences with phrases and clauses, instead of subjects. Don't forget to punctuate.

Squiggy was walking in the forest one evening. He stumbled upon a strange black lamp hidden beneath some fallen leaves. It looked like one he had seen in a storybook. He rubbed the side of it. A genie appeared, lo and behold, before his very eyes. The genie spoke in a booming voice. He said that he would grant Squiggy one wish. Squiggy thought about asking for world peace. He decided, instead, to wish for lots of cash. The genie, unfortunately, was slightly hard of hearing. He thought Squiggy had asked for a huge mustache. Hair suddenly and miraculously sprouted from above the shocked boy's upper lip and streamed down to his feet. Squiggy was very disappointed, needless to say. He walked home. The journey was difficult. Squiggy felt hogtied. He tripped along as the hair wrapped around his legs and ankles.

He finally arrived home in his very hairy condition. His mother was cooking dinner. She was irritated that he was late. She told him to bathe. Then she told him to shave and go to his room and stay. Squiggy thought in his room that night about the valuable lesson his adventure had taught him. He muttered to himself as he rubbed a soothing gel on the bumps on his razor-burned face, "Life isn't always predictable. You can ask for cash. Instead, you might get a rash."

The End

Disclaimer: Authors don't always follow the above conventional wisdom to vary sentences. When it comes to long sentences, for example, William Faulkner is a champion, a king of clauses:

Now he could hear his father's stiff foot as it came down on the boards with clocklike finality, a sound out of all proportion to the displacement of the body it bore and which was not dwarfed either by the white door before it, as though it had attained to a sort of vicious and ravening minimum not to be dwarfed by anything—the flat, wide, black hat, the formal coat of broadcloth which had once been black but which had now that friction-glazed greenish cast of the bodies of old house flies, the lifted sleeve which was too large, the lifted hand like a curled claw.

from "Barn Burning"

And, of course, if you're a Hemingway, starting all of your sentences with subjects is a sign of brilliance:

They *sat together at a table that was close against the wall near the door of the cafe and looked at the terrace where the tables were all empty except where the old man sat in the shadow of the leaves of the tree that moved slightly in the wind. A **girl** and a **soldier** went by in the street. The **street light** shone on the brass number on his collar. The **girl** wore no head covering and hurried beside him.*

from "A Clean, Well-Lighted Place"

So, the bottom line is that if you happen to be famous, you can pretty much write however the heck you please. But, you've got to learn the rules before you break them. Such is life.

7

Fragments and Run-Ons

Sentence Fragments

In Texas we have a saying: "all hat, but no cattle." Translation: a hat doesn't make someone a cowboy. Revised a little, this idea could apply to a sentence fragment—all period, but no sentence. Translation: a period doesn't make a group of words into a sentence. Sometimes, for example, a word group lacks a subject and/or verb. It might be simply a phrase or dependent clause. To be complete, a sentence must meet three simple criteria. Without any one of these three components, a sentence is a measly wannabe, a mere imposter.

1. It must contain a subject.

2. It must contain a verb.

3. It must be a complete thought.

   Take a look:

   Like bowling balls. (phrase)
   Playing the oboe. (phrase)
   When stylish cats tap dance. (dependent clause)

None of these groups of words is a complete thought (and the first two contain neither a subject nor a verb). Each needs something more to make it a complete idea.

*Curled up armadillos slowly rolled across the road **like bowling balls.*** (sentence)

*Zack is able to multi-task by juggling curled up armadillos with both hands and **playing the oboe** with his toes.* (sentence)
***When stylish cats tap dance**, they always wear colorful pants.* (sentence)

On the other hand, you might have to take out a word to make a complete thought.

*Tish **who** fries large catfish in her satellite dish.* (fragment)
Tish fries large catfish in her satellite dish. (sentence)

The vampire ***that*** ate a rare steak on his lunch break. (fragment)
The vampire ate a rare steak on his lunch break. (sentence)

Note: A true sentence won't begin with the words *"Like when"* or *"Such as when."* These words are sure-fire signals of sentence fragments.

Incorrect: *Stetson spends too much money on his pets. Like when he gave his cat an herbal body wrap to remove its excess fat.*
Correct: *Stetson spends too much money on his pets. For example, he gave his cat an herbal body wrap to remove its excess fat.*

Incorrect: *Fritz takes things too literally. Such as when he wears protective togs when it's raining cats and dogs.*
Correct: *Fritz takes things too literally. For example, he wears protective togs when it's raining cats and dogs.*

Exercise 1

Try your hand at defragging. Look at the following fragments. Change them to sentences by either adding words or cutting words out.

1. Like when hawks squawk.

2. Large-boned toads that don't float.

3. Children who chew with food in their mouths.

4. Because Cooter wears a shrimp suit.

5. Soggy dogs that frolic in bogs.

6. Twiddling your thumbs.

7. Gabbing about flabby baboons.

8. Such as when lizards hiss.

9. Before Mortimer eats more lumpy porridge.

10. Like snorkeling in Jell-O.

11. Delighted by a bright firefly.

12. Because Buzzy's sweater is covered with fuzz.

13. When snails see salt shakers.

14. Rodeo clowns that frown.

15. Around babbling babies.

Run-On Sentences

Sometimes sentences run together because they're missing a period. One of these period-deprived sentences is called, strangely enough, a run-on. Take a look:

Brutus missed his bus he had to ride a drooling mule to school.
You can fix this run-on sentence in a few different ways.

Brutus missed his bus; he had to ride a drooling mule to school.
(separate closely related sentences with a semi-colon)

Brutus missed his bus, so he had to ride a drooling mule to school.
(connect sentences using a coordinating conjunction—*for, and, nor, but, or, yet, so*—*preceded by a comma.*)

Because Brutus missed his bus, he had to ride a drooling mule to school.
(put a less important idea in a dependent—a.k.a. subordinate—clause)

Brutus missed his bus; therefore, he had to ride a drooling mule to school.
(use a semi-colon and a transitional word such as *however, nevertheless, moreover, or consequently,* followed by a comma to connect sentences.)

Exercise 2

See if you can correct the following groups of words that have sentence fragment and sentence run-on issues.

Example: *Chase annoys his teachers. Like when he erases the board with his face.*

Answer: *Chase annoys his teachers when he erases the board with his face.*

1. Cecil amused the class. Like when he put breath mints up his nose.

2. My bus driver who acts like she's crazy. Such as when she playfully drives toward pedestrians.

3. Trace thinks that space aliens hide in many places. For example, inside of the small intestines of hamsters.

4. Darlene needs dental work she eats ice she also chews on broomsticks and marbles.

5. Elvira has many talents. Such as yodeling and finger painting with vegetable extracts.

6. Fat cats that eat chocolate rats.

7. Corintha who is slightly clumsy. She always trips over air.

8. Some self-conscious warthogs get nose jobs they think that good looks will gain them more friends.

9. It's dangerous to drive on the freeway. Especially when you're blindfolded.

10. Aunt Tallulah talks to her tulips she also puts party hats on her petunias.

Exercise 3

Rewrite the following groups of words so that they are grammatically correct. If there are no mistakes, write <u>C</u> for <u>correct</u>.

1. Doritha has many beauty secrets. Such as bathing in mayonnaise for softer skin. Also, scrubbing her hair with sandpaper to remove the oily build up.

2. Uncle Herbert is famous for many things. For example, for inventing the plastic tips on shoelaces.

3. Otis always smells good. Because of the odor eaters beneath his armpits.

4. Fleas and ticks on steroids jump as high as tall buildings, and some even weigh up to twelve pounds.

5. Because Freda won the porcupine riding contest. She received a trophy of a golden quill, along with a box of bandages.

6. After he ate a pound of licorice. Larry dreamed that he was attacked by the Tooth Fairy.

7. If you swallow an apple seed, a tree will grow in your stomach if you swallow a piece of gum, it will stick to your ribs or lodge in your pancreas.

8. My English teacher who is a genius. She has a brain the size of a cantaloupe.

9. Vinnie who has strong lips. Because he plays musical instruments. Such as the tuba.

10. Some witches add extra eyeballs and newts to their brew to make it more gooey.

Note: Of course, as you might have expected, sometimes authors break the rules and use fragments for effect, to add emphasis:

Mrs. Elmo's hair sprouted in prickly gray clumps from her white onion-skin scalp, and her face looked like a prune that had been micro-waved on high. Above her lip protruded a mole. **A really big mole. A really big, hairy mole. A mole about the size of ... well, a mole ... the kind that digs.**

In English, the bottom line is this: the only rule without exception is that every rule has an exception.

Usage

8

Subject-Verb Agreement

Even when you were just a young whippersnapper, you realized that certain words fit together, and certain words didn't. You knew, for example, that a sentence like "I are a genius" isn't right because the pronoun *I* doesn't fit with the verb *are*. Instead, you were more likely to say "I am a genius" (thus proving the statement).

Now here's another one of those annoying grammar rules: the subject and verb must agree in number. Putting the right verb with the right subject is known as *subject-verb agreement*.

I'm sure you know that if a noun is *singular* in number, it refers to one person, place, thing, or idea; and if a noun is *plural* in number, it refers to more than one.

Did you know that a verb, like a noun or pronoun, can be singular or plural? Sure enough.

With a noun, you normally form the plural by adding *-s* or *-es*. Verbs, however, don't follow this pattern. Plural verbs don't end in *-s* or *-es*. Instead, the number of the verb is determined by whether its *subject* is singular or plural. A verb is singular if it takes a singular subject, and it's plural if it takes a plural subject.

Singular subject	Singular verbs	Plural subject	Plural verbs
The tarantula	*drools*	*The tarantulas*	*drool*
	stalks		*stalk*
	pounces		*pounce*

Notice that a verb generally forms its singular and plural just the opposite way a noun does. Most *singular* verbs end in -s or -es, and most *plural* verbs don't.

FYI Most verbs have the *same* form for the singular and plural in the *past tense*.

singular: *The baby burped.*   singular: *The roly-poly bug squiggled.*
plural: *The babies burped.*   plural: *The roly-poly bugs squiggled.*

Putting the right subject with the right verb is usually a matter of choosing the words that sound correct together.

Wrong: *Ludwig's earlobes **is** long.*
Right: *Ludwig's earlobes **are** long.*

Wrong: *Rude cows **moos** while they **is** chewing their food.*
Right: *Rude cows **moo** while they **are** chewing their food.*

Sometimes, though, you might encounter some tricky situations. Occasionally a sentence *sounds* correct, but it is grammatically incorrect because the subject doesn't agree with the verb. Can you find the errors in these sentences?

Wrong: ***Each** of the children **have** curly hair.*
Wrong: ***Every one** of Ida's fingernails **are** painted with rare and expensive squid dye.*

In situations such as these, it's difficult to judge by sound.

Right: ***Each** of the children **has** curly hair.*
Right: ***Every one** of Ida's fingernails **is** painted with rare and expensive squid dye.*

If you couldn't find the subject-verb agreement errors in the wrong sentences (and even if you could), here are some rules to help prevent nasty agreement accidents.

1. The agreement of a verb with its subject is not changed by interrupting words. Ignore those pesky prepositional phrases and other groups of words when determining the correct verb to use with a subject.

    Incorrect: ***One** of the bees outside my window **are** humming catchy Broadway show tunes.*

Correct: **One** of the bees outside my window **is** humming catchy Broadway show tunes.

Ignore *of the bees* and *outside my window*. These are prepositional phrases that just muddy the water. Without them, you can easily see that the subject is *one*, and, therefore, the correct verb is *is*.

A **bag** of sausages, together with a canned ham, always **makes** a lovely wedding gift.
Horatio, along with several of his friends, **suffers** from ingrown toenails.

2. When subjects are joined by *or, nor, either/or,* or *neither/nor*, the verb agrees with the closer subject.

Either a demented mole **or** jumbo **earthworms are** digging holes in the garden.

Neither Bubba **nor** his **brothers trim** their nose hair.

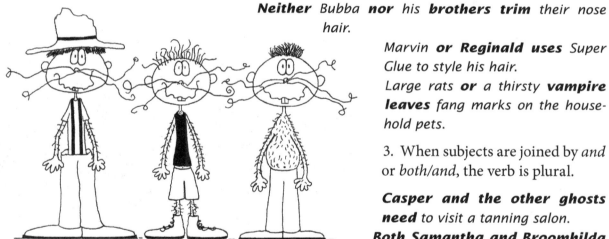

Marvin **or Reginald uses** Super Glue to style his hair.
Large rats **or** a thirsty **vampire leaves** fang marks on the household pets.

3. When subjects are joined by *and* or *both/and*, the verb is plural.

Casper and the other ghosts need to visit a tanning salon.
Both Samantha and Broomhilda play the tuba with their toes.

4. Watch out for indefinite pronouns! The following pronouns are always singular. They're tricky! When used as a subject, each of these requires a singular verb.

Singular Indefinite Pronouns

anybody	nobody	everybody	somebody	each	neither
anyone	no one	everyone	someone	either	one

One of the werewolves ***shaves*** *with a Super Gillette double-blade razor.*
Neither *of the space aliens **needs** glasses.*

5. These pronouns are plural. When one of these is used as a subject, it requires a plural verb.

Plural Indefinite Pronouns

both   few   many   several

Many *of the vicious squirrels **pelt** acorns at unsuspecting joggers along the bike path.*
Several *of the Boy Scouts **are** roasting plump, juicy possums over the campfire.*

6. These pronouns can be either singular or plural, depending on the word to which each refers. These pronouns are weird. You might actually need to look inside of a prepositional phrase for help in determining whether one of these is singular or plural.

all   any   most   none   some

Most *of the **underwear is** covered with hearts and happy faces.*
Most *of the Jockey **shorts are** pressed and starched.*

7. Use a singular verb with a collective noun thought of as a unit. Use a plural verb with a collective noun thought of as individuals.

*The **committee is** planning a National Reptile Day parade.*

The members are working together as one unit, so *committee* is singular.

*The **committee are** unable to decide who should wear the papier-mâché gila monster costume.*

The members have different opinions. Since they're not united as a unit but instead are thinking as individuals, *committee* is plural. You might say that the word *"members"* is understood here, as in *committee members.*

8. A word expressing an amount, measurement, or weight is usually considered singular.

Two thousand dollars is *the cost of Omar's snarky aardvark.*
Four tenths *of the world's population **uses** roll-on deodorant.*

9. Some nouns like *mathematics, economics, news,* and *measles* end in *-s* and look plural, but they're really singular.

   Mathematics is *difficult for crickets, aphids, and not-quite-bright ticks.*

10. Titles are singular, even if they look plural.

    The Attacks of the Killer Artichokes is *a spine-chilling movie.*
    The Trials and Tribulations of Petey the Paranoid Parakeet is *a thought-provoking* novel.

11. *Here* or *there* is never the subject of a sentence. To determine if the subject agrees with the verb in a sentence that begins with *here* or *there*, reword the sentence.

    Wrong: *There's mice frozen in the ice cubes.*

    If you rephrase this sentence, the agreement problem is pretty obvious.

    Mice is frozen in the ice cubes (there).

    Yuck, now it's easy to see that the subject, *mice*, doesn't agree with the verb, *is*.

    Right: *There **are mice** frozen in the ice cubes.*

12. To determine whether a subject agrees with the verb in a question, reword the question into a statement.

    Wrong: ***Does lizards*** *have gizzards?*

    By changing the question into a statement, you can easily see a problem.

    Lizards does *have gizzards.*

    Uggh. Subject-verb surgery is definitely needed here.

    Right: ***Do lizards*** *have gizzards?* Much better!

Exercise 1

Okay, it's show time! See if you can find the errors in agreement in the following letter. Write the incorrect word followed by the correction. A correction will sometimes involve changing more than one word. If a sentence doesn't contain an error, write C.

Dear Abby,

[1]I'm writing to you because my mother, along with my dad and my brother and my sister and my pet parakeet, are driving me crazy! [2]Neither my mom nor my dad understand me. [3]Last night we had a big fight because I want to get my nose pierced, but my parents won't let me. [4]What's the big deal about one little hole in my face? [5]My boyfriend Broderick, along with my best friend Lola, have nose and tongue piercings that look very cool. [6]I've known Broderick for almost two weeks, so he and I has a serious relationship. [7]Neither my mother nor my dad get it, though. [8]They say that Broderick and Lola is telling me what to do. [9]I'll be fourteen in February, and every one of my friends, along with, I think, maybe one of my teachers, say I'm very mature and intelligent for my age. [10]I can make my own decisions. [11]I told my parents that I want to be an individual, and, besides, everyone I know have gotten something pierced. [12]Then I asked my mom, "If they can have stuff pierced, why can't I?" [13]Now I'm grounded for the whole weekend for talking back. [14]How can I convince my mom and my dad to stay out of my life, except when one of them want to take me shopping? [15]Broderick and I really appreciates your help.

Sincerely,

An Individual Who Just Wants to be Like Her Friends

Exercise 2

Choose the correct verb in parentheses for each sentence.

1. To wake up, Bennie and Bernie (counts, count) sheep backwards.

2. Either Bart or Verne (do, does) cartwheels on windowsills.

3. To save face in the office, Doreen, along with Bernstein, (use, uses) the copy machine.

4. Either the cook or the waitresses (plan, plans) to quit because customers keep giving them orders.

5. Either deep-fried hairless honeybees or a large, bright red flea (add, adds) color and flavor to unseasoned vegetable soup.

6. Because what goes around comes around, Hermie, together with Hannah, always (wear, wears) a helmet.

7. Every day for lunch, either Livingston or Lucretia (order, orders) buffalo wings and bison toes to go.

8. Crazed grasshoppers or maniacal mosquitoes ferociously (attack, attacks) the slightly hairy legs of unsuspecting joggers.

9. In some wealthy neighborhoods, jumbo rats or a fat alley cat (feed, feeds) on scraps of broiled ostrich.

10. Flint, usually followed by his friends Brent and Trent, (march, marches) to the beat of a different percussion instrument.

11. Because Buffy and Buttercup (wear, wears) too much makeup, (her, their) eyelids are always stuck shut.

12. Because Aunt Lulu, together with Cousin Uma, (love, loves) frou-frou, (she, they) always (wear, wears) flowery muumuus.

13. Due to the risk of inflicting serious injury upon innocent bystanders, Uncle Ichabod and Aunt Ruth never (use, uses) toothpicks.

14. To get the players' attention, one of the basketball refs at the local high school (use, uses) a tuba instead of a whistle.

15. No one (want, wants) to tell colorblind Uncle Huey that his blue suede shoes are actually a light shade of puce.

16. To prepare for the holiday season, each of the elves (is, are) undergoing stress therapy.

17. (There's, There are) some rude customers in fancy restaurants who make volcanoes out of their mashed potatoes and gravy.

18. All of the macaroni (is, are) moldy.

19. Some of those cats (is, are) really jumbo rats.

20. The city council (is, are) unable to decide on the color of the new stop signs.

21. (There's, There are) some coordinated people who can hum, chew gum, and twiddle their thumbs, all at the same time.

22. (Here's, Here are) some ducks chewing on hockey pucks.

23. Why (do, does) some wacky, obsessive packrats save dirt and stiff dead gnats?

24. Either Dave or Waverly (are, is) fascinated with donuts, tires, and lifesavers.

25. Both Huxley and Heather are animal-rights activists who (refuse, refuses) to wear clothes made of feathers.

9

Pronoun-Antecedent Agreement

Everybody knows that some things (and people) just go together (Fred and Wilma, squirrels and nuts, green eggs and ham), and some don't (Superman and kryptonite, Dorothy and flying monkeys, liver and chocolate).

The same rule holds true for *pronouns* and their *antecedents*; they have to be compatible. In other words, they have to *agree*.

A quick review: An *antecedent* is the word to which a pronoun refers.

Heathcliff always takes his SPF 200 sunscreen with him to the beach.

In this sentence, *Heathcliff* is the *antecedent* to the pronouns *his* and *him*.

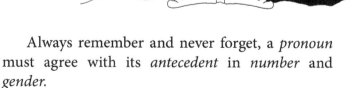

Always remember and never forget, a *pronoun* must agree with its *antecedent* in *number* and *gender*.

Wrong: *The **children** brushed **his** teeth.*

The pronoun, *his*, and its antecedent, *children*, don't agree because *children* is plural, but *his* is singular.

Right: **The children brushed their teeth.**

All right! Now the plural pronoun, *their*, matches its plural antecedent, *children*.

Wrong: **Wilma curled his eyelashes.**

Okay, the problem here is pretty obvious. Considering that *Wilma* and *his* are referring to the same person, then the pronoun, *his*, doesn't match its antecedent, *Wilma*, in gender.

Right: **Wilma curled her eyelashes.**

Here are a few little rules to help you through (or complicate) life.

1. These indefinite pronouns are singular. Therefore, be sure that words referring to pronouns on this list are also in the singular form.

Singular Indefinite Pronouns

anybody	*nobody*	*everybody*	*somebody*	*each*	*neither*
anyone	*no one*	*everyone*	*someone*	*either*	*one*

The tricky thing about pronoun-antecedent agreement is that the wrong way often sounds right. Take a look:

Incorrect: **Everyone** *should give* **their** *pennies to the Society to Help Nerdy Birds Become Socially Acclimated (SHNBBSA).*

This sentence sounds correct because people generally talk this way. However, the plural pronoun, *their*, doesn't agree with its singular antecedent, *everyone*. (Notice that *everyone* is on the list of common singular indefinite pronouns.)

If you're writing formally, you would need to correct the sentence in one of two ways: Either replace the singular antecedent, *everyone*, with a plural one; or replace the plural pronoun, *their*, with a singular one.

> Correct: **People** *should give* **their** *pennies to SHNBBSA.*
> Also correct: **Everyone** *should give* **his or her** *pennies to SHNBBSA.*

FYI When I was growing up back in the good old days, it was considered correct to use a masculine pronoun to refer to an indefinite pronoun of unknown gender. (**Everyone** *should give* **his** *pennies to SHNBBSA*). Things have changed, though, and today this practice is considered by many people to be sexist. To stay politically correct, you need to use the more awkward, but less sexist **his/her** and **he/she**.

2. Important! Ignore those pesky little prepositional phrases. The prepositional phrase does not alter the number of the antecedent.

> Wrong: **Each** *of the girls has lice in* **their** *hair.*

> Right: **Each** *of the girls has lice in* **her** *hair.*

Ignore the prepositional phrase *of the girls*. Then you can see that *each*, a singular indefinite pronoun, is the antecedent of *their*, a plural pronoun. Because one is singular and the other is plural, they don't agree.

> Wrong: **Neither** *of the boys wears* **their** *antiperspirant.*

> Right: **Neither** *of the boys wears* **his** *antiperspirant.*

Ignore the prepositional phrase *of the boys* and you can see that *neither*, a singular indefinite pronoun, is the antecedent of *their*, a plural pronoun. Because one is singular and the other plural, they don't agree.

3. Use a singular pronoun when referring to singular antecedents joined by *or* or *nor*.

Wrong: *Neither **Dudley nor Arnold** shaved **their** mustaches.*
Right: *Neither **Dudley nor Arnold** shaved **his** mustache.*

Wrong: ***Either Milly or Muffy** brings **their** pet python to class.*
Right: ***Either Milly or Muffy** brings **her** pet python to class.*

4. The following pronouns are plural. Therefore, be sure that pronouns referring to them are also plural.

Plural Indefinite Pronouns

  several   few   both   many   others

Several *of the students fed **their** spotted guppy.*
   *Others groomed **their** piranhas.*

5. Use a plural pronoun when referring to antecedents joined by *and*.

Trudy and Minny *permed **their** poodle.*
*The **shop teacher and the zookeeper** are missing several of **their** fingers.*

6. Use a plural pronoun when referring to plural antecedents joined by *or* or *nor*.

    Neither the Smiths nor their neighbors exterminated **their** roaches.

    Either the fire eaters or the sword swallowers forgot **their** throat lozenges.

7. These pronouns can be either singular or plural, depending on the meaning of each in the sentence. Unlike other indefinite pronouns, with each of these you *do* need to refer to the phrase after the pronoun to determine the pronoun's meaning.

    all   *any*   *most*   *none*   *some*

    Some of the **liver** lost **its** flavor.
    Some of the **players** laced **their** sneakers.

Exercise 1

See if you can find and correct the mistakes in agreement in these sentences. Write the incorrect word, followed by the correction. Just to make things more fun, some sentences are correct. (For these, write C.)

Example: *The dog, along with the cat, are gobbling a rat.*
Answer: *are—is*

1. A child who sticks raisins up their nose often has difficulty breathing.

2. Both Amber and Iris hope to become wealthy after they sell thousands of their solar-powered nail files.

3. Neither Frankenstein nor Dracula signs autographs for their fans.

4. In a fierce competition, one of the female mud wrestlers broke their nail.

5. Every one of the Boy Scouts gave his father a Popsicle stick tie for Father's Day.

6. All of the seven dwarfs perspire profusely while they do their work.

7. Semore, along with Dunkin, flunked the tornado drill because they stopped, dropped, and rolled, instead of dropped, sat, and tucked.

8. Neither Pixie nor Trixie could fix her potato fritter mixer, so she nixed it.

9. Goober, together with his brother Stew, surprised Mary Lou by playing "Happy Birthday to You" on their electric kazoo.

10. Huey and Louie gained fame by publishing their haiku about shoes.

Exercise 2

See if you can find and correct the mistakes in agreement in the following story. Watch out. Not every sentence contains a mistake. Write the incorrect word followed by the correct one. Write C if the sentence is already correct.

Wormville, U.S.A.

[1]The tiny town of Wormville, the earthworm capital of the world, is normally a sleepy little haven where all of the residents go about their sleepy little lives. [2]Children go to their schools, their parents go to their jobs, and all of the senior citizens rock on his or her porch or works in their garden. [3]But each year on October 27, every townsperson comes alive, for they know it's time once again for the Earthworm Festival to begin. [4]The festival is a time for all of the citizens to forget their worries and celebrate their slimy friends. [5]Generally all goes smoothly, but everyone has their own special memory of the nearly disastrous occurrence at last year's celebration.

[6]On that fateful day, the townspeople assembled for their huge parade. [7]Crowds lined Main Street, and every child was decked out in their special worm costume. [8]Some costumes were made of Styrofoam, and some were made of plastic, but each child added their own splash of creativity. [9]One little girl decorated her wormwear with flowers, and a little boy decorated his with spots. [10]With giant plastic worms adorning their caps, the Boy Scouts held their kazoos and were ready to march. [11]When a whistle sounded, each boy looked over their shoulder and saw twenty-seven worm-shaped floats ready to roll, along with the Earthworm Queen smiling and waving from a flatbed truck. [12]The high school band, dressed in their new earth-toned uniforms, tuned their instruments and prepared to perform the earthworm anthem. [13]Every young person and every parent watched with their hearts racing as the mayor, in his sporty brown Cadillac with a jumbo helium-filled worm tethered to the fender, gave the signal to march. [14]The members of the band blasted their notes, and the floats began to trundle. [15]Each Boy Scout blew their kazoo, and all was well in Wormville.

[16]But not every resident of Wormville was taking part in their town's celebration. [17]No one knew that Bubba Bigby, the twelve-year-old town brat, was waiting to thwart their fun. [18]With lightning speed, he removed the cover of the biggest manhole in Wormville, and as the scouts neared the abyss, not one of them suspected that their lives were in

danger. [19]Suddenly, PLOP, squish, PLOP, squish, PLOP, squish—each scout, clutching his kazoo, dropped into the open manhole and landed waist deep in yucky muck. [20]The parade came to a screeching halt, but no one raised their voice to volunteer for the tricky-icky job of rescuing the panicked youths. [21]Neither the mayor nor the police chief wanted to dirty their suits, and both the town founder and the grocery store owner were wearing their brand-new shoes.

[22]Finally, one courageous woman, Mary Jane Lane, the local librarian, stepped forward from the crowd to bravely volunteer to rescue the scouts. [23]Each person raised their voice in joy as the heavy equipment operator helped lower their courageous librarian into the mucky gunk. [24]The benevolent lady lifted each scout with their gooked up kazoos onto her shoulders, and Fireman Dan skillfully reached down to grab each boy and pull them to safety. [25]All of the citizens showed their relief with a collective sigh. [26]Then they all raised their voices and cheered Mary Jane Lane. [27]To honor her, either Farmer Fred or Fire Chief Keith jumped up on their truck and proclaimed that, in honor of the town hero, Main Street henceforward would have a new name: Mary Jane Lane Lane. [28]In the end, Bubba Bigby got what he deserved, for the PTA and the Quilting Club accidentally ran over him with their floats, and he received serious abrasions (although not life threatening).

[29]This year on October 27, the sleepy little town will once again awaken, and every citizen will bedeck themselves in costumes and honor their slimy friend, the earthworm. [30]Town hero Mary Jane Lane, along with Bubba Bigby (who underwent a spiritual conversion after his dastardly deed), will lead the parade down Mary Jane Lane Lane, bringing joy throughout their beloved town.

And all is still well in Wormville.

The End.

10

Some Special Pronoun Predicaments

Now here's a sentence that will change an English teacher into a temporary lunatic:

Me and him don't make much noise in the band because we both play a cymbal with one hand.

Forget the fact that only someone who is acutely musically challenged would try to play only one cymbal. The problem here is with the pronouns. When pronouns are in the wrong case, people obsessed with—uhh—I mean concerned with—correct grammar turn into basket cases. So it's important to learn about cases (pronoun cases, not basket) in order to speak and write correctly.

Pronoun Cases

Case is the form of a pronoun that shows how it's used in a sentence. Pronouns have three cases: the *nominative*, the *objective*, and the *possessive*. Take a look at these sentences:

*"**I** signed up for an advanced snake charming class,"*
*said Astor, "but **my** instructor told **me** that **I** need*
to find another pastime."

I, *me*, and *my* are all pronouns that refer to the same person, but each is in a different case because each plays a different role in the sentence. *I* is a subject, *me* is a direct object, and *my* shows possession.

Here's a chart that lists the pronouns according to case:

Nominative	Objective	Possessive
I	me	my, mine
you	you	your, yours
he	him	his
she	her	her, hers
it	it	its
we	us	our, ours
they	them	their, theirs
who	whom	whose
whoever	whomever	

The bad news is that to use pronouns correctly, you really have to know this chart. The good news is that once you know this chart, you can avoid mistakes like this:

Thank you, ladies and gentlemen. Me and my costars are very grateful for this award. Them and I are humbled that we could bring the heartwarming story of Alfie the Alligator to the big screen. This is a great honor, not only for us, but also for our colleagues who couldn't appear tonight due to severe wounds them and the director suffered while filming.

Here's some information to help you prevent pronoun meltdowns.

The Possessive Case

Pronouns in the *possessive* case (*my, mine, your, yours, his, hers, its, our, ours, their, theirs, whose*) really don't require much explanation. They show possession (hence the name, *possessive* case), or in another word, ownership. You find them in front of nouns and gerunds. Remember, a gerund is a verb form that ends in ing and is used as a noun.

*Benevolent Mr. Brittlebone gives **his** kidney stones to the neighborhood kids to use as marbles.* (before a noun)

*Because Thurston takes **his** golfing seriously, he was upset when he shot a birdie, and so was the bird.* (before a gerund)

Sometimes possessive pronouns stand by themselves:

*I think the eyelash floating in the soup is **yours**.*

Unlike nouns, pronouns in the possessive case don't require apostrophes. Adding an apostrophe would be overkill since a possessive pronoun is already possessive.

Wrong: *That kung fu fighting cockatoo is **her's**.*
Right: *That kung fu fighting cockatoo is **hers**.*

The Nominative Case

A pronoun in the nominative case (*I, you, he, she, it, we, they, who, whoever*) can be a subject of a verb, or it can be a predicate nominative. That's it. Nothing else. Period. Let's look at examples of each.

Nominative Pronouns Used as Subjects

Wrong: ***Him and I** were ready to dine when the waiter brought the baked porcupine.*

The pronouns *him* and *I* fill the *subject* slot of the sentence. The problem is that the pronoun *him* is an *objective* pronoun (*me, you, him, her, it, us, them, whom, whomever*), and only *nominative* pronouns may fill subject slots.

Right: ***He and I** were ready to dine when the waiter brought the baked porcupine.*

Superb! (The pronoun usage, not the porcupine.) The objective pronoun *him* has been bounced out and replaced with the nominative pronoun *he*. Now only nominative pronouns fill the subject slot of the sentence.

Wrong: ***Brigitte and them** eat raisins, not prunes, because they hate to spit pits.*

Brigitte and *them* are the subjects of the sentence, but *them* is an objective pronoun, and only nominative pronouns may be subjects.

Right: ***Brigitte and they** eat raisins, not prunes, because they hate to spit pits.*

I know this sentence sounds a bit goofy, but remember not to pick a pronoun just because it sounds correct.

Wrong: *Uncle Otto closed his dry cleaning shop after **him** and Aunt Lotty spent twenty years on the same spot.*

This sentence contains a main clause (*Uncle Otto closed his dry cleaning shop*) and a subordinate clause (*after him and Aunt Lotty spent twenty years on the same spot*). Because *him* and *Aunt Lotty* are in the subject slot of the subordinate clause, the pronoun *him* is incorrect because it's in the objective, not the nominative case.

Right: *Uncle Otto closed his dry cleaning shop after **he** and Aunt Lotty spent twenty years on the same spot.*

Bravo! *He*, the nominative form of the pronoun, is correct because it fills the subject slot of the clause.

Wrong: *Uncle Brett is the animal rights advocate **whom** buys hats for rats that live in sunny climates.*

Whom is incorrect because it's an objective pronoun, but it's occupying the *subject* position of a subordinate clause.

Right: *Uncle Brett is the animal rights advocate **who** buys hats for rats that live in sunny climates.*

Much better. Now the nominative pronoun, *who*, fills the subject slot of the subordinate clause.

Nominative Pronouns Used as Predicate Nominatives

Nominative pronouns are not only subjects, they're also used as predicate nominatives. Remember, a predicate nominative is a noun or pronoun after a linking verb. A predicate nominative renames the subject. (*Godzilla is a jumbo **lizard**.*)

Wrong: *The winner of the one-person synchronized swimming event was **me**.*

Me is an *objective* pronoun. Since it's in a predicate nominative position, someone needs to give *me* the boot and replace it with its nominative form, *I*.

Right: *The winner of the one-person synchronized swimming event was **I**.*

Even though the correct usage of the pronoun might sound a little wacky, it really makes sense. Suppose someone asked this question:

"Who is the world-renowned expert on the history of dirt?"

And suppose someone who's well grounded in dirt knows that Bert is a dirt expert and points him out across the room. A grammatically correct answer would be this:

"The expert on dirt is he (not him).*"*

A linking verb is a little like an equal sign since the predicate nominative simply renames the subject:

expert = he

Since the subject is always in the nominative case, it makes sense that the word that's equal to the subject is also in the nominative case. As a matter of fact, if you switch the subject with the predicate nominative, the sentence still makes perfect sense. It may even sound better and eliminate awkwardness:

He (not him) *is the expert on dirt.*

To an English teacher, *"Him is the expert on dirt"* sounds like a hawk's pointy talons scratching on a blackboard, or like a cat's cough when it's hacking up a hair ball, or like a scrappy little lapdog's yapping, or like a dentist's shrill drill carving away at a tooth. Well, you get the idea.

The Objective Case

A pronoun in the *objective* case (*me, you, him, her, it, us, them, whom, whomever*) can be a direct object, an indirect object, or an object of the preposition (hence the name, *objective* case).

Objective Pronouns Used as Direct and Indirect Objects

Remember that direct objects are nouns or pronouns that come after action verbs. A direct object answers the question *whom?* or *what?* after the verb.

Jives wrestles octopi.

To find the direct object ask yourself, "*Jives wrestles what?*" The answer is *octopi.*

Wrong: *Claude saved **he and I** from a pack of vicious wiener dogs.*

In this sentence, the nominative pronouns, *he* and *I*, fill the direct object slot, but only *objective* pronouns may act as direct objects.

Right: *Claude saved **him and me** from a pack of vicious wiener dogs.*

Now the sentence is correct because objective pronouns (*him, me*) fill the direct object slot. A helpful trick is to try each pronoun individually.

*Claude saved **him** (not he) from a pack of vicious wiener dogs.*
*Claude saved **me** (not I) from a pack of vicious wiener dogs.*

Objective pronouns are also used in indirect object slots. Remember that an indirect object answers the question *to whom? for whom? to what?* or *for what?* about the direct object:

*Wilbur gave his **frog** three warts.*

To find the direct object, ask yourself, "*Wilbur gave what?*" The answer is *warts.* To find the indirect object, ask, "*Wilbur gives warts to whom? or to what?*" The answer is *frog.* The indirect object (if a sentence has one at all) will always appear *before* the direct object.

Wrong: *Ziggy gave Mimi and **I** noogies.*
Right: *Ziggy gave Mimi and **me** noogies.*

Since the pronoun in question fills an indirect object position, it has to be in the objective case. The pronoun *me* is an objective pronoun, so it's correct. Once again, if you use the pronoun by itself in the sentence, it's easy to see the correct answer.

*Mimi gave **me** a noogie.*

If you said, "Mimi gave **I** a noogie," you would sound like a real knucklehead (get it? noogie? knucklehead? never mind . . .)

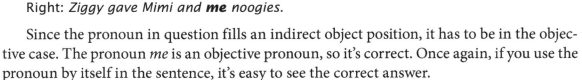

Objective Pronouns Used as Objects of the Preposition

A quick refresher course: The object of a preposition is the noun or pronoun that ends a prepositional phrase. (*A tick is on your **lip**.* The object of the preposition *on* is *lip*. See p. 75) A pronoun acting as an object of a preposition must be in the *objective* case.

Wrong: *The person **who** Godfrey was hobnobbing with has a little glob of slobber running down his chin.*

This sentence really has two problems. First, the preposition *with* is just standing by its lonesome when it *should* be starting a phrase. (Remember, a preposition always, always, always begins a phrase that ends in a noun or pronoun.) Second, once *with* is moved to where it belongs, *who* is in the object of the preposition slot, but it's a nominative pronoun.

Right: *The person with **whom** Godfrey was hobnobbing has a little glob of slobber running down his chin.*

Now it's easy to see that *with* is the preposition and *whom* is the object of the preposition.

Wrong: *Just between **you and I**, Cousin Delbert believes he's a parakeet.*
Right: *Just between **you and me**, Cousin Delbert believes he's a parakeet.*

Here you have a compound object of the preposition, and both pronouns need to be in the objective case (*you* and *me*), otherwise you'll fowl up. (Pun intended.)

Wrong: *According to **she** and Darius, that new hoity-toity restaurant serves its steaks too rare.*

The pronoun *she* and the noun *Darius* are objects of the compound preposition, *according to*. *She* is a nominative pronoun intruding into an objective slot.

Correct: *According to **her** and Darius, that new hoity-toity restaurant serves its steaks too rare.*

Now an objective pronoun correctly fills the object of the preposition position.

Exercise 1

It's time to test your pronoun prowess and choose the correct pronoun(s) in each sentence.

1. All of (us, we) neighbors know that when Irene travels to Tahiti in spring, she freezes her pets for safekeeping.

2. Dody told (him and me, he and I, him and I) to eat the toad-toe soup that was simmering on the stove.

3. (Him and me, He and I, Him and I) suggested that Aunt Ester see a therapist because she was obsessed with finding a word to rhyme with *orange*.

4. (Us, we) musicians were shocked to hear that Talula and (he, him) were booted out of band because neither could toot a lute.

5. Pearl and (her, she) surprised (him and me, he and I, him and I) by dressing up as squirrels.

6. A manufacturer hired Hector and (I, me) to be pocket-protector product inspectors.

7. After Tanner and (he, him) were stranded on a desert island, they discovered that they were allergic to sand.

8. Borack and (I, me) are going crazy because the neighbors' yak won't stop yakketty yakking.

9. Dweezle is our cousin (who, whom) believes he's being stalked by a pack of screeching monkeys.

10. (Homer and she, Homer and her) were excited to see an elf on their shelf, until they learned it was only a gnome on a tome.

Little Men

Exercise 2

Now see if you can help Muffy, who remains severely grammatically challenged, by picking the correct pronouns.

My Crush by Muffy Margaret Moppleberry

A crush, in my mind, is a strong feeling that someone like you or (me, I) has for another person. I remember that in seventh grade that every other girl in school and (I, me) had a crush on this guy. His name was Tony, and (me and him, he and I) were in the same math class. During class, (me and my best friend, my best friend and I) used to walk down the aisle and pretend we were going to sharpen our pencils just so (her and I, she and I, me and her) could stare at him. Sometimes after class, (him, he) and his football buddies would talk awhile, and then he would go to his locker, and I'd follow him. Just between (you and me, you and I), I would also try to make up excuses to get out of some of my classes. I would say I was going to the bathroom, but I would really walk by his class so I could see (he, him) and his friends talking. Once (me and my friend Darlene, my friend Darlene and I) were walking behind him in the hall, and he stopped to talk to me. While (me and Darlene, Darlene and I) were standing there, he looked right into my eyes and said, "Are you some kind of stalker?" Then I said to (he, him) and his friend, "What do I look like? A piece of celery?" This was a joke because I was referring to stalks like the ones that (us, we) vegetarians buy at grocery stores. Then he said that I was weird in this sort of affectionate way, and (he, him) and his friend walked off. He was probably in a bad mood because (he, him) and his teammates lost their game the day before. (Him and me, Him and I, He and I) are very much alike because I get in bad moods too, when my face breaks out, for example. A week later (he, him) and his family moved to Dallas, Texas. I think the phones in Dallas are messed up because (me and him, he and I, him and I) always have a bad connection, and I get cut off. (Me and Darlene, Darlene and I) are going to Dallas this summer with her family, and I'm going to try to visit him. I know (he, him) and his new friends will be happy to see me. Who knows. Someday (he and I, me and him, him and I) might be together forever.

Pronouns in Incomplete Constructions

Suppose you have a sentence like this:

Ogden lifts overweight hogs more easily than Dotty.

Now suppose you wanted to substitute a pronoun for *Dotty*. Which sentence is correct?

Ogden lifts overweight hogs more easily than she.
Ogden lifts overweight hogs more easily than her.

Okay . . . trick question. Both sentences are correct; they just mean different things. Each of these sentences ends with a subordinate clause that begins with *than*. The problem is that the clauses have parts missing, and the way you finish each clause determines the correct answer:

Ogden lifts overweight hogs more easily than she (lifts over-weight hogs).
Ogden lifts overweight hogs more easily than (he lifts) *her.* (Dotty).

Apparently plump porkers weigh less than *Dotty.*

So, with these kinds of incomplete *than* clauses, you can determine the correct pronoun by simply finishing the clause.

Wrong: *"The moldy porridge in the fridge is older than **me**," said twelve-year old Midge.*
Right: *"The moldy porridge in the fridge is older than **I** (am)," said twelve-year old Midge.*

Wrong: *Floe is planning to go to the international oboe contest in Tokyo, and no one is more ready than **her** for a solo.*
Right: *Floe is going to the international oboe contest in Tokyo, and no one is more ready than **she** (is ready) for a solo.*

Exercise 3

Now here's your chance not only to test yourself on pronoun proficiency, but to also learn some words that might be fun to slip into a conversation.

1. According to Eustacious and (her, she), when Nate's blind date announced that she was a mutated space alien, he absquatulated (absquatulate-to flee in a hurry).

2. When Mrs. Cledhopper, the neighborhood flibbertigibbet, fixed my brother and (me, I) dinner, she dropped the meatloaf in the cat litter (flibbertigibbet-a silly, scatterbrained, or talkative person).

3. Chuck and (I, me) always wear our mukluks when we hunt ducks (mukluk-a waterproof boot).

4. Bob told (we, us) and his doctor that he had swallowed a thingamabob, and he was feeling discombobulated (discombobulate-to throw into a state of confusion).

5. Smitty, a sniveling lickspittle, makes (us, we) office workers prickle when he brings the boss coffee and pumpernickel (lickspittle-a fawning underling; a flatter; a toady).

6. After the boxing match, Oscar and (he, him) had sweaty oxters (oxters-armpits).

7. Little Holly, (who, whom) is mollycoddled by the entire family, received a Lamborghini when she turned three (mollycoddle—to surround with an excessive degree of attention).

8. By (who, whom) should Uncle Hewitt sit so that his doppelganger doesn't have a fit (doppelganger-a ghostly counterpart of a living person)?

9. After the mayor and (he, him) were caught with oodles of loot in their freezer, they tried to bamboozle their way out of the ballyhoo with their flap-doodle (bamboozle-hoodwink;. ballyhoo-noisy shouting or uproar.; flapdoodle-foolish talk; nonsense).

10. When Uncle Mort's eyes are stuck shut with gound, everyone can ski better than (he, him). (gound—the icky stuff that forms in your eye when you sleep).

Unclear Pronoun Reference

Scientists have recently discovered huge parrots, and they're living off the coast of Australia on a small deserted island. Some of them are six feet tall and they have unusual diets. They are also quite intelligent, and they hope to collect the data for their future research on behalf the International Society for the Preservation of Really Big Birds (ISPRBB).

This big-bird blurb is mighty confusing because clear pronoun reference has flown the coop and is nowhere to be seen. Is the article about six-feet-tall scientists who live on a deserted isle and are quite intelligent, or is it about big, brainy parrots?

A few corrections in fuzzy pronoun reference help to clarify the message:

Scientists have recently discovered huge parrots that are living off the coast of Australia on a small deserted island. Some of the birds are six feet tall, and they have unusual diets. These giant parrots are also quite intelligent, and scientists hope to collect the data for their future research on behalf of the International Society for the Preservation of Really Big Birds (ISPRBB).

Here are a few simple rules to make your pronoun reference clearer:

1. The pronoun *who* refers to people and animals with names. The pronouns *which* and *that* refer to animals and things. *That* can also refer to people in anonymous groups.

   *Broderick, **who** won the art contest with his imaginative sculpture of a rock, received a lifetime supply of chicken stock.*

   *After a debate **that** lasted days, the senators decided to clean up their states by passing gum control legislation.*

   *I think the new law **that** requires pedestrians to wear helmets and padding will result in lots of sweaty people in the southern states.*

   *The people **that** (or **who**) are planning to stop procrastinating have decided to wait until tomorrow. (People is an anonymous group.)*

2. Make sure that a pronoun refers to one specific antecedent. (Remember that an *antecedent* is a word to which the pronoun refers.)

Confusing: *As Erlene and her mom were driving along,* **she** *swerved into a ditch to avoid flattening a frolicking squirrel.*

Does the pronoun *she* refer to Erlene or her mom?

Better: *As Erlene was driving along with her mom in the car, she swerved into a ditch to avoid flattening a frolicking squirrel.*

3. Make sure that the pronouns *which* and *that* refer to *definite* antecedents.

Confusing: *Thadeus didn't get much sleep before participating in the National Spelling Bee, and he forgot the seventh i in* floccinaucinihilipilification, *which made him really mad at himself.* Was Thadeus mad about his sleep deprivation, or his sudden memory loss?

Better: *Thadeus didn't get much sleep before participating in the National Spelling Bee. and he was mad at himself for forgetting the seventh i in* floccinaucinihilipilification.

Confusing: *"Vincent, the boy next door, picks fights with everyone," said little Squiggy. "Last week he left stink bombs by all of the neighbors' doors. Sometimes he steals kids' lunch money.* **That's** *why my mom won't let me play with him."*

Does the pronoun *that* refer to Vincent's penchant for bullying, stink bombs, or theft?

Better: *"Vincent, the boy next door, picks fights with everyone," said little Squiggy. "We go to the same school, but he doesn't ride my bus. Last week he left stink bombs by all of the neighbors' doors. Sometimes he steals kids' lunch money. Because he's a creep, my mom won't let me play with him."*

4. Make sure *it* and *they* refer to specific antecedents.

When we talk, we use idioms like "It's raining," or "It's about time." These types of expressions have just become accepted. Sometimes, though, *it* without a clear antecedent pops up too many times in the same sentence.

Informal: *"*It *said on TV that* it's *going to rain today," announced inane Aunt Maimy, "so I cut a hole in the roof so* it *will drain."*

Formal: *"The weatherman forecasts rain for today," announced inane Aunt Maimy, "so I cut a hole in the roof so the water will drain."*

Informal: *If* it *doesn't rain,* it *will be fun when all of the relatives get together to decorate the traditional holiday cactus with colorful fruits and vegetables.*

Formal: *If it doesn't rain (or if the weather is clear), getting together with all of the relatives to decorate the traditional holiday cactus with colorful fruits and vegetables will be fun.*

Sometimes the pronoun *they* pops up as a sort of catch-all indefinite pronoun for a nameless, faceless antecedent.

Informal: *"I called the Beef O Rama," sputtered Lombard, "and asked **them** to deliver five triple-sized lump-of-beef burgers with double cheese and a diet drink, but **they** never came."*

Formal: *"I called the Beef O Rama," sputtered Lombard, "and ordered the delivery of five triple-sized lump-of-beef burgers with double cheese and a diet drink, but my food never arrived."*

5. In formal essay writing, students often misuse the pronoun *you*. Always keep your audience in mind. If your audience expects formality—as many English teachers do—then be sure that you use the pronoun *you* to mean *you, the reader*. (Sorry about all of the *you*s in the preceding sentence.)

Informal: *When **you're** walking on a circus tightrope with a marsupial on **your** head, **you** should always hold **your** arms away from **your** body to keep **your** balance.*

The problem here is pretty obvious. *You* should refer to *you, the reader*, so unless the reader is an acrobat (and, personally, I never plan to walk a tightrope, and I've never had the urge to balance a marsupial on my head), the sentence needs to be reworded.

Formal: *When an **acrobat** is walking a circus tight rope with a marsupial on his or her head, the performer should extend his or her arms for balance.*

FYI Replacing *you* with the nonsexist *he/she* or *his/her* can become awfully awkward, especially in lengthy papers. Sometimes you can avoid this problem by using plural references. The following paragraph is mighty awkward.

*When a person walks down a sidewalk of a seemingly peaceful neighborhood, **he or she** should be aware of hidden dangers. Many times things fall from trees and can cause serious damage to the head of an unsuspecting pedestrian. When **his or her** guard is down, **he or she** might be hit by a branch, a pine cone, or—the most devastating culprit—a falling squirrel. For this reason a person should always wear a helmet when **he or she** goes strolling.*

Now, check out the revised version.

*When people walk down sidewalks of seemingly peaceful neighborhoods, **they** should be aware of hidden dangers. Many times things fall from trees and can cause serious damage to the heads of unsuspecting pedestrians. When **their guards are** down, **they** might be hit by branches, pine cones, or—the most devastating culprits—falling squirrels. For this reason, people should always wear helmets when **they** go strolling.*

6. Be sure that a pronoun is close to its antecedent.

Confusing: *Thadeus told his friends, "The best part of the movie was the scene where the giant grapefruit people from outer space were rolling really fast down the hill, and the townspeople were running in front of them, trying to escape with their lives. Then **they** couldn't stop and they ran into a huge cement wall, and **their** insides splattered all over the place."*

Hmm . . . Were seeds and pulp splattered everywhere, or did the poor townspeople suffer a rather horrible fruit-induced fate?

Better: *Thadeus told his friends, "The best part of the movie was the scene where the giant grapefruit people from outer space were rolling really fast down the hill, and the townspeople were running in front of them, trying to escape with their lives. Then the townspeople jumped aside, but the grapefruit people couldn't stop. They hit a huge cement wall, and their grapefruit insides splattered all over the place."*

Exercise 4

The following sentences have pronoun problems (or perhaps I should be more politically correct and say pronoun *issues*). Rewrite each sentence to make the pronoun reference clearer. Some sentences might require some major tinkering. You might have to add words, take away words, and/or shuffle a few words around.

1. "I like going to English class because there you can catch up on your sleep," said Harley. (author's note: Harley, no doubt, will someday fall into a life of crime.)

2. Cindy Lou's little brother always borrows her Barbie dolls and uses them for sling shot practice, which makes her cry.

3. When you have a job as an elevator operator, you have to be ready for the ups and downs.

4. For job security, the tooth fairy placed a bag of jawbreakers and a piece of taffy under little Wilbur's pillow, and he found it there in the morning.

5. After work, Mrs. Doobledorfer, boiled the water, put up the groceries, chopped up the chicken, let the cat in and dropped it in the pot to simmer for several hours.

6. During dinner, Uncle Beamer kept coughing on the roast beef and sneezing in his tea, and that made me queasy.

7. Nadine wakes up at 2:30 every morning to do her hair and nails so that she can be at work by eight, which she hates.

8. Marguerite and her girlfriends always swim around man-eating sharks because they know they won't devour them.

9. In school, they always tell you to wear clothes.

10. Milly called Molly to announce that she was dating her old boyfriend again.

11

Tense About Verbs?

Verbs tenses and moods need not make you tense and moody. This chapter explains some of the verb basics: *parts of the verb, tenses, mood,* and some *special problems.*

Principal Parts of the Verb

An ample worm wiggled out of Latimer's apple.

Every verb has four principal parts: *present, present participle, past,* and *past participle.* The four principal parts of the verb *wiggle,* for example, look like this:

Present	*wiggle*
Present Participle	*(is) wiggling*
Past	*wiggled*
Past Participle	*(have) wiggled*

Regular Verbs

Regular verbs form their past and past participles by adding *-d* or *-ed.* The four parts of regular verbs follow these basic patterns:

1. The **present** is the no-frills base form of the verb.

    squeak   yodel   babble

FYI When the base form is preceded by *to*, it's called the *infinitive* form (*to squeak, to yodel, to babble*).

2. The **present participle** ends in *-ing*. When the present participle is used as a part of the verb, it shows continuing action, and it always follows a helping verb (a present form of *be*).

> *(is) squeaking   (is) yodeling   (is) babbling*

3. The **past** ends in *-d* or *-ed*.

> *squeaked   yodeled   babbled*

4. The **past participle**, like the past form, ends in *-d* or *-ed*. Unlike the past form, the past participle, when used as a verb, always follows a form of the verb *have*, which acts as a helping verb.

> *(have) squeaked   (have) yodeled   (have) babbled*

FYI Present and past participles don't actually function as verbs unless they follow helping verbs. Instead, they might function as adjectives that are simply called *participles*. (See p. 81.)

> A ***rolling*** (participle) *stone gathers no moss, but it collects a lot of dirt.*
>
> ***Frustrated*** (participle) *students tried for hours to make origami fruit flies.*

A present participle that doesn't follow a helping verb might also function as a noun known as a *gerund*.

> ***Wearing*** (gerund) *shoelaces way-too-long can be dangerous for people and pets.*

Here are the four principal parts of some regular verbs:

Principal Parts of Some Common Regular Verbs

present	present participle	past	past participle
chortle	*(is) chortling*	*chortled*	*(have) chortled*
dabble	*(is) dabbling*	*dabbled*	*(have) dabbled*
doodle	*(is) doodling*	*doodled*	*(have) doodled*
flutter	*(is) fluttering*	*fluttered*	*(have) fluttered*

present	present participle	past	past participle
gawk	(is) gawking	gawked	(have) gawked
giggle	(is) giggling	giggled	(have) giggled
gobble	(is) gobbling	gobbled	(have) gobbled
jiggle	(is) jiggling	jiggled	(have) jiggled
mutter	(is) muttering	muttered	(have) muttered
nibble	(is) nibbling	nibbled	(have) nibbled
scratch	(is) scratching	scratched	(have) scratched
skip	(is) skipping	skipped	(have) skipped
sniffle	(is) sniffling	sniffled	(have) sniffled
sputter	(is) sputtering	sputtered	(have) sputtered
tattle	(is) tattling	tattled	(have) tattled
twitch	(is) twitching	twitched	(have) twitched

Irregular Verbs

Some goofy verbs, wouldn't you know, don't always fit the mold. A verb that forms its past or past participle in an *irregular* way is called, surprisingly, an *irregular* verb. Here are some of the gazillions of irregular verbs:

Principal Parts of Some Common Irregular Verbs

present	present participle	past	past participle
begin	(is) beginning	began	(have) begun
bid	(is) bidding	bid	(have) bid
bite	(is) biting	bit	(have) bitten or (have) bit
blow	(is) blowing	blew	(have) blown
buy	(is) buying	bought	(have) bought
bring	(is) bringing	brought	(have) brought
burst	(is) bursting	burst	(have) burst
catch	(is) catching	caught	(have) caught
come	(is) coming	came	(have) come
cost	(is) costing	cost	(have) cost
cut	(is) cutting	cut	(have) cut
dive	(is) diving	dived or dove	(have) dived
do	(is) doing	did	(have) done

present	present participle	past	past participle
draw	(is) drawing	drew	(have) drawn
dream	(is) dreaming	dreamed or dreamt	(have) dreamed or (have) dreamt
drive	(is) driving	drove	(have) driven
drink	(is) drinking	drank	(have) drunk
eat	(is) eating	ate	(have) eaten
fall	(is) falling	fell	(have) fallen
feel	(is) feeling	felt	(have) felt
find	(is) finding	found	(have) found
fly	(is) flying	flew	(have) flown
freeze	(is) freezing	froze	(have) frozen
get	(is) getting	got	(have) got or (have) gotten
give	(is) giving	gave	(have) given
go	(is) going	went	(have) gone
grow	(is) growing	grew	(have) grown
hold	(is) holding	held	(have) held
hurt	(is) hurting	hurt	(have) hurt
hit	(is) hitting	hit	(have) hit
know	(is) knowing	knew	(have) known
lose	(is) losing	lost	(have) lost
leave	(is) leaving	left	(have) left
lead	(is) leading	led	(have) led
let	(is) letting	let	(have) let
make	(is) making	made	(have) made
meet	(is) meeting	met	(have) met
pay	(is) paying	paid	(have) paid
prove	(is) proving	proved	(have) proven
put	(is) putting	put	(have) put
ride	(is) riding	rode	(have) ridden
rise	(is) rising	rose	(have) risen
run	(is) running	ran	(have) run
say	(is) saying	said	(have) said
see	(is) seeing	saw	(have) seen
set	(is) setting	set	(have) set
sew	(is) sewing	sewed	(have) sewn
shake	(is) shaking	shook	(have) shaken

present	present participle	past	past participle
show	(is) showing	showed	(have) shown
shrink	(is) shrinking	shrank	(have) shrunk
sing	(is) singing	sang or sung	(have) sung
sink	(is) sinking	sank or sunk	(have) sunk
sleep	(is) sleeping	slept	(have) slept
slide	(is) sliding	slid	(have) slid
spit	(is) spitting	spat	(have) spat
speak	(is) speaking	spoke	(have) spoken
spring	(is) springing	sprang or sprung	(have) sprung
stand	(is) standing	stood	(have) stood
steal	(is) stealing	stole	(have) stolen
swim	(is) swimming	swam	(have) swum
ring	(is) ringing	rang	(have) rung
take	(is) taking	took	(have) taken
tell	(is) telling	told	(have) told
throw	(is) throwing	threw	(have) thrown
win	(is) winning	won	(have) won
wear	(is) wearing	wore	(have) worn
write	(is) writing	wrote	(have) written

Exercise 1

Now see if you can find the incorrect verb in each of in the following sentences. Write the correct form of each incorrect verb. If a sentence is correct, write C.

1. When Graham swimmed in Amsterdam, he rammed into a dam.

2. Wellington has recently sang a bouncy song about Ping-Pong.

3. Last night Otis dreamt about croaking toads.

4. Instead of eating his tomatoes for supper, Tupper drunk a bottle of ketchup.

5. Cousin Nell, who always pretends she's a pail, has fell into the well.

6. Hank's bloated goldfish has sank to the bottom of the tank.

7. Nate always wears deodorant on dates.

8. The play has been postponed because all of the actors have broke their legs.

9. Paddington has never wrote with a new pencil because he believes it would be pointless.

10. Look! The Easter Bunny has came and left lots of tasty tofu!

Verb Tense

Time is a very important concept, and it's been the subject of many great philosophers. As Groucho Marx once said, "Time flies like an arrow; and fruit flies like a banana"; and, of course, who can forget the words of the great philosopher Kermit the Frog: "Time flies when you're eating flies."

In the world of verbs, time is conveyed by *tense*. Every verb has six tenses: *present, past, future, present perfect, past perfect,* and *future perfect.* Let's look at each one.

1. The **present tense** simply refers to action that's happening in the present.

   *Moe **swallows** minnows.*
   *Dee **dreams** about bucktoothed ducks.*

2. The **past tense** refers to an action that took place in the past and ended in the past.

   *Moe **swallowed** a minnow.*
   *Dee **dreamed** about bucktoothed ducks last night.*

3. The **future tense** indicates action that will take place at some time in the future. It requires the helping verb *shall* or *will*.

   *Moe **will swallow** a minnow.*
   *Dee **will dream** about bucktoothed ducks.*

FYI *Shall* has almost become a dinosaur (the shallasaurus?); you don't hear it spoken much. Nowadays it sounds a little highfalutin. (*I shall call the waiter, for my sushi is crawling.*) It's used with the pronouns *I* and *we*, and you hear this construction occasionally in polite or formal situations.

4. The **present perfect tense** consists of *has* or *have* used as a helping verb, followed by the past participle. This tense has a confusing name. Even though it's called the *present* perfect, it actually refers to action that has happened in the *past*. It's a shade different from just the plain past tense, though, because it indicates that the action occurred at an *indefinite* time in the past:

*Moe **has swallowed** minnows on several occasions.*
*Dee **has dreamed** about bucktoothed ducks many nights.*

The present perfect can also refer to action that began in the past but still continues:

*Moe **has eaten** minnows all day.* (He began eating them earlier, and he's still eating them.)
*Dee **has dreamed** about bucktoothed ducks for the past six years.* (She began dreaming about them six years ago, and she's still dreaming about them. I guess she's quacking up).

5. The **past perfect tense** uses the helping verb *had* followed by the past participle. This tense is a little tricky. It refers to something that happened in the past before some point of time or some other action in the past. I guess you can say it's the pre-past tense.

*Moe **had swallowed** twelve minnows before he had to sing the national anthem.* (He sang the anthem in the past, and he swallowed the minnows *before* that time in the past.)

*Dee **had dreamed** about ducks twelve times by morning.* (Morning occurred earlier, and Dee dreamed about the quackers *before* that time in the past.)

6. The **future perfect tense** should really be called the pre-future tense. It indicates an action (that happens in the past, present or future) that is completed before some other time or action in the future. It's formed by using *will have* or *shall have*, followed by the past participle.

*Moe **will have eaten** 1,756 minnows by Friday.* (He began eating in the past or present, and he will finish eating in the future—on Friday.)
*Dee will begin dreaming about ducks tonight, and she **will have dreamed** (or **dreamt**) about thousands of her feathery friends by morning.* (She will begin dreaming about ducks in the future—*tonight*, and she will finish dreaming about them before another time in the future—*morning*.)

Since minnows and ducks are getting a little old, let's use the different tenses to discuss Finnegan's growth spurt:

*Finnegan **grows** several inches each year.* (present)
*Finnegan **grew** two inches last fall.* (past)
*Finnegan **will grow** two inches this fall.* (future)
*Finnegan **has grown** several inches since last fall.* (present perfect)
*On the first day of school, Finnegan's friends were flabbergasted to see that he **had grown** a foot over the summer.* (past perfect—Finney's friends were flabbergasted in the past, and he began growing before that time in the past.)
*By the time he starts college, Finnegan **will have grown** several feet, and he will need to shop for fashionable footwear.* (future perfect—Finney starts college in the future, and he will stop growing in the future before that time.)

Now let's look at Maddie's bad habit:

*Maddy always mistakenly **vacuums** up the cat.* (present)
*Yesterday Maddy mistakenly **vacuumed** up the cat.* (past)
*Maddy probably **will vacuum** up the cat again tomorrow.* (future)
*Maddy **has** mistakenly **vacuumed** up the cat for years.* (present perfect—She began vacuuming up the cat in the past, and she continues sucking up the feline in the present.)
*Maddie vacuumed up the doormat after she **had** accidentally **vacuumed** up the cat.* (past perfect—Maddie vacuumed up the doormat [in the past], and she vacuumed up the cat [before that time in the past].)

*By the end of next year, Maddy **will have** mistakenly **vacuumed** up the cat 2,746 times.* (future perfect—The end of the year occurs in the future, and Maddie will have vacuumed the cat 2,747 times before that future time.)

Conjugating Verbs

Let's take a moment to concentrate on conjugating. To *conjugate* a verb simply means to list or recite the verb as it's used in first, second, and third persons singular and plural in the six tenses. The conjugation of a typical verb like *wobble*, for example, looks like this:

Present Tense

Singular

I wobble
you wobble
he, she, or it wobbles

Plural

we wobble
you wobble
they wobble

Past Tense

Singular

I wobbled
you wobbled
he, she, or it wobbled

Plural

we wobbled
you wobbled
they wobbled

Future Tense

Singular

I will wobble
you will wobble
he, she, or it will wobble

Plural

we will wobble
you will wobble
they will wobble

Present Perfect Tense

Singular

I have wobbled
you have wobbled
he, she, or it has wobbled

Plural

we have wobbled
you have wobbled
they have wobbled

Past Perfect Tense

Singular

I had wobbled
you had wobbled
he, she, or it had wobbled

Plural

we had wobbled
you had wobbled
they had wobbled

Future Perfect Tense

Singular

I will have wobbled
you will have wobbled
he, she, or it will have wobbled

Plural

we will have wobbled
you will have wobbled
they will have wobbled

The verb *be* has a conjugation that's weird even among irregular verbs. It's a species unto itself:

Present Tense

Singular	Plural
I am	*we are*
you are	*you are*
he, she, or it is	*they are*

Past Tense

Singular	Plural
I was	*we were*
you were	*you were*
he, she, or it was	*they were*

Future Tense

Singular	Plural
I will be	*we will be*
you will be	*you will be*
he, she, or it will be	*they will be*

Present Perfect Tense

Singular	Plural
I have been	*we have been*
you have been	*you have been*
he, she, or it has been	*they have been*

Past Perfect Tense

Singular	Plural
I had been	*we had been*
you had been	*you had been*
he, she, or it had been	*they had been*

Future Perfect Tense

Singular	Plural
I will have been	*we will have been*
you will have been	*you will have been*
he, she, or it will have been	*they will have been*

Exercise 2

Check time! See if you can identify the tenses of the underlined verbs in these sentences. Write the letter of the correct tense.

a) present   b) past   c) future   d) present perfect   e) past perfect   f) future perfect

1. Covington <u>has</u> always <u>entertained</u> himself on elevators by talking to the passengers with his lovable hand puppet.

2. Nine out of ten doctors <u>recommend</u> frequent hand washing, and one out of the ten dies of an infectious disease.

3. Before last year, Mona <u>had</u> never <u>been</u> on a date, but one time she did stand on a raisin.

4. Toby <u>has</u> always <u>played</u> tic-tac-toe with his toes.

5. Last week Tiff miffed Cliff because she <u>had said</u> that he smelled like a fish.

6. Yesterday, Hazel the witch <u>mixed</u> witch hazel and basil to cure her postnasal drip.

7. By next year, Cooper <u>will have made</u> oodles of loot by selling his super-duper pooper scooper.

8. Walter <u>will</u> always <u>waffle</u> when he orders breakfast.

9. Muffy's scruffy earmuffs <u>look</u> like two mangy mutts.

10. For several weeks the neighbors <u>have seen</u> Zigby taking his dog for a walk and his snake for a slither.

11. Little Hue <u>will ask</u> his teacher if it's true that centipedes need one hundred shoes.

12. Perpetually positive Patty <u>has</u> never <u>had</u> a bad hair day; she has only had an occasional twenty-four hour follicle challenge.

13. Louise <u>shaved</u> her Pekinese's knees because they were covered with fleas.

14. Because Templeton's elephant <u>has developed</u> a pimple, he made an appointment with a pachydermatologist.

15. Double-jointed Cousin Zack <u>claps</u> backwards.

Exercise 3

In this passage from *James and the Giant Peach* by Roald Dahl, the author relies on the past perfect tense to describe the scene. He tells of an incident in the past—the chaotic scene inside of the peach—and uses the past perfect tense to describe the events that occurred before that incident in the past. In other words, the past perfect describes the pre-past. List the past perfect verbs you see in each sentence. (Hint: Some sentences have none, and some have more than one.)

¹At this moment the scene inside the peach was one of indescribable chaos. ²James Henry Trotter was lying bruised and battered on the floor of the room amongst a tangled mass of Centipede and Earthworm and Spider and Ladybug and Glow-worm and Old-Green Grasshopper. ³In the whole history of the world, no travelers had ever had a more terrible journey than these unfortunate creatures. ⁴It had started out well, with much laughing and shouting, and for the first few seconds, as the peach had begun to roll slowly forward, nobody had minded being tumbled about a little bit. ⁵And when it went BUMP! and the Centipede had shouted, "That was Aunt Sponge!" and then BUMP! again, and "That was Aunt Spider!" there had been a tremendous burst of cheering all around.

Progressive Verb Forms

Now that you know the four principal parts of the verb and the six tenses, it's time to progress to the progressive form.

The progressive form of a verb isn't exactly a tense. It's . . . well . . . let's call it a condition. Each tense has a *progressive form* that's used to express ongoing action. The progressive consists of a combination of a form of *to be* followed by the present participle. (Remember that the present participle is one of the four forms of the verb. It always ends in -*ing*.)

Every verb tense has a progressive form:

present progressive	Mort ***is chortling***
past progressive	Mort ***was chortling***
future progressive	Mort ***will be chortling***
present perfect progressive	Mort ***has been chortling***
past perfect progressive	Mort ***had been chortling***
future perfect progressive	Mort ***will have been chortling***

Let's look at each progressive form:

1. The **present progressive** shows an ongoing action that is taking place now:

   *Dudley **is doodling** pictures of doodlebugs.*

2. The **past progressive** shows an ongoing action that took place in the past:

   *Dudley **was doodling** pictures of doodlebugs.*

3. The **future progressive** shows an ongoing action in the future:

   *Dudley **will be doodling** doodlebugs.*

4. The **present perfect progressive** shows an action that started in the past but is ongoing in the present:

   Dudley ***has been doodling*** *pictures of doodlebugs for years.* (He started doodling when he was younger, and he continues to doodle today.)

5. The **past perfect progressive** shows an action that took place in the past that was interrupted by another action in the past:

   *Dudley **had been doodling** pictures of doodlebugs when his English teacher asked him to conjugate a verb.*

6. The **future perfect progressive** shows a future ongoing action that will have occurred before a stated time in the future.

   Dudley **will have been doodling** doodlebugs for seventy-two hours by Friday.

Exercise 4

See if you can change the verbs in these sentences using the progressive form in parentheses:

1. Moby picks his nose with his toes. (present progressive)

2. The crabby zookeeper harangues the orangutans. (past progressive)

3. Uncle Humford hopes to make a fortune by selling recycled gum. (past perfect progressive—Caution! *Make* is not the main verb. It's part of the infinitive *to make*.)

4. Just for kicks, Derrick writes catchy limericks about ticks. (future progressive)

5. To flee stampedes of evil weasels, unstable Aunt Mable will hide under the coffee table for days. (future perfect progressive—Be careful! *Flee* is not the main verb. It's part of the infinitive *to flee*.)

6. Ella tries to balance her diet by eating chocolate and vanilla. (present perfect progressive—Be careful again! *Eating* is a gerund; it isn't the verb. Remember, if the present participle isn't preceded by a helping verb, it doesn't function as a verb.)

7. Topper hopes to sell many copies of his pop up book of the digestive system. (past progressive)

8. Some gleeful young frogs play leap people. (past perfect progressive)

9. Cubby is making a fortune with his rubber shrubbery boutique. (future progressive)

10. Margie knits warm sweaters for her cold-blooded buddies. (present progressive)

Exercise 5

The following passage from *Winnie-the-Pooh* by A. A. Milne has several examples of the past progressive. The author describes action in the past that did not occur at one specific moment in time. The progressive label shows that the past action was continuing. See if you can pick out all of the past progressive verbs in these rather long sentences. (The author uses some creative capitalization and punctuation, probably to give the writing a more childlike tone.)

Beware Remember that not all words ending in *-ing* are verbs. For an *-ing* word to be a verb, it must be preceded by a helping verb (*was blubbering, is drooling, has been sniffling*).

"Yes!" said Roo, "Look at me sw—!" and down he went over the next waterfall into another pool.

¹Everybody was doing something to help. ²Piglet, wide awake suddenly, was jumping up and down and (was) *making "Oo, I say" noises; Owl was explaining that in a case of Sudden and Temporary Immersion the Important Thing was to keep the Head Above Water; Kanga was jumping along the bank, saying "Are you sure you're all right, Roo, dear?" to which Roo, from whatever pool he was in at the moment, was answering "Look at me swimming!" ³Eeyore had turned round and hung his tail over the first pool into which Roo fell, and with his back to the accident was grumbling quietly to himself, and* (was) *saying, "All this washing; but catch on to my tail, little Roo, and you'll be all right"; and, Christopher Robin and Rabbit came hurrying past Eeyore, and were calling out to the others in front of them.*

Exercise 6

Now identify the tense of each underlined verb (including whether or not the verb is progressive) in this excerpt from *Harry Potter and the Chamber of Secrets* by J. K. Rowling. If part of the underlined verb is in a contraction, I've underlined the letters that represent the verb, for example, <u>can</u>'t <u>squiggle</u>, you<u>'re</u> <u>twiddling</u>.

The squat ghost of a girl <u>had glided</u>¹ over. She <u>had</u>² the glummest face Harry <u>had</u>³ ever <u>seen</u>, half-hidden behind lank hair and thick, pearly spectacles.

"What?" she <u>said</u>⁴ sulkily.

"How <u>are</u>⁵ you, Myrtle?" said Hermione in a falsely bright voice. "It's nice to see you out of the toilet."

Myrtle <u>sniffed</u>⁶.

"Miss Granger <u>was</u>⁷ just <u>talking</u> about you—" said Peeves slyly in Myrtle's ear.

"Just saying—saying—how nice you look tonight," said Hermione, glaring at Peeves.

Myrtle <u>eyed</u>⁸ Hermione suspiciously.

"You<u>'re</u> <u>making</u>⁹ fun of me," she said, silver tears welling rapidly in her small, see-through eyes.

"No—honestly—didn't I just say how nice Myrtle's looking?" said Hermione, nudging Harry and Ron painfully in the ribs.

"Oh, yeah—she did."

"Don't lie to me," Myrtle <u>gasped</u>¹⁰, tears now flooding down her face, while Peeves chuckled happily over her shoulder. "D'you think I don't know what people <u>call</u>¹¹ me behind my back? Fat Myrtle! Ugly Myrtle! Miserable, moaning, moping Myrtle!"

"You've forgotten pimply," Peeves hissed in her ear.

Moaning Myrtle burst into anguished sobs and fled from the dungeon. Peeves shot after her, pelting her with moldy peanuts, yelling, "Pimply! Pimply!"

"Oh, dear," said Hermione sadly.

Shifts in Tense

You always need to watch out for those pesky little troublemaking verbs that change tense when they're not supposed to, just at the time that you're not paying attention to what you're writing.

In other words, when you write, it's important that you avoid shifts in verb tenses unless you really do mean to indicate a shift in time. You hear this mistake often when people talk: For example:

*Yesterday I was driving along, minding my own business, when I almost **run** into this chubby chicken sittin' there in the middle of the road. I **don't** exactly know what to do, so I **yell** for it to move, but it just **sits** there like it's sort of plumb tuckered out. So I get out of my pickup and give it a little boot and watch it roll on across to the other side of the road.*

One grammatical problem in this little monologue is a shift in verb tense. The action happened *yesterday* when the speaker *was* driving down the road, but then the tense miraculously changes to present. In a perfect world (for grammar sticklers, anyway) the fowl talk would read like this:

*Yesterday I was driving along, minding my own business, when I almost **ran** into a chubby chicken sitting in the middle of the road. I **didn't** know what to do, so I **yelled** for it to move, but it **continued** to sit there like it was exhausted. So I stepped out of my pickup and gave it a little boot and watched it roll across to the other side of the road.*

Sometimes you *do* have shifts in verb tense when you really *do* want to show a change in time:

*Yesterday Elmo **said** (past) that Floe **is** (present) a so-so sewer of trousers for sows, but she **is** (present) a bigwig maker of wigs for pigs.*

Exercise 7

Now see if you can rewrite the following story to correct the flubs in verb tense consistency. Write each incorrect verb, followed by the tense correction. If a sentence is correct, write *C*.

Example: 1. wants — wanted

[1]*Once upon a time there lived a beautiful princess who had everything that she wants.* [2]*Her closet was full of thousands of expensive gowns and shoes, and she lives in an enormous palace with servants who tend to her every wish.* [3]*As a matter of fact, many people in the kingdom believe that she is a spoiled brat because they would often see her throwing tantrums in public.*

[4]*One day the princess, escorted by her entourage, goes out for a burger and fries.* [5]*She could have had the meal delivered, of course, but periodically she liked to see how the poor denizens of her kingdom lived so that she could feel superior to them.* [6]*Surrounded by pal-*

ace guards, she sat in a shabby diner, munching on a double-decker and super-sized fries, when a peasant woman rushes into the diner shouting, "Please, someone help! [7] A wild bear has carried away my child! [8] My baby will surely die if I do not have help to save him!" [9] All of the customers in the diner, young and old, jump from their chairs and run out to help the poor peasant recover her child, leaving their burgers behind. [10] All run, that is, except for the princess and her guards.

[11] "Silly peons," she sputtered as she chewed. [12] "They let their food go to waste because of a careless child." [13] As she says these words, an asteroid shoots down from the sky and crushes the princess before she can finish her last fat fry.

Moral: It's safer to run to save a small fry than to stay and eat a large one.

Passive and Active Voice

Pretend you're sitting in an auditorium listening to a lecture. Would you be more attentive if the speaker were droning on behind a podium, acting as lively as a frozen fish stick, or if he or she were illustrating points by leaping around the stage and doing somersaults into the audience? Performance number two has my vote.

Action makes a situation more exciting, and when you write, it's *generally* a good idea to stay in the *active voice* as opposed to the *passive voice*. So what's the difference?

A verb is *active* if the subject of the sentence *performs* the action, and a verb is *passive* when the subject *receives* the action. Generally speaking, a sentence is stronger and less wordy when the subject is the *doer* and not the *receiver*. Take a look:

Active: *The audience gave Octavius a huge hand after the recital.*

The subject, *audience*, performs the action.

Passive: *Octavius was given a huge hand by the audience after the recital.*

The action is performed upon the subject, *Octavius*.

Active: *Because Cousin Wainwright wears underwear that's too tight, his face is always white.*

Cousin Wainwright, the subject of the subordinate clause, performs the action.

Passive: *Because underwear that's too tight is worn by Cousin Wainwright, his face is always white.*

Underwear, the subject of the subordinate clause, receives the action.

Notice that when the verb is in the *passive voice*, the sentence is wordier because the main verb requires a helping verb, and the performer of the action is banished to a tacked-on prepositional phrase.

The passive voice isn't all bad. As a matter of fact, sometimes it's better to use the passive voice instead of the active. For example, sometimes the performer of the action isn't known or isn't the most important element of the sentence.

*"Attention all shoppers! A finger **was found** in the power tools department. To claim it, please report to the courtesy booth.*

The finger finder is unknown.

*Orpal's pet scorpion **has been found**, so the class can relax.*

The main focus is on the scorpion; no one cares who caught the critter.

Sometimes the passive voice hides blame. When the government discovers that it's spending $650 a piece for thumbtacks, an official might announce one of the most well-known passive sentences:

Mistakes have been made.

Also, you often find the passive voice in legal documents and official reports.

Exercise 8

This excerpt from *Harry Potter and the Goblet of Fire* refers to an official report. If an underlined verb is active, write *A*, and if a verb is passive, write *P*.

The police were summoned, and the whole of Little Hangleton had seethed with shocked curiosity and ill-disguised excitement.

The police had never read an odder report. A team of doctors had examined the bodies and had concluded that none of the Riddles had been poisoned, stabbed, shot, strangled, suffocated, or (as far as they could tell) harmed at all. In fact (the report continued, in a tone of unmistakable bewilderment), the Riddles all appeared to be in perfect health—apart from the fact that they were all dead.

As there was no proof that the Riddles had been murdered at all, the police were forced to let Frank go. The Riddles were buried in the Little Hangleton churchyard, and their graves remained objects of curiosity for a while.

Exercise 9

Rewrite each of the following sentences, changing the verb from passive to active.

1. Indigestion was suffered by several guests after someone found a mildewed shoe in the fondue.

2. At the party, balloon rutabagas were made for the children by Quirky the clown.

3. A seamster was sued by Sue for mending her bathing suit with glue.

4. An air guitar was given to Billy by his parents for his birthday, but he cried because the box was empty.

5. Carrion is carried by stylish vultures in carry-on luggage.

6. Because of a typo, a proposal was signed by the governor creating a twenty-thousand-acre skate park.

7. In a tragic accident, a concussion was suffered by Fifi when her doggy door stuck shut.

8. The clam chowder was thickened with foot powder by Uncle Howard.

9. Scientists announced that global warming is caused by fireflies.

10. A backache was suffered by Oberone the gnome when he tried to play the trombone.

Mood

People are moody (maybe I should speak for myself), so it makes sense that the verbs we use express mood. Verbs have three moods:

1. The **indicative** mood expresses statements or questions of fact.

    Waiter, there's a fly in my soup.
    Hefty Aunt Gretchen gives bugs the jitters when she jitterbugs in the kitchen.

2. The **imperative** mood expresses a command or a request. The subject of a sentence in the imperative mood is *you*, and it's usually omitted. This invisible *you* is called the *understood you*.

    Watch out for those stampeding squirrels!
    Please send donations to the Foundation for Victims of Stampeding Squirrels.

3. The **subjunctive** mood expresses speculation and contrary-to-fact statements (among other things). It's trickier than the other moods, because the verbs are ... well ... weird.

The subjunctive form is only used in subordinate clauses. There are two types of subjunctive:

The **present subjunctive** uses the base form of the verb. This means that you drop the *s* on the third person singular form of the verb. Generally this type of construction occurs in a subordinate clause beginning with *that* when the main clause contains a verb showing command, such as *insist, recommend, demand,* and *order*.

> *Mrs. Wiggleberry insisted that her cat **quit** adjusting the thermostat.* (Normally you would use the verb *quits* with the subject *cat*.)

Another quirky thing about the present subjunctive is that for the present form of *to be*, the verb *be* is used, instead of *am, is,* or *are*, with every subject, whether singular or plural.

*Whether the occasion **be** (instead of is) a formal gathering or a child's birthday party, painted mothballs always make attractive party favors.*

*Aunt Maybelline recommended that this year the turkey and the ham **be** (instead of are) stuffed with baked beans.*

*The Society for the Prevention of Cruelty to Parasites demanded that Herby **be** (instead of is) kinder to fleas.*

The **past subjunctive** is used in *what if* and *if only* types of sentences. The past subjunctive is only a troublemaker with the *past tense* form of *be (was)*. As weird as it sounds, you use *were* for the past tense form of *be*, even with singular subjects.

*"If I **were** (not was) president, I would give everyone a billion dollars and a puppy," declared Clarence.*

*"If you **were** a potato chip," blurted mean Irene, "you would probably be the green one."*

*"If a dog **were** (not was) a person, would it be its own best friend?" asked Wendell.*

*"If humans **were** dogs, would a ten-year-old be a septuagenarian?" ruminated little Eustasius.*

Exercise 10

Here's some mood for thought (sorry-bad pun). Identify the mood of each of these sentences. (Note: The preceding sentence is in the imperative mood).

> a) *indicative*   b) *imperative*   c) *subjunctive*

1. Uncle Tyrone has found that ammonia makes a fragrant, yet inexpensive, cologne.

2. Never try to start the wave in an elevator.

3. Simon enjoys talking to mimes.

4. Clem intends to cash in when he invests in a chain of drive-thru gyms.

5. Trish sent back her fish dish because it was squishy.

6. Myrtle, you must quit using turtles for hurdles.

7. "If I were a cold goose, would I get people bumps?" asked Lumpy.

8. Rapunzel is letting down her hair and getting out more often.

9. Trixy insisted that her tabby lose fat by eating low-fat rats.

10. For a more stylish look, Ray wears the pelt of a small animal for a toupee.

Sit or Set?

Some people get these two words confused, but they're really not difficult. *Set* means *to place or put*, and it's always followed by a direct object. *Sit* is what you do in a chair, and it's never, ever, ever followed by a direct object. In other words, *set* is transitive, and *sit* is intransitive.

It's easy to remember the difference because you tell Fido to *"sit,"* not *"set"*—that is, unless Fido is a highly intelligent dog, and you're ordering him to *set* the table, or to *set* out your clothes for the next day—but I digress. Here are the principal parts of the verb for *sit* and *sat*.

Present	Present Participle	Past	Past Participle
sit	*(is) sitting*	*sat*	*(have) sat*
set	*(is) setting*	*set*	*(have) set*

Sit

*When Tad's chameleon **sits** on plaid, it suffers a panic attack.* (present)
*Tad's chameleon is skittish when it **is sitting** on plaid.* (present participle)
*Yesterday when Tad's chameleon **sat** on plaid, it felt deeply inadequate.* (past)
*Because Tad's chameleon **has sat** on plaid so many times in the past, it's brain is badly addled.* (past participle)

Set

*When Tad **sets** his pet chameleon on plaid, it becomes radical.* (present)
*Tad **is setting** his chameleon on plaid, and it's going mad.* (present participle)
*Yesterday Tad **set** his chameleon on plaid, and it felt a tad sad.* (past)
*Because Tad has **set** his chameleon on plaid so many times in the past, it's a basket case.* (past participle)

Lie or Lay?

I've saved two of the most unnerving verbs for last: *lie* and *lay*.

Lie is what sleeping dogs do, and *lay* is what you do when you put your cards on the table. (Sorry about the clichés. I know they're a dime a dozen.) In other words, the present form of *lie* means *to recline*, and the present form of *lay* means *to put*. *Lie* doesn't require a direct object, but *lay* does.

An explanation of the correct use of these two bugaboos is really quite simple. Just follow along with me as I make things perfectly clear. You see, the past form of *lie* is *lay*, but the past form of *lay* is *laid*, and the past participle of *lie* is *lain*, and the past participle of *lay* is the same as its past form, *laid*, and the present participle of each is actually what you would expect it to be. Uhh—bottom line is that you just have to memorize this chart:

Present	Present Participle	Past	Past Participle
Lie (to recline)	(is) lying	lay	(have) lain
Lay (to put)	(is) laying	laid	(have) laid

Lie

*Rats that **lie** in the middle of highways should be called "splats."* (present)
*The rats that **are lying** in the middle of the highway should be called "splats."* (present participle)
*The rats that **lay** in the middle of the highway yesterday are now "splats."* (past)
*Rats that **have lain** in the middle of the highway for days are very flat "splats."* (past participle)

Lay

Aunt Gabby, lay your delicious battered wombat on the platter. (present)
*Aunt Gabby **is laying** her tasty battered wombat on the platter this very moment.*
  (present participle)
*Ten minutes ago, Aunt Gabby **laid** the enticing battered wombat on the platter.* (past)
*Aunt Gabby **has laid** the battered wombat on the platter, but her dinner guests have
  scattered.* (past participle)

Exercise 11

   With the nifty little charts on pages 180 and 181 to clarify things (maybe), choose the correct verb forms.

1. "I will (lay, lie) on a bed of coals to prove my love for you," Gomer told Dot, "unless they're hot."

2. After Santa's little elves helped (set, sit) presents under all of the trees, Elf Number Three had to have knee surgery.

3. When Aunt Hedda saw Cousin Ray's toupee (laying, lying) on the bed, she thought the cat had come back from the dead.

4. Dirk (sets, sits) for hours in front of the TV watching the Vegetable Network.

5. Tootsie, the family's cat, always (lays, lies) on Matt because she thinks he's a mat.

6. Sometimes just to see fur fly, mischievous Joel (sets, sits) the catnip toys in the dog food bowl.

7. Thumbelina was glum because she couldn't remember where she (had laid, had lain) her gum.

8. After Blanch (laid, lay) on the beach all day, she still looked pasty.

9. Jane (sat, set) next to a brat on the plane who stole her peanuts and drove her insane.

10. The tomcat, which (sat, set) on the napkin in Maddie's lap, lapped up the splotches of grease and fat.

11. Quigby (is laying, is lying) on the couch, munching on chips to exercise his mouth.

12. Fred (lay, laid) awake all night because he was certain that a severed head was under his bed.

13. When Garp rides his magic carpet, he wears his Velcro robe so that when he (sets, sits), he sticks.

14. The nearly extinct garpadoodlelopidus has just (laid, lain) an egg on Doreen's head.

15. After she slept, Tilly regretted (laying, lying) her face on a corduroy pillow.

16. When Gus (sets, sits) in class, he passes the time pretending he's a mollusk.

17. The Bummbletons (laid, lay) new carpet in their house because they disliked the sound of toenails clicking on linoleum.

18. The spider that was (setting, sitting) by the wheel of that truck is now guts.

19. Thank goodness someone stopped Uncle Dave from (setting, sitting) his pet ferret to dry in the microwave.

20. Vampire moms always remind their tykes to (lay, lie) down their stakes before they go skating.

FYI The *lie* that means *tell an untruth* is a completely different creature from the *lie* that means *recline*. The forms of the *lie* that means *fib* look like this:

*Bad children who **lie** have to eat guppies' eyes.
(present)*

*Bad children **are lying**, but soon they'll be crying. (present participle)*

*Yesterday the bad children who **lied** had to eat an entire cup of eyes. (past)*

*Bad children who **have lied** many times in the past must eat the eyes of squids and bass. (past participle)*

I guess the moral is not to lie . . . or don't forget the ketchup.

12

More Adverb and Adjective Tips and Tidbits

When I go to the local grocery store and stand in the line where the sign reads "Ten Items or Less," I become slightly agitated. The source of my anxiety isn't the person ahead of me with fifteen items instead of ten (I count). Nope. It's that darn sign. I have to squelch the urge to mark a huge X through the word *less* and write *fewer*. TEN ITEMS OR FEWER. (Some people have suggested that the problem lies with me, not with the sign. Shows what they know.)

Likewise, when I hear the idiom "put your best foot forward," I have to quell the urge to ask how many feet the person has. Grammatically speaking, anyone with only two feet should put his or her "better foot forward." (Maybe I do need to seek help.)

So that you can keep the neurotic English teachers of the world from developing nervous tics and twitches, it's a good idea to learn how to use adjectives and adverbs—also known as modifiers—correctly when you make comparisons.

Degrees of Comparison

Adverbs and adjectives have three degrees of comparison: *positive, comparative,* and *superlative.*

The *positive degree* is the base form of the adjective or adverb.

*Rippley's kitten is **nitpicky** about its brand of catnip.*
*Maggie's eyebrows are **shaggy**.*
*Bucky **often** pops his knuckles.*
*Hannelore wears **high** heels.*

The *comparative* degree is used when two things are being compared.

*Tipper's kitten is **more nitpicky** than Rippley's kitten.*
*Tad's eyebrows are **shaggier** than Maggie's eyebrows.*
*Chuck pops his knuckles **more often** than Bucky.*
*Hildegarde's heels are **higher** than Hannelore's heels.*

The *superlative* degree is used to compare more than two things.

*Of the three kittens, Kizzy's kitten is the **most nitpicky**.*
*Among Tad, Agatha, and Bagby, Bagby has the **shaggiest** eyebrows.*
*Among Jen, Bucky and Chuck, Jen pops her knuckles **most often**.*
*Compared to Hannelore's and Hildegarde's heels, Heidi's heels are the **highest**.*

Forming Degrees of Comparison

The general way an adjective or adverb forms its *comparative* and *superlative* degrees depends on its number of syllables. Here are some guidelines:

1. Add *er* to form the comparative degree, and add *est* to form the superlative degree of most one-syllable modifiers:

Positive	Comparative	Superlative
tall	taller	tallest
mad	madder	maddest
weird	weirder	weirdest

2. There are two ways to form degrees of two-syllable modifiers: either add *er* for the comparative or *est* for the superlative; add *more* for the comparative, *most* for the superlative.

Positive	Comparative	Superlative
fuzzy	fuzzier	fuzziest
snooty	snootier	snootiest
frazzled	more frazzled	most frazzled

The best way to decide whether to add *er/est* or whether to use *more/most* is to play it by ear. Sometimes adding *er/est* makes a two-syllable modifier awkward to pronounce. Just try hitching a comparative or superlative ending to a modifier like *overpriced*.

Right: *Aunt Thelma believes that rubber bands are **overpriced** at office supply stores.*

Right: *She believes that they are **more overpriced** at shops in the mall.*

Right: *She believes that they are the **most overpriced** at The Rubber Band Boutique.*

Really Goofy Sounding: *Aunt Thelma believes rubber bands are **overpriceder** at shops in the mall.*

Really Goofy Sounding: *She believes that they are **overpricedest** at The Rubber Band Boutique.*

See what I mean? Adding *more/most* sounds a heck of a lot less awkward. Sometimes, though, the form that sounds better is a toss up. For instance, with words like *steady* (*steadier, steadiest* or *more steady, most steady*) and *handsome* (*handsomer, handsomest* or *more handsome, most handsome*), either method of forming the comparison is correct. When in doubt, always check the trusty dictionary.

FYI Always use *more/most* with adverbs that end in *ly*.

> *Fruity always walks **snootily** when she wears her faux emu-skin boots.*
> *When she wears her faux emu-skin boots, Fruity always walks **more snootily** (not snootilier) than her friends.*
> *Compared to all other boot wearers in town, Fruity walks the **most snootily** (not snootiliest).*

3. For modifiers with three or more syllables, use *more* to form the comparative degree and *most* to form the superlative degree:

> *Aunt Tasha has a **cockamamie** idea to sell galoshes in Oshkosh.*
> *Granddad Irving has a **more cockamamie** (not cockamamier) scheme to open a Bingo parlor in Beijing.*
> *Grandma Alexandra has the **most cockamamie** (not cockamamiest) plan; she's going to join a rock band and tour Japan.*

4. To show that a modifier has *less* or the *least* of its quality, use *less* before the modifier to form the comparative and *least* to form the superlative..

> *Horace found that his mail-order solar-powered nail clippers were **not useful**.*
> *His double-sided playing cards from a home shopping network were **less useful** than the clippers.*
> *His **least useful** purchase, however, was a do-it-yourself dental surgery and cyst removal kit that he ordered from a late-night infomercial.*

Exercise 1

Now try this exercise. If a sentence contains an incorrect form of an adverb or adjective, write the incorrect form, followed by the correct form. Write *C* if a sentence is correct as it is.

1. Of all of the vegetables, Brussels sprouts make the loveliest holiday decorations; and because they're edible, they're the more practical, too.

2. Because Tracy wanted to be the most stylish spectator in the New Year's Day Parade, she tied several colorful balloons to her braces. (Tracy is loitering back on p. 188!)

3. Among all types of insects, tarantulas are the more affectionate.

4. "I can remember facts I learned in college more quickly than my friend Egbert," said Della, "but Pavlov's dog just doesn't ring a bell."

5. Truman, the most talented twin, plays amazing tunes by rubbing together two balloons.

6. When hunting their prey, the sneakiest snakes wear the more sly disguises for an element of surprise.

7. Greta is most irritable when she finds grub worms in her grits.

8. Mary Lou is the more qualified person in her field of accounting, but she's having trouble finding an employer who won't prosecute for embezzlement.

9. Bridgette likes prunes, but she likes raisins better because she hates to spit pits.

10. The new company president, who seems to be intelligenter than the last one, vowed to put the *K* back in *quality*.

Degrees of Irregular Adjectives and Adverbs

Everyone knows that when it comes to the English language, the only rule without exception is that no rule is without exception. Some irregular comparisons are just plain wacky, and you have to memorize them. On page 190, there are some modifier misfits.

Positive	Comparative	Superlative
good	better	best
well	better	best
bad	worse	worst
far	farther	farthest
many, some, much	more	most

Double Negatives

A double negative is a grammar error that occurs when two negative terms are used to express a negative idea. This is a list of some of the most common negative words:

Negative Words

never	none	barely
no	not	hardly
nobody	nothing	scarcely

I hate to show my age, but I remember a couple of songs from years ago. One by a little group called the Rolling Stones had these lines:

I can't get no satisfaction.
I can't get no good reaction.

Another, by a group called Pink Floyd, featured these lyrics:

We don't need no education.
We don't need no thought control,
No dark sarcasm in the classroom . . .

Unlike errors on checkout lane signs, blatant grammar errors in lyrics, for some odd reason, don't bother me. Taking the bad grammar out of some lyrics would destroy the whole attitude thing.

I can't get satisfaction.
I can't get a good reaction.

We don't need education.
We don't need thought control
or dark sarcasm in the classroom . . .

See what I mean?. The whole rebellious tone is a little . . . well . . . toned down, to say the least.

A funny thing is that when someone uses a double negative, he or she is really saying the opposite of the statement's intended meaning. Two negatives equal a positive. In other words, the negatives cancel each other out. When Mick Jagger sings that he can't (can **not**) get **no** satisfaction, he's really saying that he's a pretty happy guy; and when the children's choir in the Pink Floyd song sings that they don't (do **not**) need **no** education, they're actually announcing their need for some heavy-duty schooling, (a point made obvious by the use of the double negative).

Therefore, if someone says, "I didn't hardly have time to sit down today," you know he or she is pretty well rested. Likewise, if someone announces, "I don't need none of your advice," the poor individual is actually crying out for your help.

Illogical Comparisons

Sometimes it's easy to fall into the trap of making comparisons that sound perfectly clear to you, but they don't quite pass the logic test. These are some examples of some illogical statements. See if you can find the flaws:

Wrong: *My cat Straggly's whiskers are longer than your cat Scabs.*

The two or more things that are compared have to be comparable. In this sentence, Straggly's whiskers are being compared to Scabs, a cat. The sentence should compare whiskers to whiskers:

Right: *My cat Straggly's whiskers are longer than your cat Scabs's whiskers.*

Wrong: *At the beach, Phebe wears sunglasses that are bigger*
than anyone else.
Right: *At the beach, Phebe wears sunglasses that are bigger*
than anyone else's sunglasses.

This next sentence is a little trickier:

Wrong: *Aretha can spin around and catch a baton in her teeth better than any twirler in her class can.*

Aretha is being compared to her class. Since she's *part* of the class, she's actually being compared to herself. This error has a quick fix. By adding the word *other*, Aretha stands apart from the group:

Right: *Aretha can spin around and catch a baton in her teeth better than any **other** twirler in her class.*

The word *else* can also correct this type of error:

Wrong: *Although Peabody ran the car into a tree, he still steers better than anyone in his driver's ed class.*

Right: *Although Peabody ran the car into a tree, he still steers better than anyone **else** in his driver's ed class.*

Also, avoid changing a modifier to a comparative form when it has no comparative form.

Wrong: *Holden's goldfish was **deader** than Trish's goldfish.*

Right: *Holden's and Trish's goldfish have bit the dust* or *have gone to that big fishbowl in the sky.* (Forget the euphemisms. They're just plain **dead**.)

Wrong: *Foster, who dresses like a lobster, is the **most unique** child in class.*

Right: *Foster, who dresses like a lobster, is a **unique** child.*

Double Comparisons

A double comparison is one of the easiest mistakes to catch. This mistake occurs when two methods are used instead of one to form the comparative or superlative degree of an adjective or adverb.

In other words, it's incorrect to combine *er* and *more* to form the comparative of a modifier. It's also incorrect to combine *est* and *most* to form the superlative:

Wrong: *"I'm going to be **more better** at making decisions," Squiqqly announced, "or maybe not."*

Right: *"I'm going to be **better** at making decisions," Squiqqly announced, "or maybe not."*

A double comparison is overkill. It's redundancy. It's a form of repetition. It's just adding stuff that you don't need.

Good or Well?

A valuable piece of information is about to appear before your eyes. To use *good* and *well* correctly, remember the following: *good* is an *adjective*, and *well* is an *adverb*. Therefore, *good* describes a noun, and *well* modifies a verb. *Well* can also be an adjective that means *"in good health"* or *"satisfactory."*

Wrong: *"I can ride a unicycle **good**," said Dory, "as long as it has two wheels." (The adjective **good** is modifying the verb, can ride, but adjectives only modify nouns and pronouns.)*

Right: *"I can ride a unicycle **well**," said Dory, "as long as it has two wheels." (The adverb, **well**, is modifying the verb, can ride, just as it should.)*

Wrong: *I did **good** on my grammar test. (The adjective **good** is modifying the verb, did, but adjectives only modify nouns and pronouns.)*

Right: *I did **well** on my grammar test. (The adverb, **well**, is modifying the verb, did, just as it should.)*

FYI *"I feel good"* means *"I feel happy or satisfied,"* but *"I feel well"* means *"I feel in good health."*

*Fester **felt good** after his larva costume won first prize at the County Pest Festival.*

*I hope Stella **is feeling well** after her bout with salmonella.*

Further or Farther?

Question: Which of these sentences is correct?

*Because Mitchell pitched his chip the **farthest**, he won first place in the Fifth Annual Cow Chip Pitch Contest.*
*Professor Furgleburg will talk **further** about the furry-bellied jellyfish.*

Answer: Both

Farther refers to physical distance, and *further* refers to non-physical distance. So, a person would walk *farther*, throw *farther*, ride *farther*; but he or she would read *further*, talk *further*, think *further*. In other words, if the distance is measurable, use *farther*; if not, use *further*.

Less or Fewer?

I can't let this chapter end without further (not farther) explanation about my checkout-line irritation. (See p. 185.) Why should the sign read *TEN ITEMS OR FEWER and not TEN ITEMS OR LESS?*

The answer is (and I hope that stores across the country are listening) that *fewer* refers to items that can be counted, and less refers to items that can't be counted. So, someone might buy *less* gas, but fewer gallons; or someone might eat *less* of the cake, but *fewer* pieces of the cake; or someone might chew *less* tutti-frutti bubble gum, but chew fewer pieces of tutti-frutti bubble gum, or someone might read less of the news, but *fewer* headlines in the news.

*Even though Gomer constantly gobbles gummy worms, he has **fewer** cavities than Tavis.*
*Appleton, who stuck his tongue in a bug zapper, has **less** common sense than Vincent.*

Exercise 2

Now you get to show what you know (about comparisons, that is). Once again, if a sentence contains an error in comparison, write the incorrect adverb or adjective followed by its correct form. Some sentences have more than one error. Write *C* if a sentence is correct as it is.

1. "The further you travel, the further you are," said not-so-deep-thinking Binkly.

2. At camp, Wellington thought that he did good on his swim test; but instead of being grouped with the Minnows or Sharks, he was placed with the Plankton.

3. "I don't need no help with English from nobody," announced Othello.

4. Gin raised more money to buy little wool hats for penguins than anyone in her school.

5. Boyd threw an oyster further than any other contestant in the International Shellfish Pitch.

6. The most dumbest thing that Runyan has ever done is to stick his tongue on a frozen flagpole.

7. Uncle Fester's left nostril is his hairiest one.

8. Uncle Dewitt, who has more credit debt than anyone else in the family, foolishly bought solid gold pants for all of his siblings.

9. Between Heda's hedgehog and Henrietta's hedgehog, Heda's weighs more.

10. "If it looks like a duck, walks like a duck, and quacks like a duck," said Bucky, "it's probably someone who imitates a duck really good."

11. "Out of all of the jobs I've held," said Tess, "I had to deal with the most stickiest situations as a Krazy Glue hotline operator, and I never got no respect."

12. Rosemary bought the least inexpensive garage door opener not knowing it wasn't a closer.

13. Priscilla, the most devoted animal rights activist in her group, refuses to wear polyester because she's against cruelty to parrots.

14. Little Grace plays the tuba better than anyone else in the band when she wears her lucky back brace.

15. Eveline has the most loveliest hat I've ever seen.

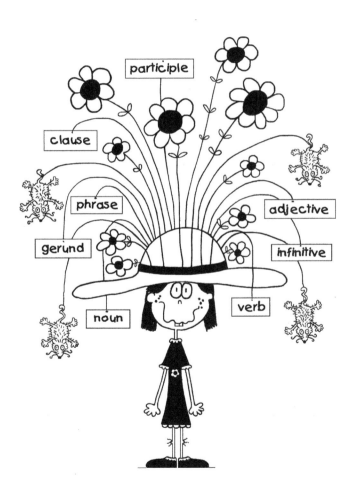

Mechanics

13
Capitalization Consternation

Most people don't realize the importance of capitalization rules. Capitalization, along with seemingly unimportant marks of punctuation, can change the meaning of a few words. Take a look:

dot spots big spots little spots everywhere

This plain little group of words sounds like something a toddler would say about a freckly face. But add some punctuation and capitalization, and the meaning suddenly changes:

Dot spots big Spot's little Spots everywhere.

Amazing! Now the picture is transformed from speckles and freckles to a plethora of puppies. These rules are guaranteed to add sense to your sentences:

1. Capitalize names of specific persons (a real tough one to remember).

   Examples: Wilma Flintstone, Miss Piggy, Norman Bates

2. Capitalize specific geographic locations.

   Cities: *Houston, Bedrock, Gotham City, New York City*

States: *Texas, Florida, North Carolina, California, New Jersey*
Sections of the country: *the North, the Southwest*

FYI Don't capitalize the words *north, south, east, west, southwest,* etc. when referring to direction. Do capitalize a direction word if it refers to a section of the country.

> *In a small town in the* **South** *(a section of the country), surprised residents sighted giant possums* **north** *(direction) of the Roadkill Grill.*

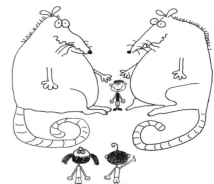

Countries: *the United States of America, Germany, Poland*
Continents: *North America, Africa, Asia, Europe*
Islands: *Long Island, Philippine Islands*
Mountains: *the Rocky Mountains, Mount McKinley, the Alps*
Bodies of water: *the Pacific Ocean, the English Channel*
Roads: *Highway 45, Chughole Avenue*

FYI Now here's a really picky rule. In a street name that contains a hyphenated number, the second number begins with a small letter:

> *Weird Uncle Ernie sells paintings of Elvis on velvet on the corner of* **Thirty-third Street** *and Maple Avenue.*

3. Capitalize the names of organizations, businesses, institutions, and government bodies.

> *American Red Cross,* the *National Broadcasting Company, Homer Simpson High School,* the *House of Representatives,* the *National Acne Prevention Society*

4. Capitalize the names of historical events and periods, special events, and calendar dates. However, don't capitalize seasons (*winter, spring, summer, fall*).

> *Middle Ages, World War II, Mother's Day, Groundhog Day, Australian Fruit Bat Day*
> *Every* **Halloween** *confused little Thadeus dresses like an* **Easter** *bunny, and every* **Christmas** *he cries to go trick-or-treating.*

*In the **winter** he wears his swim trunks, and in the **summer**, he insists on wool underwear.*

5. Capitalize the names of nationalities, races, and religions.

   American, German, Negro, Caucasian, Mormon, Buddhist

6. Capitalize brand names, but not the product.

   ***Dell** computers, **Levi's** jeans, **Clearasil** acne cream*

7. Capitalize the names of ships, planets, monuments, awards, and any other particular places, things, or events:

   Ships and aircraft: the *Mayflower*, the *Enterprise*
   Monuments, memorials: *Washington Monument*
   Buildings: the *Empire State Building*, *Rockefeller Center*
   Awards: the *Grammy*, the *Nobel Peace Prize*
   Planets, stars: *Mars*, *Saturn*, the *Milky Way*, the *Big Dipper*

FYI Planets, constellations, asteroids, stars, and groups of stars are capitalized; however, *sun* and *moon* are generally not capitalized, and *earth* is not capitalized if it is preceded by *the*.
   *In **the** fertile **earth**, Theodore planted mutant sunflower seeds.*

8. Only capitalize a school subject if it is a language or a course title followed by a number.

   speech, homemaking, drama, biology, Speech II, Drama 301, English, French, German, Latin, Toenail Painting 101

FYI Don't capitalize *freshman*, *sophomore*, *junior*, or *senior* unless the word is part of a proper noun such as the *Junior-Senior Prom*.

   *Matilde became ill in **English**, and later she threw up while dissecting a toad in **biology**. Unfortunately she'll miss the **Sophomore Talent Show** where she intended to sing a medley of Beatles tunes in **German** and **Latin**.*

9. Capitalize the title of a person when it comes before a name.

Examples: *Dr. Doolittle, Captain Crunch, Sergeant Pepper, Mr. Kiddlehopper*

10. Do not capitalize a title used alone or following a person's name unless it refers to a high official (such as the President or Vice President of the United States) or to someone to whom you wish to show special respect:

*The **President** brushed and flossed before meeting with the **Prime Minister** of **England**.* (high titles)

*Digby was elected **president** of the Caterpillar Growers of America.* (not a high title)

*The **Vice President** met with several governors to discuss emu exploitation in America.* (high title)

*The **vice president** of the liposuction support group resigned.* (not a high title)

FYI When a title is used alone in a direct address (in other words, when a person is spoken to directly), it's usually capitalized:

*Are these your false eyebrows, **General**?*
*You really should consider a nose job before the election, **Senator**.*

11. Capitalize the first word and all important words in titles of books, magazines, poems, stories, movies, paintings, and other works of art. (Unimportant words in a title are *a*, *an*, *the*, and short prepositions that are fewer than five letters. However, the first and last words of a title are always capitalized, even if they're unimportant words.)

Reader's Digest; *The Grapes of Wrath*; *Alexander and the Terrible, Horrible, No Good, Very Bad Day*; *Mona Lisa*; *The Little Mermaid*; "*Sarah Cynthia Sylvia Stout Would Not Take the Garbage Out*"

12. Capitalize words referring to the Deity and holy books.

God** and **His** universe, the **Koran**, the **Bible

FYI The word *god* is *not* capitalized when it refers to gods of ancient mythology.

*The Greeks worshiped many **gods**.*
*When he flexes his muscles, Wilbur thinks he looks like a Roman **god**.*

13. Capitalize a word showing family relationship when used with the person's name (as part of the name), but not when the word showing relationship is preceded by a possessive pronoun (my, your, his, her, its, their, our).

Aunt Erma, my aunt, Cousin Verne, your cousin, Grandfather Scabs, their grandfather, my uncle Joe

*Because incorrigible Reginald was angry at **his mother**, he stepped on cracks.*

FYI When family-relationship words like *aunt* and *cousin* are thought of as part of a name, capitalize them even after a possessive.

My *talented **Uncle Buford** is a frog-calling champion in five countries.*

FYI (again) Capitalize a word showing family relationship when used in a direct address.

*"Gosh, **Mom**," whined Lionel, "why can't I wrestle crocodiles? Stumpy's **mom** lets him!"*

14. Capitalize abbreviations for degrees that follow a person's name: M.D., Ph.D., D.D.S., A.B.C.D.E.F.G. (just kidding)

15. Capitalize the abbreviations *Jr.* and *Sr.* when they follow a person's name.

16. Abbreviations *A.D., B.C., C.E., B.C.E.* are capitalized, but *am, fm* (radio frequencies), and abbreviations for measurements are not (*ft., sec., kg.*). For the times of day, do whatever strikes your fancy: *A.M.* or *a.m., P.M.* or p.m.

17. Capitalize the first word and each noun in the salutation (opening) of a letter. However only the first word in the closing of a letter is capitalized:

Dear Miss Dimpsy, Sincerely yours, Yours until crawdads fly,

Exercise 1

It's time to show what you know. Find the capitalization mistakes in the following sentences and correct them. Some words need to be capitalized, and some need to be in lower case and not capitalized. If a sentence has no capitalization mistakes, write *C* for correct.

1. Last year coach Waddle, my Math Teacher, let us try to shoot paper-wad baskets in the trash can for extra credit, but this year I'm failing Algebra II because my teacher isn't a sports fan.

2. To look her best, Prudy used Clairol hot rollers, Maybelline mascara, and Clearasil before her date with the vice president of the filmore high school chess club.

3. Every Mother's Day, little beings from Pluto send postcards to earth.

4. This year I'm taking english, basket weaving, Geography, history II, and plastic surgery III.

5. In a televised speech, the president of the United states spoke to congress about the country's need for every american to wear deodorant during the summer while attending the olympics.

6. "Hey, mother, come quick! I think that the static electricity from TV has interfered with uncle Charlie's pace maker."

7. The *National Scientific Enquirer*, a well-respected magazine, reported that dirty sweat socks cover the surface of some planets in distant solar systems.

8. Although many athletic armadillos prepare for the Gulf Coast track and field tournament in the spring, most are too slow to qualify.

9. "Hey, mom, I need to take my hawaiian shirt to acme cleaners to have the spot of liver casserole removed before the dance tonight."

10. During the industrial revolution, a brilliant scientist from the south invented the first eyebrow tweezers.

Exercise 2

Now try these. As in Exercise 1, correct the words with capitalization errors. If a sentence has no errors, write *C*.

1. On our vacation, we will visit the caribbean islands and go shark diving with my one-legged aunt Mildred.

2. Every year pranksters drop watermelons and kiwi fruit off of the Golden Gate bridge that sometimes splatter on passing vacation liners like the *princess*.

3. After careful observations, professor plimp at Boston university believes that one of jupiter's moons has a marshmallow filling.

4. On saint patrick's day, my lucky grandmother received the nobel peace prize, and then she won thirty dollars playing the slot machine.

5. Some people in the polar regions smear their faces with mayonnaise and whale blubber to protect their skin from the sun.

6. On every birthday and christmas, Petunia gives Aunt Hulga a refreshing dinner mint.

7. In May, mice munch on melons that grow north of the museum of national history.

8. Sally Mae is President of students against students who are always against stuff (SASWAAAS), a new organization at her high school.

9. The *Houston Chronicle* reported on Tuesday that seventy-five percent of students at Van Winkle high school spend ninety-eight percent of their time everyday dreaming in class.

10. In the movie *the attack of the alien gophers* which is showing at the theater at the corner of twenty-second street and avenue B, three-eyed rodents nibble on new yorkers.

11. During the press conference, the new football coach announced that he planned to turn the losing team around 360 degrees.

12. In a presentation before the houston bar association, a talented contortionist twisted his body into the form of a pretzel.

13. A group of students in Miss Tremble's freshman geography class is doing a report on baboons that eat bananas in Bangkok.

14. Yuck, dad, you're shedding on the couch!

15. Because Mabel's mom has eyes in the back of her head, she carries two pairs of glasses.

Exercise 3

See if you can find the capitalization mistakes in Muffy's letter. She needs a little help (in more ways than one). Write each incorrectly capitalized word in its correct form. Write *C* if the sentence is correct.

Hi, Buff!

[1]I'm sitting in english, and my weird teacher is talking about herself again. [2]She's even more boring than my History teacher. [3]I always tune him out because all he talks about is how some president, I think Eisenhower, won the civil war and held the country together. [4]I'm really impressed. [5]Anyway, the best part of this class is the guy from London, which is a place in england—you know—the place where they have the London bridge and famous stuff like that. [6]I swear he looks like a statue of a greek god. [7]I'm drooling all over my copy of health and glamour magazine. [8]By the way, I'm learning how to do a proper sit up. [9]I can already do two of them—in a row! [10]Anyway, I think his Dad is a famous senator or Congressman or athlete or something who won some kind of important award, like the purple heart or medal of Honor or grammy or something. [11]And I think his mom is a sophomore teacher or a counselor or a principal or something like that at Einstein high school on forty-third street. [12]Speaking of Einsteins, I forgot to tell you that my brilliant Mom grounded me for accidentally driving the Porsche through the garage wall while she and Dad went to a meeting of their support group, you know, parents with children of challenging teens. [13]I was practicing driving because I get my license in the spring, which is only 11½ months away! [14]My Birthday is the day after Easter, so I always get a bunch of stale candy. Whoopee. [15]Would you believe

mom said I can't go anywhere for six months? ¹⁶The good thing is she'll forget by friday. ¹⁷If she doesn't, mother's day is this weekend, and I bought her a piece of godiva chocolate to soften her up. ¹⁸I accidentally ate half of it, but I don't think she'll notice. ¹⁹I have to go to Algebra next, and the teacher is such a dork. ²⁰Monday he had this big green thing hanging from his nose and he didn't even know it. ²¹He looked like someone from that movie The Revenge Of the Slime People. ²²Speaking of dorks, my english teacher is walking over here. ²³I'll see you in Biology tomorrow, and I just hope we don't have to cut up a frog because guts are so gross! ²⁴I think the president of the country should make cutting up stuff illegal, don't you?

²⁵Your Friend,

Muffy

14

A Few Comma, Semicolon, and Colon Rules to Know and Love

Commas can make a big difference when it comes to precision in writing, or comma-munication (made up word). Just take a look:

In the cabinet of the old house, Norman keeps a hand towel, finger paint, and carving knife.

What a difference a bit of comma switch-a-roo can make:

In the cabinet of the old house, Norman keeps a hand, towel, finger, paint, and carving knife.

Aaaaahhhhh! Norman probably isn't the type of guy you'd want to ask to feed your dog while you're on vacation.

So don't let commas make you comma-tose (another made up word). To avoid distorting your message, or just to make your writing more comma-pre-hensible (another made up word. Okay, I know this is annoying. I'll quit.), you just need to know a few simple rules. What a coincidence! Here they are. I'll even throw in some colon and semicolon rules for free.

Commas

1. Use a comma to separate words or groups of words in a series.

   Buffy bought cookies, tofu, tortillas, and a kumquat to snack on during the movie.
   Disturbed people nibble, lick, and gnaw on telephone poles.

2. Use a comma to separate two adjectives when the conjunction *and* makes sense between them.

   Lionel's lion loves to lap vanilla, chocolate, strawberry, and antelope ice cream cones.

   (Don't place a comma between ice and cream.)

3. Use a comma to separate two sentences joined by a coordinating conjunction (*for, and, nor, but, or, yet, so*—FANBOYS for short).

   The laundry was not dry by school time, so Emmett cleverly put his jockey shorts in the toaster.
   Milly performed electrolysis on her teddy bear, and she completed brain surgery on her favorite doll.

4. Use a comma to separate words in direct address from the rest of the sentence.

   A direct address refers to a name used when you speak directly to a person.

   Thorton, why did you name your dog Spot?
   Please toss me a cantaloupe, Wilbur.
   Oh, Full Moon, why do you cause loony goons to croon in June? (Great poetry, if I do say so myself.)

   Beware Don't confuse a direct address with a simple mention of a name in a sentence:

   Wrong: *Wanda, lost her head, but the cat found it under her bed.* (Since no one is speaking to Wanda directly, a comma isn't necessary after her name.)

Right: *Wanda lost her head, but the cat found it under the bed.*

Right: *Wanda, you've lost your head.* (Someone is speaking directly to Wanda, so a comma is necessary after her name.)

5. Use a comma to separate short introductory words from the rest of the sentence.

   Gee, I think I sat on your miniature chihuahua.
   Yes, I will have another Spam milk shake.

6. Use a comma to separate two or more introductory prepositional phrases from the rest of the sentence. Also, use a comma to separate one long introductory prepositional phrase (four words or more) from the rest of the sentence.

   For favors at her birthday party, Wilma passed out guppy eggs dyed in attractive pastel colors. (two short prepositional phrases at the beginning of the sentence)
   In the bug-filled flower bed, Doug dug up a hyperactive slug. (one long prepositional phrase at the beginning of the sentence)

Beware Never place a comma after a phrase or phrases followed by a verb.

   *In the basement of the house on the corner **live** millions of mutant millipedes.*

The verb, *live,* directly follows the prepositional phrase, so no comma is necessary.

7. Use commas to separate transitional words (*however, therefore, nevertheless, thus, consequently, besides . . .*) from the rest of the sentence.

   *Horace, **for instance**, enjoys molding clay statues of giant flying monkeys.*

8. Use a comma after an introductory adverb clause or an introductory participial phrase.

   ***When Squiggly grows up**, he wants to be either a nuclear physicist or a shepherd.* (introductory adverb clause)
   ***Hoping to win the election for class president**, Egbert gave every student a pony.* (introductory participial phrase)

9. Use a comma to enclose most appositives (words that rename nouns) and their modifiers.

> *The parakeet,* ***a popular house pet****, has a brain the size of a shriveled pea.*
> *JellO wrestling,* ***my favorite hobby****, requires great skill and coordination.*
> *The National Globe,* ***a well-respected magazine****, reports that ferocious fireflies are attacking children between the ages of six and twelve.*

10. Use commas to enclose parenthetical expressions (expressions such as *of course, to tell the truth, I believe,* and *I think* that are used as side remarks and could be omitted from the sentence).

> *Everyone knows,* ***of course****, that eating large amounts of red M&M's increases a person's intelligence.*
> *Some earthworms in the North Pole grow to a length of fifty feet,* ***I think****.*

11. Use a comma to set off contrasting expressions beginning with *not*.

> *Use flour,* ***not sawdust****, to make cupcakes.*
> *Freda brought a tick,* ***not a goldfish****, for Show and Tell.*

12. Titles or degrees that follow a person's name should be set off by commas.

> *Barney Trembles,* ***M.D.****, removed my appendix.*
> *Phil Filling,* ***D.D.S.****, gives each patient a free pedicure.*

13. Use commas to separate the elements in dates and addresses.

> *On Feb. 11, 2002, Goober rode his gnu to Timbuktu.*

FYI A comma is also used to separate a date or address *from the rest of the sentence.* Also, do not use a comma to separate the state from the zip code.

> *Mrs. Dittleberry mailed a million-dollar check to the Save the Ferret Foundation, 657 Rodent Road, Los Angeles, CA 90410, although she refused to buy a box of Girl Scout cookies.*

Notice that the comma after the last element of the address, *90410*, is necessary to separate the entire address from the rest of the sentence.

14. Use commas to separate *nonessential* participial phrases and *nonessential* clauses from the rest of the sentence. An *essential* phrase or clause is necessary to identify a person or thing and tells *which one*. It's *not* set off by commas. (See page 83.)

> *People **who are trying to lose weight** should not snack on sticks of butter.* (essential)
> *Mr. Peabody, **who recently underwent a costly hair transplant operation**, suffers from split ends.* (nonessential)
> *The crispy caterpillars **that you ordered** look delicious!* (essential)

15. To use, or not to use, a comma is sometimes simply a judgment call, so the final rule is simple: Use a comma to avoid confusion.

In 2004, 352 million people received emergency care for paper cuts.

Now you can put an end to your comma trauma! On to semicolons . . . but check yourself first.

Exercise 1

For each of the following sentences, write the word that precedes each comma. If a sentence needs no comma, write *C* for correct.

Example: *Little Gwendolyn sleeps with Fluffy her favorite dust bunny every night.*
Answer: *Fluffy, bunny,*

1. Dr. Robert Driller a slightly demented dentist rewards his good little patients with taffy peanut brittle and jawbreakers.

2. On crowded elevators in plush office buildings Arnold sometimes pretends he's a hyperactive chihuahua.

3. Across the slippery arctic ice and into a thirty-one flavors ice cream shop waddled the pudgy penguins.

4. Hippity-Hoppity a confused Easter bunny brought children Spam and tacos not baskets full of candy.

5. Little Mortimer failed kindergarten for he could not find Waldo.

6. During extremely mild winters furry polar bears shave their tubby bodies before they tan in the Arctic sun.

7. Paper clips in my opinion are deadly weapons that should be banned from schools.

8. Muffy filed a lawsuit against a major aspirin company for she broke a nail on a tamper-proof bottle.

9. Semore always falls asleep during class and annoys other students with his gurgling and drooling.

10. Thadeus was expelled from school on Wednesday March 10 for wearing his heavily starched boxer shorts on his head.

11. Maybelle a musical genius plays the kazoo not the tuba in the school band.

12. No you may not use your father's power tools to play dentist Timmy.

13. Goober did you know that thousands of children are injured every year by out-of-control Slinkys?

14. Thelma won the Olympic silver medal in underwater belly dancing and she hopes someday to win the gold medal in synchronized tight-rope ballet.

15. Many professional bikers I believe pick bugs from their teeth with sharp Swiss army knives.

16. Mrs. Dweeble my strange neighbor decorates her front yard with ceramic monkeys and weasels.

17. Ronald mailed a five thousand dollar check to The Hair Club for Men Box 456 Seattle Washington 90543 for dreadlocks and matching sideburns.

18. Dancing doodlebugs for example are an endangered species.

19. Mr. Theodore Snodgrass Jr. has accumulated a fortune from producing marketing and selling high-quality whoopee cushions.

20. In December of last year desperate vampires were fitted with expensive retainers to correct their embarrassing overbites.

Semicolons:

1. Use a semicolon to connect closely related sentences.

   Lyda, who is in a constant state of denial, refuses to believe her tire is flat; she insists that the other three are bloated.

2. Use a semicolon to connect two sentences when the second sentence begins with a transitional expression such as *however, nevertheless, moreover, in addition, furthermore, consequently, for instance, for example, on the other hand,* etc.

   Lolita was startled to find bugs in her begonias; furthermore, she was astounded to see menacing monkeys in her mimosa.

3. Use a semicolon (instead of a comma) to separate items in a series when one (or more) of the items contains commas.

   Theodore brushed his teeth on January 7, 2006; March 5, 2007; and February 10, 2008.
   Norton won tiddlywinks contests in Detroit, Michigan; Houston, Texas; Miami, Florida; and a small town in Antarctica.

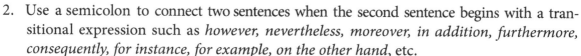

4. Use a semicolon (instead of a comma) between the clauses of a compound sentence if one of the clauses contains commas.

   In his spare time, George plays the xylophone, wrestles his python, and practices ballroom dancing; but his favorite pastime is designing potholders.

Exercise 2

Try these. For each missing comma or semicolon, write the word that precedes the error, followed by the correct punctuation. If a sentence is correct, write C.

Example: *Morty has held forty-two jobs in the last three months but he's not a quitter he's just been fired a lot.*

Answer: *months, quitter*;

1. Buzzy was struck by lightening on February 3 1992 November 18 1993 and June 1 1994.

2. Morris Raymond Thistledown Jr. left part of his two billion dollar estate to his wife and children however he left most of his money to Skippy his affectionate weenie dog.

3. In the making of the movie *The Attack of the Killer Baboons* many of the actors suffered from serious fang wounds on their earlobes legs and ankles.

4. No Semore you may not practice acupuncture on your little sister.

5. Samantha contracted a mild case of bubonic plague consequently she was unable to complete her homework.

6. You should in my opinion have liposuction performed on your face Hulga.

7. Gomer sent a check to Dr. I. B. A. Quack Box 231 Hollywood CA 90211 for a correspondence course in brain surgery.

8. Ramona recently opened a new Italian restaurant-mortuary her customers receive a free pizza with every burial.

9. Thadeus is too pudgy to play football nevertheless he is the cow-throwing champion of his school.

10. In the midst of Mildred's frizzy hair live several species of birds and bats.

11. Some people think that Quimby is strange he enjoys the study of infectious diseases.

12. Boomer often harasses his little sister for example he put Mr. Potato Head's eyes in her breakfast cereal.

13. Horatio my brother clips his bristly back hair with sharp garden clippers.

14. Grandma received tickets on January 8 1962 October 9 1968 and March 12 2008 for driving under the speed limit.

15. By the end of the holiday season twelve of Santa's elves suffered from exhaustion back pain and carpal tunnel syndrome.

16. Muffy's gerbil received a severe head wound on March 15 2008 when it fell off of its exercise wheel.

17. The Surgeon General advised that wool underwear causes chafing and skin rashes therefore most brands will soon carry warning labels.

18. The Pillsbury Doughboy I believe is currently undergoing treatment for obesity and high cholesterol.

19. After a two thousand dollar phone call to the Psychic Friends Hotline Marvin learned that financial difficulties were in his future.

20. Reginald ordered french fries not toads' eyes.

Colons

Because there aren't very many of them, colon rules are pretty easy to learn.

1. A colon is used to mean, "Hey, notice what follows." Use a colon to show that a list is about to popup.

   Thadeus received the following gifts from his parents on his birthday: an electric train set, a complete set of action figures, an electric car, twenty model airplanes, an aquarium, an electric guitar, a baseball glove, and an ant farm. However, he cried because he wanted a sock puppet.

Beware Never put a colon after a verb or preposition. In other words, a colon should be preceded by a sentence.

Wrong: *Opey's biggest fears are: ghosts, monsters under his bed, werewolves, vampires, and hangnails.*

Right: *Opey fears many things: ghosts, monsters under his bed, werewolves, vampires, and hangnails.*

Wrong: *Haggardy is annoyed by: knuckle poppers, bubble gum blowers, ice crunchers, food smackers, and breathers.*

Right: *Several types of people annoy Haggardy: knuckle poppers, bubble-gum blowers, ice crunchers, food smackers, and breathers.*

2. Use a colon to set off a quotation, especially a long one.

   When it comes to America's healthcare system, Homer Simpson has this unique perspective: "America's health care system is second only to Japan's . . . Canada's, Sweden's, Great Britain's . . . well, all of Europe. But you can thank your lucky stars we don't live in Paraguay!"

3. Use a colon to draw attention to an appositive.

   Bing finds one type of person the most irritating: the individual who refuses to pick up his or her toenail clippings.

4. Use a colon in some conventional situations:

   Hours and minutes: *According to Uncle Howarth, the space aliens should drop the giant match that will heat the earth and melt the ice caps at approximately 4:30 A.M.*
   Biblical chapters and verses: *Genesis 27:28 John 3:16*
   Salutations in business letters: *Dear Professor Quigglebottom:*

Exercise 3

Challenge! In the following exercises, you get to test what you know about commas, semicolons, and colons. As in the previous exercises, write the words that should be followed by punctuation, and write the correct punctuation after each word. If a sentence is correct, write *C*.

   Example: *My favorite hobbies are the following high wire walking skydiving bungee jumping and knitting.*
   Answer: *following: walking, skydiving, bungee jumping,*

1. During the construction and remodeling of some houses termites generally speaking suffer severe head wounds.

2. In 1996 345 million teachers suffered nervous breakdowns and many others are currently receiving therapy for nail biting and panic disorders.

3. Fiona often uses tape not tweezers to remove straggly eyebrows.

4. Buford mailed two thousand dollars to the following address Scammers Corporation of America Box 123 Hollywood CA 90210 for information on how to raise sea monkeys for fun and profit.

5. Milly's Great Dane died tragically on Saturday March 8 1997 when it choked on a plump weenie dog.

6. The main character in the novel *Wilbur Goes to High School* is hospitalized with a terminal case of acne I think.

7. Except for the open sores and boils Muffy's blind date is quite attractive.

8. To protect his identity Mr. Twipple the school's strangest substitute always wears a fake nose and mustache.

9. During the talent portion of the Miss America Pageant one of the contestants adroitly cleaned a fish to the music of *Saturday Night Fever.*

10. Horatio Thadeus Bumgarden Jr. recently donated fifty million dollars to the Save the Trees Foundation furthermore he hopes the government will one day outlaw the use of paper pencils and toothpicks.

11. In my opinion you should not wear a string bikini to your job interview with the bank president Nadine.

12. Off of the diving board and into a large vat of pineapple pudding gracefully jumped the sumo wrestler.

13. Misty molds attractive candles out of large lumps of ear wax and she makes provocative mosaics out of unusually shaped toenail clippings.

14. Vincent began to worry when his girlfriend wanted something besides flowers she wanted one of his ears.

15. For breakfast Matilda always consumes the following a hard boiled egg, a piece of toast, and a pitcher of fresh cod-liver oil.

16. Petunia bought thirty boxes of chewy monkey sausage to give as holiday gifts.

17. No you may not take Grandpa's dentures or oxygen mask for Show and Tell Jerome.

18. Buzzy has a serious addiction to chewing pen caps he has recently joined a twelve-step program.

19. Vivian sighted Elvis buying peanut butter and bananas on Monday December 10 2007 Wednesday December 19 2007 and Tuesday January 29 2008.

20. Cicero is too short to play basketball however he is the National Limbo Champion.

Exercise 4

More fun ahead. Once again, write the word that should be followed by punctuation, and write the correct punctuation after each word. If a sentence is correct, write C.

1. Mrs. Peabody spotted young playful vampires chatting chortling and drinking cherry-flavored Kool Aid in her flower garden.

2. Little Parker perplexes his parents because he thinks he's a pinecone.

3. Marvin panicked when he awoke from surgery and found his nose attached with Velcro.

4. Neurotic Mr. Gompers avoids the following telephone poles ducks and dirty dish towels.

5. Marvin lifts weights to develop his biceps and he watches cartoons to stimulate his mind.

6. Matilda did you wash the dishes take out the trash and feed the iguana?

7. Sometimes heavily sedated pets make attractive centerpieces for baby showers birthday parties and holiday dinners.

8. Some of Santa's elves have secretly undergone costly ear reduction surgery and many of them are taking growth hormones.

9. After several hours of trick or treating little Prudence received twelve pieces of gum two chocolate bars nineteen jaw breakers and twelve frozen dinners.

10. Few people realize that some cost-cutting restaurants serve tadpoles in their seafood platters and they mix rat lips in their taco meat.

11. Trent Tremble M.D. lost his contact lens in a patient's chest cavity while assisting in open-heart surgery.

12. Grandmother Furby mailed ten dollars to the Acme Tools Company 700 Wayside Drive Seattle Washington 77003 for a new pair of electric nose-hair clippers.

13. According to the great philosopher Groucho Marx "Outside of a dog, a book is a man's best friend. Inside of a dog, it's too dark to read."

14. Although Donald can't sing he can play the cello with his toes teeth and tongue.

15. My sister is a brain surgeon and my brother is a successful mime.

16. Generally speaking short people with high foreheads are extremely intelligent I believe.

17. Frederick don't stick your finger in those dangerous electrical sockets.

18. Mr. Norman Bittleman Sr. sent a check to the National Halitosis Foundation for $2,027.

19. Little Lola could not sleep for a week after seeing the flying monkeys in the movie *The Wizard of Oz.*

20. Hilda traveled to Juneau Alaska so that she could meet her Cousin Ernie a millionaire penguin breeder.

15

Those Crazy Little Apostrophes

Apostrophes are little marks of punctuation, but they can have a big effect on meaning. Just take a look at the difference in these sentences:

Those old bags in the corner are my grandmothers.
Those old bags in the corner are my grandmothers'.

In the first sentence, someone's poor grandmothers certainly get no respect. In the second sentence, the grannies could simply use some new Samsonite.

Poor confused apostrophes must have serious identity problems because they have several very different functions. Let's take a look at each.

Apostrophes to form the possessives of nouns

An apostrophe is used to show that a noun owns something. For instance, instead of saying that the bunny possesses ears, it's much easier to say the *bunny's* ears.

Here are some simple rules to remember when making a noun possessive:

1. To form the possessive of a singular noun, simply add *'s*.

   the monster's proboscis (nose)   *the ant's antennas*

2. If a noun is *plural* and ends in *s*, just add an apostrophe at the end of the word.

   the monsters' proboscises   *the ants' antennas*

3. If a noun is *plural* and does not end in *s*, add *'s* at the end of the word.

   the children's candy   *the mice's whiskers*

FYI If a singular noun with two or more syllables ends in *s*, you may choose to form the possessive by adding just an apostrophe or *'s*. Play it by ear. If you hear too many *s* sounds (Odysseus, Dickens, Delores) or the *ez* sound (Euripides, Xerxes, Achilles), you may opt to add only an apostrophe.

Dolores's Doberman or Dolores' Doberman   *Achilles's mutt or Achilles' mutt*

4. Use an apostrophe to form the possessive of indefinite pronouns (*anyone, anybody, no one, nobody, everyone, everybody, someone, somebody*).

    *Has **everyone's** picture been taken with the giant badger?*

5. Don't use an apostrophe with possessive pronouns (*his, hers, its, ours, theirs, yours*). This makes sense. These words already indicate possession. Adding an apostrophe would be going a little overboard.

    Wrong: *That cornflake-shaped purse is **her's**.*
    Right: *That cornflake-shaped purse is **hers**.*

Apostrophes to show joint possession

When two or more people (or things, or whatever) own the same thing, the last name mentioned is in possessive form. However, if two or more people (or things, or whatever) own different things, *both* names are in possessive form. I know this sounds like mumbo jumbo. Maybe the following example will help.

Milly and Trudy's gerbil

(The girls own the gerbils together.)

Milly's and Trudy's gerbils

(Each girl owns her own gerbil)

If one word showing joint ownership is a pronoun, put an *'s* on the other word.

Milly's and my gerbil is learning to tap dance.

FYI If you want to make a compound noun possessive, add *'s* to the last word.

*My **sister-in-law's** facial mole is growing rapidly.*

Other Uses of Apostrophes

Apostrophes to form contractions

You probably already know that one of the main uses of apostrophes is to form contractions. In a contraction, the apostrophe usually takes the place of a missing letter.

isn't (is not)
I'm (I am)
you're (you are)
can't (cannot)
don't (do not)
Won't (will not—I admit that *won't* is a little weird. Beats me how someone came up with this one.)

Also, use an apostrophe when stating time: four o'clock (four of the clock)

Apostrophes to form some plurals

Suppose young Einstein made an A in each of his classes: science, math, and underwater whistling. If you write that he made four *As*, the plural of the letter *A* looks like the word *As*.

Add *'s* to form the plural of capital letters, numbers, and symbols. However, it's acceptable in these cases to just add *s* (without the apostrophe) if doing so presents no confusion.

*The winning lottery number has five **7s** (or 7's) in it.*
*In the **1800s**, people wore fur underwear when the temperature dropped into the **20s** (or 20's).*

For some odd reason, you don't use an apostrophe when forming the plural of centuries—for example, *1700s, 1800s, 1900s, etc.*

Always add *'s* to form the plural of lower case letters, and of words and expressions used to represent themselves.

*The word arachnophobia has three **a's** in it.*
*Ya know, you use too many **ya know's** when you speak.*

Exercise 1

See if you can choose the correct word in parentheses.

1. My brother Branford had been saving (his, his') money for months to buy a pet flea.

2. Branford and I read a book about pet (fleas, fleas'), and then we went to examine Pet Emporium's selection.

3. (Everyone's, Everyones) preferences are different when it comes to fleas.

4. However, since a large (fleas, flea's) life span can be over fifty years, caring for one is a big commitment.

5. If (your, you're) looking for a less demanding species, you might consider a tick or a tapeworm instead.

6. In my (grandmother's, grandmothers) yard, some ticks grow to be the size of small rodents.

7. One (ticks', tick's) sociability won Branford and me over, and we adopted it as our own.

8. Whether you pick a flea or a tick for a pet, be sure not to get (its, it's) feet wet.

9. If a (flea's, fleas') feet get wet, rush it quickly to the vet.

10. (Its, It's) easy to fall in love with the friendly little bloodsuckers.

Exercise 2

Write each word with an apostrophe mistake in its correct form by either adding or deleting an apostrophe. If a sentence is correct, write *C*.

1. Are Mr. Potato Heads kids called tater tots?

2. Why aren't ducks bills called *bobs*?

3. Tods toad croaked, so he buried it.

4. Because he crosses his *is* and dots his *t*s, Titinius has a signature that is hard to read.

5. Aunt Irmas underwear is always itchy because its covered with too much tacky ric-rac.

6. Some fleas fangs cause pain when they stick into skinny peoples veins.

7. A persons I.Q. is generally equal to his height in inches added to his shoe size.

8. A guppys brain will fit on the head of a pin.

9. Norman's and Broomhilda's poodle is an amazing tap dancer.

10. The mice's lice look like tiny grains of rice.

Exercise 3

Once again, write the words that need apostrophes, and place the apostrophes where they belong.

1. Marvins sister is a brilliant brain surgeon; however, Marvin works as a human pin cushion in his Cousin Vinneys circus.

2. In a box in his room, Timmy keeps a squids eye, a vampires' fang, and three pigs brains.

3. Against his doctor's advice and his mothers' warning, Thadeus pierced his nose and tattooed his earlobes.

4. In Mrs. Peabody's and Mr. Snodgrass's front yards, wild, rabid weasels' are running in circles and gnawing on tree trunks.

5. After he made four Ds and an F on his report card, Reginald's parents' took away the keys to his new jet.

6. Smitty and Petunia's Uncle Ulric amuses the family every Christmas by clinking along to carols with his' false teeth.

7. My eccentric aunt keeps my uncles' kidney stone in a jar on her coffee table next to my grandmother's appendix.

8. In the National Honor Society's talent show, Marvin thrilled the audience by playing "Stairway to Heaven" with his armpits'.

9. In a recent election, the students' decided that their school's colors would be chartreuse and mauve, and their mascot would be a loveable earthworm.

10. This holiday season hundreds of elves will collect money in front of grocery stores to pay for Santa's liposuction, Rudolphs' nose job, and Mrs. Clause's aerobic's classes.

Exercise 4

Warning. The following story is a very trifling turkey tongue twister. Please ignore the absurdity. Also, please overlook the fact that I seem to have some weird kind of tick fixation.

Write the words that need apostrophes, and place the apostrophes where they belong. If a sentence has no apostrophe error, write C.

Tillie's Turkeys

¹Once upon a time there lived a woman named Tillie who raised turkeys in tents. ²She fed the turkeys tofu, and she sprinkled the tofu with tea leaves so that the tofus taste was tart. ³Tillie charged tourists and their toddlers two dollars to see the turkeys. ⁴To amuse the tourists tykes, Tillie painted all of the turkeys toenails turquoise and topped the birds heads with toupees. ⁵Unbeknownst to Tillie, many of the turkeys toupees were tainted with ticks. ⁶These ticks had teeth, and the ticks teeth tormented the turkeys. ⁷To rid the turkeys of ticks, Tillie fed the birds taffy instead of tofu because she hoped the ticks would stick to it. ⁸The ticks didn't stick, and the turkeys grew sick from too much taffy. ⁹Tillie sold her tubby turkeys to a trapeze artist who taught the turkeys and the turkeys ticks to tap dance. ¹⁰In twenty years, Tillie plans to retire and teach tiger taming to tots in Tennessee, if they have their parents permission.

The End

Now you can avoid all of those embarrassing apostrophe catastrophes!

16

Quotation Marks and Italics

Like all marks of punctuation, quotation marks are important to clarify meaning; a few quotation marks in the wrong places can make a big difference. Suppose, for example, you plop down with a novel. Suppose in the novel, Wilma and Gertrude are friends who work together, say . . . as office assistants at a modeling agency. Suppose they're both in love with one of the agency's most in-demand models, Heathcliffe. Now suppose on page 73 these words appear:

Gertrude blurted Wilma said Heathcliff is in love with me.

The way the words are punctuated can make a big difference in who knows what about whom.

Gertrude blurted, "Wilma said Heathcliff is in love with me."

or

Gertrude blurted, "Wilma said, 'Heathcliff is in love with me!'"

or

"Gertrude," blurted Wilma, "said Heathcliff is in love with me!"

or

"Gertrude," blurted Wilma, "said, 'Heathcliff is in love with me'!"

Aha! Several questions arise: Are Wilma and Gertrude still friends? Has Gertrude betrayed Wilma? Has Wilma betrayed Gertrude? Will Heathcliff jump off a cliff?

So much for examples that go on way too long (and for my career as a novelist). I hope with the following information at hand, quotation mistakes will haunt you—to quote a famous bird in poetry—"Nevermore."

Quotation Marks

1. Use quotation marks when giving a speaker's exact words (a direct quotation).

   Right: *"Sometimes I like to enhance my eyebrows with fuzzy caterpillars," declared Hillary.* (direct quotation—These are Hillary's exact words.)

   Right: *Hillary declared that sometimes she likes to enhance her eyebrows with fuzzy caterpillars.* (indirect quotation—The sentence doesn't include Hillary's *exact words*, so no quotation marks are needed.)

   Wrong: *Hillary declared that "Sometimes she likes to enhance her eyebrows with fuzzy caterpillars."* (Quotation marks aren't used with an indirect quotation.)

2. A direct quotation usually begins with a capital letter:

   *Esther questioned, "**W**hy doesn't Super Glue stick to the inside of the tube?"*

3. Commas and periods always, go inside of closing quotation marks.

   Right: *"A duck with udders," muttered Cubby, "would be utterly ridiculous."*

   Wrong: *"A duck with udders", muttered Cubby, "would be utterly ridiculous".*

4. When a speaker tag (the *somebody said* part of a quotation) or other types of words *interrupt* a quoted sentence, punctuate the sentence in the following way:

   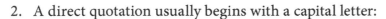

   - Enclose the first part of the sentence in quotation marks.

   - Place a comma before and after the interrupting words.

- Enclose the second part of the sentence in quotation marks.

- Begin the second part of the sentence with a lowercase letter.

Right: *"I consider myself very lucky," said Sally Mae, "that I have good hair every day."*

Wrong: *"I consider myself very lucky," said Sally Mae. "That I have good hair every day."* (That I have good hair every day is a sentence fragment.)

Wrong: *"I consider myself very lucky." said Sally Mae. "That I have good hair every day."* (Ahhh!—too many periods!)

5. When the speaker tag or another type of expression comes at the end of a quoted sentence, punctuate the sentence like this:

- Enclose the directly quoted sentence in quotation marks.

- Put a comma, not a period, at the end of the directly quoted sentence.

- Place a period after the tag.

- Begin the next sentence with a capital letter.

Right: *"A bird dropping landed in my eye," exclaimed Tyson. "I'm certainly glad that hippopotami don't fly."*

Wrong: *"A bird dropping landed in my eye," exclaimed Tyson, "I'm certainly glad that hippopotami don't fly."* (Ahhh! a comma splice!)

6. If a direct quotation includes several uninterrupted sentences, place quotation marks only at the beginning and end of the quote, not around every sentence:

Right: *Reginald sputtered, "My favorite class is Handcrafts 101. Yesterday the class made potholders out of cat fur. Last week we carved figures of jumbo garden insects out of blocks of processed meat."*

Wrong: *Reginald sputtered, "My favorite class is Handcrafts 101." "Yesterday the class made potholders out of cat fur." "Last week we carved figures of jumbo garden insects out of blocks of processed meat."* (Ahhh! too many quotation marks!)

7. Place single quotation marks around a quote inside a quote:

   Right: *"My favorite short story is 'The Cats of Amarillo' by Edgar Allan Poe," announced Moby.*

   Wrong: *"My favorite short story is "The Cats of Amarillo" by Edgar Allan Poe," announced Moby.*

8. In dialogue, begin a new paragraph every time the speaker changes:

   "I need you to knead the bread," said Ed, "because we'll need a fresh loaf in the morning."

   "Hey, I'm no loafer," shot back Fred, "so quit stewing and stir the stew."

   "Just simmer down and turn up the heat on the turnips," said Ed.

   "Okay," replied Fred, "but I just wish you'd quit bugging me and squash the bug on the squash."

   Gosh darn. Aren't (bad) puns fun.

9. If a direct quotation is several paragraphs long from one speaker, put quotation marks at the beginning of each paragraph and at the end of the quote. Don't place closing quotation marks at the end of each paragraph.

   "Timmy, why don't you show the class what you brought for Show and Tell?" asked Miss Pimpleton, a slightly frazzled third grade teacher.

   "Uh, this is my ant farm," stammered Timmy, standing and holding a plastic container in front of the class. "Ants are fascinating creatures. They are actually very strong. An ant can carry about ten or a million times its own weight. Ants have antennas and some legs.

"My ant farm doesn't have any ants in it 'cause I knocked it over this morning and they went all over the kitchen. My mom was kind of mad. She sprayed them and they all died. Which I don't think is right 'cause she didn't spray my hamster when it got loose.

"In conclusion, ant farms are very fascinating to watch, especially if they have ants in them."

"Thank you, Timmy," muttered Miss Pimpleton, "and tell your mother she has my sympathy."

Exercise 1

Now test your quotations intelligence quotient (Q. I. Q.). See if you can correctly punctuate these sentences. If a sentence is correct, write *C*.

1. I collect jellyfish on the beach said Ralph because they make excellent erasers.

2. How did pioneer women fix their hair asked Dody I don't think they had blow dryers.

3. My favorite song is Tomorrow said Opie I wish I could play it on the xylophone.

4. I prefer to play jumbo golf said Durwin not miniature.

5. I got a part in the school play! exclaimed Bula I'm going to be a pitted olive!

6. Horace observed I can't believe those mutant gnats actually attacked a rhino.

7. I think the reason Maude is a starving artist remarked Dodson is because she only paints pictures of cephalopods.

8. As a member of the Ferret Preservation Society remarked Waldo I've learned to appreciate rodents.

9. Doctor said Donald to his psychiatrist sometimes I think I'm a turnip.

10. A pushy officer pulled me over blurted Prissy and I was only going ninety-five in a school zone!

11. I've noticed observed Egbert that clocks always run clockwise.

12. I just heard a cow bark remarked Opal it sounded like a chihuahua.

13. Wilamena excitedly told her mother, for Halloween, I'm going to be a grilled cheese sandwich!

14. I bought a new mouse for my computer muttered Mortimer Duncely but it crawls all over my monitor.

15. The psychic said that she was late for a reading because she had lost her car keys.

Exercise 2

Now try these. Correctly punctuate each sentence. If a sentence is correct, write C.

1. Large roaches Hubert noted sometimes feed on cattle.

2. Timmy cried I want a pony for my birthday! however his parents gave him a pack of gum instead.

3. I have insomnia yawned Ronald but it doesn't keep me up at night.

4. Ostriches with fleas remarked Louise are often ostracized by their peers.

5. I have a pet turtle announced Roland and he looks just like my grandfather.

6. I wish Christmas would come in July whined Lizzy so the shops wouldn't be so busy.

7. The reason my bulldog's face is flat admitted Barker is because he chases parked cars.

8. Sometimes I wish I were the windshield, not the bug moaned Dudley.

9. Instead of wearing a hat with my outfit said Rhoda sometimes I prefer to wear a matching toad.

10. Neil said that his favorite meal is eel on a stick.

11. I was shocked said Holly when the principal shouted We're having a meteorite storm! Take cover.

12. For my poetry presentation said Scuzzy I would like to read a selection entitled Dustmites.

13. Vinnie inquired why is it impossible to tickle yourself?

14. I was so excited when Arnold looked into my eyes Zoey recalled I was crushed, though, when he told me that I had a piece of spinach between my teeth.

15. The guide shouted watch out for the killer chiggers!

Exercise 3

Now see if you can use quotation marks in a situation with more than one speaker. (Hint: Rule 8, Rule 8, Rule 8)

At the County Fair, Senator Sham was campaigning furiously for his shaky reelection bid. Senator, asked one reporter, will you raise taxes if you're reelected? That's a good question, the senator replied, trying to look thoughtful. So let me give you a straight answer. I don't intend to raise taxes unless, of course, in case of a serious situation like war or rain or something. However, even then I won't, unless I do. The reporter looked puzzled but continued. Will you support education? Of course, I think that every young person should be illiterate enough to read and write. Also, Senator, how do you intend to handle the budget? Simple. Let me give you some concrete ways. I'll make a detailed budget that's within budget. First, I'll clean out the attic and sweep out the dust. Then I'll budget for the budget with funds from various funds. And one last question, Senator. How do you explain your recent criminal conviction? The senator's tanned face turned slightly pale. I'm sorry. I couldn't hear that last question, he finally stammered, and in a flash he was off to kiss a nearby baby and hug a retired person.

Exercise 4

Now try to punctuate this dialogue that has no speaker tags. (Just remember: Rule 8, Rule 8, Rule 8!)

Good evening. Welcome to The Jay O'Casey Show. Our guest this evening is Mr. Noah Life who has spent the last several years reading the complete fifty-volume set of the Oxford English Dictionary. Welcome, Mr. Life. Thank you, Mr. OKC. Call me Jay. Now tell me, what motivated you to read the entire dictionary? Well, Mr. OKC, I mean J, because it was there. I see. J, those happen to be two of my favorite letters. Okay. Those, too, J. Let's move on. Let me ask you this. In addition to I, C, O, and K, what are some of your other favorite letters of the dictionary? Well, I'd have to say P because it has plot, but the A section was pretty good too because it has action. I see. Do you like T? No, I prefer coffee, thank you, J. You know, Mr. Life, some people say that you're quite a shallow person. How do you respond to these critics? I enjoy deep sea diving, J. I see. Well, unfortunately we're out of time. Thank you for joining me. Uh, J, before I go, I'd just like to say hello to my kids, Dee, Bea, and Kay. Join me tomorrow night when our guest will be the great-great grandson of the inventor of the paper clip. Good night for now, America.

Exercise 5

Now try to place quotation marks in the right places when the same speaker goes on for several paragraphs. To simplify things, only write the words that need quotation marks before or after, and place the marks where they belong

Example: *"I,*

"Later,

me."

Muffy, not exactly a model student, is giving her book report in front of the class.

Over the summer I read a book called The Old Man and the Sea. It was about an old man and a fish. That is why the book is called The Old Man and the Sea because the fish was actually in the sea. I don't remember the author's name. Anyway, I chose this book because it was 102 pages long.

I really couldn't relate to any of the characters. The old man is really old, and he's a man, and I'm not. I also could not relate to the fish. However, I could relate to some of the book. I have an aquarium. I think my fish are probably a lot smaller than the old man's, but they swim around and stuff.

The first few pages of the book were wonderful. I didn't like or dislike the ending because I never really finished the book. I was going to, but I lost it, and then I forgot about it. I hope you won't count off points since I'm at least being honest.

I didn't experience many obstacles while reading the book, except that I got kind of confused in the beginning and middle. This book was definitely one of the best books I have ever almost read in my whole life.

Quotation Marks and Italics in Titles

In addition to indicating a person's exact words, quotation marks are also used to enclose titles of short published works: (magazine and newspaper articles, short stories, poems, songs, chapters, song titles, and other short works.)

"Scientists Discover Tiny Space Aliens in Breakfast Cereal"—article
"The Dog That Bit People"—short story
"Mr. Speds and Mr. Spats"—poem
"Some Where Over the Rainbow"—song

If a work is longer (the work itself, not the title), instead of using quotation marks, you write the title in *italics*. Italics, by the way, are those *goofy slanting letters*. If you're writing instead of typing, you would underline to indicate that something should be italicized.

Longer works include the following: books, long plays, movies, magazines, newspapers, and some long musical works. In addition to italicizing titles of long works, for some strange reason you italicize names of air and sea ships, and works of art.

FYI Only italicize the words *a*, *an*, and *the* if they're actually part of the title.

The Velveteen Rabbit (book)
My Fair Lady (long play)
The Houston Chronicle (newspaper)
Time (magazine)
Beethoven's *Pastoral Symphony* (long musical work)
the *Nina*, *Pinta* and *Santa Maria* (ships)
the starship *Enterprise* (airship)
the *Mona Lisa* (work of art)

Also, use italics for words, letters, and numbers when you're referring to the word, letter, or number itself. Since that explanation is about as clear as mud, take a look at these examples:

The word *sesquipedalian* has one **q.**
Unfortunately, nearsighted Mrs. Bittlebottom thought the **7**s in her winning lottery number were actually **3**s.

Finally, use italics for foreign words or phrases that will likely be unfamiliar to those who speak only English.

Arnold committed a terrible *faux pas* when he sneezed in his date's face.

FYI Use either underlining or italics with a title, but not both. This would be overkill. Doing so would be redundant. It would also be repetitious.

Wrong: <u>*How The Grinch Stole Christmas*</u>
Right: *How The Grinch Stole Christmas* or <u>How The Grinch Stole Christmas</u>

Exercise 6

Now, here's a little examination so that you can test your degree of elucidation and try to exceed expectations by providing the underlining and quotations for clarification in the following sentences. (I should be a government poet.)

1. Biffy read the poem Mossy Artichokes on a Psychedelic Tundra to the class from the book, The Poetry of the Insane.

2. After watching the movie The Revenge of the Killer Roly-Poly Bugs, Waldo read a copy of Field and Stream to calm his nerves.

3. Evonne was shocked by the headline in the National Enquirer: Customer Spontaneously Combusts in Mexican Food Restaurant.

4. When Barney was a contestant on Wheel of Stuff, his favorite game show, he won lovely gold-plated, squid-shaped bookends.

5. Doreen's painting, entitled The Flight of Sniffling Ferrets, hangs in the city museum.

6. Sigfried's incorrigible little brother drew a mustache on the Mona Lisa.

7. Buford had nightmares after reading the chapter Fear the Dark from the book Vampires, Goblins, and Mutant Lice.

8. Ralph's new boat The Unsinkable sank after a crazed seagull crashed into the hull.

9. Lileth read the novel Great Expectations, but she prefers nonfiction—for example, The Ultimate Guide to Eyebrow Waxing.

10. The Bells and The Raven are Pogo's two favorite Poe poems.

11. The word aardvark has three a's.

12. In the Denver Post, the headline reads Aliens Found in Frito Bags.

13. In Spanish, tu madre esta loca means your mother is crazy.

14. A sculpture called Pollen and Mold Spores will soon be unveiled at North Shore Park.

15. Semore finished reading Pain in the Night, the last chapter of the book Vampires with Cavities and Gum Disease.

16. Marvin's painting entitled Hangnails, Cuticles, and Toe Hair hangs in the Museum of Modern Art.

17. Dóndé está el baño? are the only words Gertrude remembers after taking twelve years of Spanish.

18. Orvil, a precocious three year old, wrote his first opera: Big Bird and the Existential Truth.

19. For extra credit, Meldrick performed the entire play Julius Caesar for his first grade class using only sock puppets.

20. After muttering bon voyage, Gustave flushed his dead goldfish down the toilet.

17

Hyphens, Dashes, Parentheses, and Ellipses

(a.k.a. the Leftovers)

For most people, the last four marks of punctuation fall into the "other" category. In other words, they aren't given much attention. People often use them in creative ways, but these poor, neglected marks actually have rules that apply to formal writing. So, in the interest of fairness, this chapter is devoted to the leftover four.

Hyphens

1. Hyphens are used mainly to divide words into syllables. I've already hinted that grammar sticklers are a little neurotic, and here's one more thing that drives an English teacher (namely me) slightly bonkers—incorrect syllable division. Take a look.

Wrong:

Snakes

by Muffy Marguerite Moppleberry

Snakes are very interesting creatures. Most snakes are long. They are a-

lso limbless, so they don't have disposable thumbs like humans. Some snakes are poisonous and some snakes aren't. Snakes aren't fur- ry because they aren't mammals. They're also cold blooded, so they lie in the sun a lot. This is probably why they have such wrinkl- y skin. They would probably live longer if they used sunscreen.

Even though few people aren't as hyphenally (made-up word) chal- lenged as Muffy, it's always good to know a few guidelines. These rules will help if, when you reach the end of a line, you're faced with that daunt- ing decision—to divide, or not to divide.

- Divide words ONLY between syllables. Thank goodness for a nifty book called a dictionary. It actually shows you how to divide a word if you're unsure.

- Never divide a one-syllable word.

  Wrong: to-oth   no-se   po-och

- Never have one letter hanging out there all by itself, even if the letter is a complete syllable.

  Wrong: *itch-y   gass-y   e-mus*

- Don't carry a two-letter word ending over to the next line.

  Wrong: *wrink-ly   gang-ly   gullywash-er*

- Divide hyphenated words only at the hyphens.

  Right: *mother-in-law   merry-go-round*
  Wrong: mo-ther-in-law   me-rry-go-round

- Don't divide capitalized words (proper nouns or proper adjectives).

  Wrong: *Grace-land   Mr. Fribble-berry   Rocky Moun-tains*

2. Use a hyphen when writing out the numbers twenty-one to ninety-nine.

   *Quidley, who saves money by buying toilet paper in bulk, was disappointed to find that his package of **one hundred** rolls only contained **ninety-nine**.*

3. Use a hyphen with fractions that are used as adjectives, but not with ones that are used as nouns.

   *Morticia graduated in the top **one third** of her embalming class.* (noun)
   *Zeffy always begins the morning with **one-half** cup of bran and a smoked ham.*
      (adjective)

4. Now this rule is goofy. Use a hyphen when a compound adjective comes *before* a noun, but not when a compound adjective comes *after* a noun.

   *Thisleberry was too hungry to wait, so he ate a **half-baked** rattlesnake.*
   *After Thisleberry ate the rattlesnake **half baked**, he started rattling and shaking.*

FYI If a compound adjective before a noun is *capitalized*, don't use a hyphen unless the adjective already requires a hyphen.

   Smellsville's Annual Limburger Cheese Celebration
   The Self-Help Book Writers' Issue Resolution Convention

FYI (again) If an adverb ending in *-ly* and an adjective come before a noun, don't use a hyphen.

   Wrong: *a slightly-scuzzy buzzard*
   Right: *a slightly scuzzy buzzard*

5. Hyphens are used to separate prefixes from proper nouns or adjectives.

   *"I think my mother was born in the **pre-Victorian** era," said Ditzy, "which was a long
      time ago."*
   *"The Loch Ness Monster lives someplace in Lake Michigan," said not-so-worldly Appleton,
      "and I think Bigfoot lives in the **mid-Atlantic**."*

6. Use a hyphen with the prefix *self-*. *Don't use a hyphen with selfish, selfhood, or with pronouns such as himself or herself.*

   *For **self-protection**, Marlowe, a **self-described** innovator, built a moat **himself** around
      his home for **self-defense**, despite the complaints of his **selfish** neighbors.*

7. Use a hyphen to separate a title from the suffix *-elect*.

   *The **governor-elect** requested that the state bird be changed to the snipe.*

8. Use a hyphen after the prefix *ex-* when it means *former* or *formerly.*

   *Mr. Bittlehopper, soon to be the **ex-governor**, graciously suggested that the new bathroom facilities in the capitol be named after the **governor-elect**.*

9. *Sometimes*—emphasis on *sometimes*—a prefix is separated from a word to prevent confusion, or to prevent identical vowels or too many vowels from coming together. If you're unsure about whether or not to include a hyphen, then resort to rule 10.

   re-creation   anti-intellectual   co-authorship

10. The dictionary is your friend. Take advantage of it. (That didn't come out quite right.)

Exercise 1

Time to check out what you know. Find the mistakes in hyphen usage in these sentences. Write the words with hyphen errors correctly, and write *C* if a sentence has no hyphen errors.

1. The mayor elect decided that to curb indecency in the city all tree squirrels should be clothed.

2. Aunt Posie has no regrets about ordering her forty seven pieces of exercise equipment because they make quaint clothes hangers.

3. Ermine's self improvement plan includes consuming fewer calories by substituting one half gallon of parsley for her usual tub of ice cream.

4. Beenie thought that his ex neighbors were slightly strange when they insisted that the spaceship like contraption in their backyard was merely an extremely large sprinkler.

5. Because Cousin Dwight keeps a well waxed kitchen floor, the roaches have fun slipping and sliding all night.

6. Hoping to grow sunflowers, confused Mrs. Zipple carefully planted all of her light bulbs.

7. Because Archie likes to keep a stiff upper lip, he makes sure his mustache is always well starched.

8. When Axle went through his mid life crisis, he traveled the mid European countries, bought a bright red sports car, and had his back waxed.

9. Lester was voted the best dressed pest in the Annual Fire Ant Festival Costume Contest.

10. Because Edgar's freckles run together, they look like one big cow spot, not dots.

11. A self motivated scientist has finally discovered the gene that's responsible for singing in the shower.

12. Uncle Jenkins was self employed making plastic yard flamingos, but he quit his business and bought a rinky dink skating rink that he painted light pink.

13. The plucky chicken ducked in and out of traffic to get to the other side of the newly constructed superhighway.

14. Because Blanche always wears appropriate colors, she went to the nine to midnight Halloween party dressed as a traffic cone.

15. One of Mitsy's little pitfalls occurred last fall when she slipped on the spit of some crude mannered nitwit and slid across the just polished floor of the mall.

Dashes

Dashes and commas have a lot in common. They both show pauses, but a dash shows a greater pause. Dashes are handy in these situations:

1. Use a dash when you want to show a change of thought, a very deliberate pause.

   "I called the Addict Hotline," divulged Kibby, "and I had to admit that I'm—I'm—I'm hooked on phonics!"

2. Use a dash for emphasis.

   Oh, my! Look what the cat, dragged in—a seventy-pound rat!

3. You can use dashes to set off appositives that have commas. Otherwise, you end up with too many commas in a row.

"I know what type of car I'm going to buy—either a blue one, a green one, or a yellow one—and I hope the dealer has a fifteen-year finance option," said Trixie.

4. Use dashes to separate appositives from the rest of the sentence, when they are introduced by phrases such as *for example, that is,* and *for instance.*

An intimidating guard animal—for example, the snaggle-toothed gopher—requires months of training.

Vacationers should rule out certain places—for instance, villages near active volcanoes—when making their travel plans.

Parentheses

I know this is sort of a no-brainer, but the first thing to know about parentheses is that they always come in pairs.

FYI *Parentheses* is plural, and *parenthesis* is singular.

You use parentheses to set off side comments, or information that's not closely related to the sentence. Anything that you place in parentheses, as with hyphens, you should be able to lift out of the sentence and have the sentence still make sense.

If the shoe fits, wear it (but make sure the other one fits too because sometimes two sizes get mixed up in the box).

The winner of the Anti-Air Pollution Award (a prize that's coveted in the scientific community) was the inventor of the minty breath spray.

How do you decide whether to put the period inside or outside of a closing parenthesis? Good question.

Gertrude runs every race with her lucky rabbit's foot (but for some reason she always comes in last).

Since the material in parentheses belongs to the sentence, a period follows the closing parenthesis. When the material becomes an addition to the sentence, the period goes inside the closing parenthesis.

Fletcher quit his job as a dogcatcher. (He grew tired of being hounded by the opposition.)

Ellipsis

Points of ellipsis (like these dots . . .) are generally used to show that words have been omitted. There are different methods of using ellipses, but the three-dot method is the simplest. Here are a few ellipsis tipsis.

FYI *Ellipsis* is singular, and *ellipses* is the plural form of the word.

1. An ellipsis mark consists of three periods with a space after each period. (Also, put a space before the first period.)

2. You generally don't need to put points of ellipsis (dots) at the beginning or end of a quote, unless the quote begins or ends mid-sentence.

3. The three dots may be preceded or followed by a period, comma, semicolon, colon, exclamation mark, or question mark if one appears in the original manuscript. Take a look at this passage from *Alice in Wonderland*.

They were standing under a tree, each with an arm round the other's neck, . . . one of them had "DUM" embroidered on his collar, and the other "DEE." . . .

They stood so still that she quite forgot they were alive, and she was just looking round to see if the word "TWEEDLE" was written at the back of each collar, when she was startled by a voice coming from the one marked "DUM."

"If you think we're wax-works," he said, "you ought to pay, you know . . . !"

4. Always make sure that the quote makes sense after you've left some of it out.

    Wrong: *They were standing . . . "DEE."* (huh?)

5. Ellipses are sometimes used to show hesitation or deliberation.

    "Hmm, . . ." ruminated Beasly, "I think for my vacation I'll travel to Egypt to see the pyramids, . . . or maybe I'll go to New Jersey. . ."

*I would describe my neighbor as . . . well . . . a little strange
. . . but ambidextrous. She uses her long, sharp fingernails
to nail annoying, flying insects.*

Exercise 2

If the following sentence is punctuated correctly, write *C*. If it's
punctuated incorrectly, write *I*.

1. Opal sold her stock in the bowling ball manufacturing company. (The business was in the gutter).

2. Flintly who is the weirdest kid on the block collects navel lint.

3. The newlyweds suffered serious pre honeymoon concussions because the guests threw: canned goods instead of rice.

4. The angry fans with no self control threw hamburgers, hot dogs, corn dogs, and a small wiener dog at the umpire.

5. "Gosh," . . . I wonder if I should order the buzzard burger . . . or the seaweed sandwich . . ." Josh cogitated.

6. Griswald is always grasping for straws. (No wonder no one wants to sit by her in a movie theater.)

7. According to Dave Barry: "In modern America . . . airplanes."

8. Morticia plans to quit her job in the mortuary—a grave decision since she's had the job for the past twenty years—because she's tired of having a bunch of stiffs for clients.

9. For some reason, (in the Senate hearing on cloning,) no one seemed to notice that all of the scientists looked alike.

10. "I—I—I've fallen in love with a circus clown!" Stacy Mae finally had the nerve to say to her shocked fiancé.

18

A Little Help with Spelling: Words Often Confused and Spelling out Numbers

After years of teaching, I've learned the importance of precision when it comes to words. One little slip, one little mix-up, and the whole meaning of a sentence can be altered into something unintentional, and even quite astonishing. Papers from students have provided me a wealth of examples:

At the top of my aunt's old house is a gloomy **addict**.

I guess everyone's family is dysfunctional in some way.

After chasing down the criminal, the citizen was honored for his amazing **feet**.

Actually, this sentence might be intended as is since, considering their probable speed and dexterity, the hero's feet most likely were amazing.

Odysseus threw a steak at the Cyclops and hit him in the eye.

I couldn't help but wonder where Odysseus found the steak, what he was doing with it in the cave, and more importantly, why the heck he and his men didn't eat the thing instead of aggravating Polyphemus with it.

The wild **bore** *attacked the dog.*

Talk about an oxymoron.

*I hate getting **close** on special days like my birthday.*

For the longest time I worried about this student, thinking he had some kind of attachment disorder. I thought this was odd because he seemed so personable in class. It wasn't until weeks later that I discovered that he actually meant shirts and socks, and he had nothing against bonding.

So much for the examples. I hope this chapter will help you choose the right words to give your reader the right massage . . . uh, make that message.

Frequently Confused Words

accede   [verb] to agree

Howie acceded to pay Bertha $20 after his pet boa swallowed her beagle.

exceed   [verb] to go beyond

Nora exceeded her parents' expectations when she became an eyebrow groomer to the Hollywood stars.

◎   ◎   ◎

accept   [verb] to receive willingly

At the school talent show, Kiwi accepted kudos from the crowd after she performed a tap dance on the tight rope to the bouncy tune of "Tomorrow."

except   [preposition] but (not including)

All of the football players, except Egbert, grew sideburns shaped like puffy poodles.

[verb] to leave out or exclude

Hoping to win reelection, Senator Keester announced that he would exempt every citizen with a vowel in his or her name from paying taxes.

◎   ◎   ◎

adapt   [verb] to adjust; to change to meet new requirements

With the help of an SPF 50 sunscreen, Petunia's penguins were able to adapt to the prairie.

adopt   [verb] to accept and take as one's own

Penelope adopts every playful platypus on the playground.

◎   ◎   ◎

advice   [noun] counsel

Following his doctor's advice to exercise more, Freddy increased the rate and intensity of his chewing.

advise   [verb] to give advice

After Freda's friends advised her to *fight fire with fire*, she accidentally burned down the house.

◎   ◎   ◎

affect   [verb] to influence

Finding a roach in the rice did not affect Alfred's appetite.

effect   [noun] consequence; result

In a recent government study, scientists observed the effects of caffeine and jelly-beans on porcupines' dreams.

[verb] to accomplish

By giving up lard, Elvira hopes to effect a quick weight loss.

◎   ◎   ◎

all right   [adjective] correct; okay (note: This is the only correct spelling. Even though *alright* appears in the dictionary, it's labeled as slang.)

It is not all right to write *all right* as *alright*.

◎   ◎   ◎

all ready   [pronoun plus adjective] everyone is ready

The children were all ready to collect money to give to the Foundation for Cows with Cooties.

already   [adverb] previously

Shirley has already donated to the Baths for Bovines movement.

⊚ ⊚ ⊚

allusion   [noun] an indirect reference

Ainsley's report on primates contained an allusion to the flying monkeys in *The Wizard of Oz*.

illusion   [noun] a false idea or appearance

Elmer was startled by the illusion of eighteen elves eating olives on top of his armoire.

⊚ ⊚ ⊚

altar   [noun] structure at which religious rites are performed

The guests were surprised when the bride jumped on the altar and belted out the theme from *Saturday Night Fever*.

alter   [verb] to change

Alpha underwent plastic surgery to alter her appearance before her wedding, but her fiancé refused to marry her because he didn't recognize her at the altar.

⊚ ⊚ ⊚

all together   [pronoun plus adverb] everyone in the same place

When the family is all together, we like to barbecue barnacles.

altogether   [adverb] entirely

Bertha ate altogether too many buttered beans with her barbecued barnacles.

⊚ ⊚ ⊚

bear   [noun] a big furry creature; [verb] to carry

Some overweight bears (noun) that can barely bear (verb) their own weight bear (verb) signs urging park visitors to feed the bears (noun).

[verb] to endure

Mrs. Felini crochets frilly little coats for all of her kittens because she can't bear to see them chilly.

bare   [adjective] having no clothing or cover; unadorned

Because he believes that every citizen has the right to bare arms, Dirk always wears sleeveless shirts to work.

◉   ◉   ◉

boar   [noun] a wild hog

That short-legged, beady-eyed, bristly backed boar bears an uncanny resemblance to Uncle Norton.

bore   [noun] a tiresome or annoying person

"Aunt Dora is such a bore," droned Lenore, "because she only talks about her foot sores."

         [verb] to cause weariness or tedium

"When Squiggy talks in clichés," said Ingrid, "he bores me to tears."

◉   ◉   ◉

board   [noun] a wooden plank

With his new buzz saw, Buzzy cuts boards to build birdhouses for buzzards.

         [noun] a group of officials acting together

The school board voted 9-0 to provide all teachers with primal scream therapy.

bored   [adjective] feeling weary from lack of stimulation

During his psychiatrist's lecture on how to cure insomnia, Buzzy grew bored and fell asleep.

◉   ◉   ◉

brake   [noun] stopping device

Stan slammed on the brakes of his van to avoid flattening the flamingo flitting in the freeway.

break   [verb] shatter

If you're hungry, Unger, don't chew on screws, or you'll break a tooth!

☉   ☉   ☉

breath   [noun] the air inhaled and exhaled in respiration

After struggling to open a bag of pork-rinds, Potsy was too out of breath to exercise.

breathe   [verb] to draw air into the lungs and expel it

"It's not easy to breathe when a chimpanzee sleeps on your face," squeaked Louise.

☉   ☉   ☉

capital   [noun] city

"No, Herman, Transylvania is not the capital of Texas," said Rex, quite vexed.

[noun] money used by a business

Jacqueline was itching to lend Zack capital to invest in a back scratcher factory.

capitol   [noun] chief building that houses a government body

The citizens were shocked when the governor painted the dome of the capitol the color of a cantaloupe.

☉   ☉   ☉

choose   [verb] (rhymes with whose) to select

Freda suffered an anxiety attack when she had to choose between small curd and large curd cottage cheese.

chose   [verb] past tense of choose—rhymes with hose

After pondering the question of whether to be a bee, or not to be a bee in the school play, Hamlin chose to be a bee.

"To be a bee, or not to be a bee? That is the question."

☉   ☉   ☉

coarse   [adjective] rough, crude

The coarse horse costume caused Fritz's skin to itch.

course   [noun] unit of study

Because he's an underachiever, Redmond Remmington, Jr., took a correspondence course to be a crash test dummy.

[noun] track or way

The Scouts lost their course in the forest because their eager leader packed a microwave in his backpack, but he forgot the compass on the bus.

[noun] path of action

After hours of debate on the course to take, the legislature decided to tax toothpicks.

◎   ◎   ◎

complement   [noun] something that completes or makes perfect

When Gramps receives his new dentures, he'll finally have a full complement of teeth.

[verb] to fill out or complete

Many people compliment Nigel on the way his dog Fido complements his unique style.

compliment   [noun] a remark that says something flattering about a person

Connie received many compliments on her unusual partridge-shaped purse.

[verb] to say something flattering

The neighbors complimented Bernice on her lovely yard gnome.

◎   ◎   ◎

council   [noun] a group called together to accomplish a job

The school council is planning to raise money for neglected parents.

consul   [noun] the representative of a foreign country

The Chinese consul presented the President with a platinum-plated egg roll.

councilor [noun] a member of a council

The city councilors voted unanimously to help fight global warming by lowering the thermostat in City Hall to fifty-eight degrees.

counselor [noun] someone who gives advice

After administering several aptitude tests, the school counselor advised Morton to become a turkey farmer.

⊚   ⊚   ⊚

desert   [noun] a dry region

Dwayne was pained when his plan for a chain of sock shops in the Sahara Desert unraveled.

desert   [verb] to leave or abandon

Captain Cotter was distraught when he caught his crew planning to desert his yacht with his polyglot parrot.

dessert   [noun] a sweet food served after dinner

No one mustered the courage to try to taste Uncle Buster's new mustard custard dessert.

⊚   ⊚   ⊚

die   [verb] to stop living [died-past tense]

When Gordy's goldfish died, he simply replaced it with an orange slice.

dye   [noun] a substance used to change the color of something [dyed-past tense]

Lacking imagination, Doritha dyed her dark-red hair dark red.

⊚   ⊚   ⊚

emigrate [verb—followed by the preposition *from*] to leave a country or region to settle elsewhere

People in distress who detest jumbo flying pests emigrate from rain forests.

immigrate [verb—followed by the preposition *to*] come to settle in a new habitat or country

Rain forest residents who like to ice skate immigrate to arctic straits.

◎ ◎ ◎

farther   [adverb] a reference to measurable distance

At the Annual Fish Toss Tourney in Tulsa, Thoreau threw a tadpole ten feet farther than Elmo.

further   [adverb] a reference to an extension that does not involve measurable distance

After further debate, the noncommittal committee finally decided to paint the courthouse clear.

Exercise 1

Choose the word that makes sense in each set of parentheses.

1. Because Donald didn't follow his mother's (advice, advise) not to swallow the apple seed, he later underwent surgery to remove the tree so he could (breath, breathe).

2. Saul wrapped himself in a (bare, bear) skin rug and attended the dance as a giant hair ball.

3. After Elenore was elected to the city (council, counsel, consul), she proposed to (die, dye) all of the squirrels around the courthouse green so that they would (complement, compliment) the grass.

4. Because she doesn't believe in signs, Faith never (brakes, breaks) at intersections.

5. Winnie became (board, bored) and quit school, and now she's illiterate in more than twelve languages.

6. To calm her nerves, Minerva is taking (coarses, courses) in meditation, metaphysics, and mechanics.

7. Because he doesn't want to be arrested, the (councilman, counselman) uses only legal-size paper.

8. People in this country who love fresh jalapenos (emigrate, immigrate) in droves to Mexico.

9. When he was stranded on a (deserted, desserted) island, Roland had trouble (adapting, adopting) to the sun because his skin was (bare, bear), (accept, except) for his camel-hair active wear.

10. Most social scientists (accede, exceed) that three out of four people make up seventy-five percent of the population.

11. The school (councilor, counselor) (accepted, excepted) a new, less stressful job disarming bombs.

12. Art choked on an artichoke, but he's (all right, alright) now.

13. The mayor's speech included an (allusion, illusion) to his dogged hero, Lassie.

14. Reginald tried to (altar, alter) his appearance with a head transplant.

15. Because he insists on driving defensively, Horace (choose, chose) to buy a tank.

16. Alvin tried to create the (allusion, illusion) of pulling a rabbit out of his hat, but he mistakenly retrieved a humongous gnat.

17. Biff (boars, bores) his friends because he discusses nothing (accept, except) his postnasal drip.

18. After debating (farther, further), the city (council, counsel, consul) decided to name the new building *The New Building*.

19. Florence has (all ready, already) fed her flounder.

20. With a government grant, scientists are studying the (affects, effects) of peanut butter on jellyfish.

⊚   ⊚   ⊚

feat   [noun] an accomplishment

Uncle Wheezy performed the amazing feat of eating an entire side of beef without his false teeth.

feet [noun] plural of foot

Because Claude has two left feet, he has twice as many pairs of shoes as most people.

◎ ◎ ◎

formally [adverb] properly; according to the strict rules

The party invitation said to dress formally, so Lockwood wore clean socks.

formerly [adverb] previously; in the past

Dr. Anguine, a nuclear physicist, was formerly a snake charmer.

◎ ◎ ◎

hair [noun] stuff that grows on the top of most people's heads (and various other places)

"You have hairs in your nose," said little Rose.

hare [noun] a fluffy animal with long ears that hops around; rabbit

Fluvia flabbergasts her friends with the fantastic feat of balancing a large, long-haired hare on her single long hair.

◎ ◎ ◎

hear [verb] to receive sounds through the ear

"Did you hear the news?" blurted Betty Lou. "I'm going to raise gnus!"

here [adverb] the opposite of *there*

Persephone pleaded, "Do you mind if I leave Petey my pet piranha here with you while I vacation in Sweden?"

◎ ◎ ◎

hole [noun] a perforation or cavity

"I need a pet mole like a hole in the head," muttered Dole.

whole   [adjective] entire

Pearson spent a whole year writing his first book, but he had to start over when he realized an autobiography was not about cars.

⊚   ⊚   ⊚

its   [pronoun] the possessive form of *it*

Quentin's finicky kitten only nibbled at its food, and it refused to eat its after-dinner mint.

it's   [pronoun plus verb] it is

An ostrich becomes ornery when it's ostracized for its odor.

⊚   ⊚   ⊚

lead   [verb] to go before; to take charge (rhymes with seed)

Morton volunteered to lead the Save the Snails March in his community.

led   [verb] past tense of *lead*

The Save the Snails Society led the movement to outlaw salt.

lead   [noun] graphite (the stuff in pencils); [noun] a type of metal

When dropped from the top of the Empire State Building, a ball of lead and a snail fall at the same rate.

⊚   ⊚   ⊚

loan   [verb] to lend

loan   [noun]something lent

For a science project, Ramona agreed to loan Lawrence her pet leeches.

lone   [adjective] solitary; isolated

Lawrence lost eleven leeches in the lunchroom, and he recovered a lone one.

⊚   ⊚   ⊚

loose   [adjective] (rhymes with goose) the opposite of tight; not fastened or tied down

Tracy suffered fourteen loose teeth when a nearsighted duck that had lost its way collided with her face.

lose   [verb] (rhymes with ooze) to not know where to find

Because Toya was afraid she would lose her tuba, she tied it to her toe.

   [verb] to suffer defeat

Because he practices six hours a day, Binky never loses at tiddly-winks.

◎   ◎   ◎

moral   [adjective] having to do with good or right; [noun] a lesson on how to act

Miss Prickles, a moral (adjective) woman, announced to her first graders, "The moral (noun) of the story, students, is never to wear wool undies in the summer."

morale   [noun] mental condition; spirit

The team's morale was high after winning the first round of the National Turnip Tossing Tourney.

◎   ◎   ◎

pain   [noun] suffering

"My husband is a pain in the neck," complained Mrs. Dracula.

pane   [noun] piece of glass in a window

For Halloween, Francine painted Frankenstein's brain on her window pane.

◎   ◎   ◎

passed   [verb] past tense of pass (to move by)

When flying piglets passed by Petunia's window, she passed out.

past   [adjective] gone by in time

In his past life, Barney believes he was a stalk of broccoli.

   [noun] time gone by

Because Mortimer was reared by monkeys, he is secretive about his past.

[preposition] beyond

Jasper sprinted past his friends in the fifty-yard dash, but his chance to win vanished when he tripped on an ant.

☺ ☺ ☺

peace [noun] opposite of strife or turmoil

Every night little Lucretia prays for peace on earth and a pony.

piece [noun] a part of something

"If you swallow a piece of gum, does it really take seven years to digest?" choked Festus.

☺ ☺ ☺

plain [adjective] not fancy; [adjective] understandable; [noun] a flat piece of land

As the airplane flew over the plains (noun) of Kansas, the pilot made the evacuation procedures plain (adjective) while the passengers ate plain (adjective) yogurt.

plane [noun] airplane; [noun] a flat surface; [noun] a tool for smoothing or shaping a wood surface

Mr. Jitters, the three-fingered shop teacher, demonstrated to the class how to safely use a buzz saw, a drill, and a plane to make a model plane.

☺ ☺ ☺

principal [noun] the head of a school; [adjective] main or most important

The principal [adjective] point of the announcement made by the principal [noun] was that every student who makes straight A's will receive a case of tasty fruitcakes.

principle [noun] a role of conduct

"A principle for good health," sputtered Dr. Flabosky, "is never to eat more than you can power lift."

[noun] a law or main fact

Little Semore enjoys reading books about purple dinosaurs, super-heroes, and the principles of hydro-nuclear physics.

⊚   ⊚   ⊚

quiet   [adjective] silent

The students were stunned and quiet when their science teacher lost his head, and it slowly rolled to the back of the class.

quite   [adverb] to a great extent or degree; completely

Sigmund was quite saddened when his imaginary friend disappeared.

⊚   ⊚   ⊚

shone   [verb] past tense of *shine*

As the sun shone brightly over the bay, Samantha sang a sad song about salmon.

shown   [verb] revealed

Pheodora has shown many friends her extraordinary collection of laundry lint.

⊚   ⊚   ⊚

stationary   [adjective] in a fixed position

Crazy Uncle Ernie collapsed from exhaustion trying to ride his stationary bike to California.

stationery   [noun] writing paper

Aunt Erma wrote the city council an angry note on fancy stationery complaining about the sinkhole that swallowed her house.

⊚   ⊚   ⊚

than   a conjunction used to make comparisons

"I'm happier than a bloated tick," blurted Mick.

then   [adverb] soon after that; next in order of time

Every morning Brunella brushes her chattering baboons, and then she shampoos her persnickety poodles.

⊚   ⊚   ⊚

their　[pronoun] the possessive form of *they*

After the Seven Dwarves began taking growth hormones, they lost their jobs.

there　[adverb] a place; the opposite of here

Look up there! That cloud is shaped like a three-headed, buck-toothed duck!

they're　[pronoun plus verb] a contraction for *they are*

"People who eat lots of seafood are never flabby," babbled Abbie, "but they're always crabby."

◎　◎　◎

threw　[verb] past tense of *throw*; hurled

When Uncle Scooter threw his new computer out his office window, it was snared in midair by a prodigious passing pigeon.

through　[preposition] in one side and out the other

When Wally walked through the door, he had to pay for the damages.

◎　◎　◎

to　[preposition] indicating motion or purpose toward something

Heat turns gum to goo.

[part of the infinitive form of the verb]

Luna loves to savor pork-flavored Popsicles.

too　[adverb] also

"I'd like a crispy fried bat's wing too!" blurted Burton.

[adverb] more than enough

The students who were talking too much in class bungled their science experiment and caused their chemistry teacher to spontaneously combust.

two　[adjective] a number

Two heads are better than one, but 1½ heads are worse.

◎　◎　◎

wait   [noun] remain; expecting something

Tate had to quit his job as a waiter so that he could wait in line for hours to audition for a part in a play about a waiter who had to quit his job so that he could wait in line for hours to audition for a part in a play about a waiter.

weight   [noun] heaviness

"The secret of my quick weight loss," Ralph bragged to his dinner guests, "was acute food poisoning."

◎   ◎   ◎

waist   [noun] the middle part of the body

Squib's friends knew he was spending too much time in the gym because his neck was eight times bigger than his waist.

waste   [verb] to squander

To her dismay, Macy learned that she had wasted her money on paintings by Shakespeare.

   [noun] useless material

Eventually Macy threw all of her Shakespearean paintings into a pile of waste.

◎   ◎   ◎

weak   [adjective] not strong; lacking energy

Elvin knew he had to start exercising more when blinking left him weak and winded.

week   [noun] seven days

Active rats reek unless they shower once a week.

◎   ◎   ◎

weather   [noun] atmospheric conditions

In rainy weather, Lizzy goes into a tizzy because her hair gets the frizzies.

whether   [conjunction]

Paloma pondered, "I don't know whether I should go to the party dressed as Queen Elizabeth I or a possum."

◎　◎　◎

who's   [pronoun plus verb] who is, who has

"Who's (who is) squeezing the toothpaste from the middle of the tube?" bristles Miles every morning before he brushes.

"Who's (who has) been eating my hot dog?" barked Frank.

whose   [pronoun, possessive]

"Whose tooth is this in my chewy ratatouille?" wondered toothless Uncle Louie.

Exercise 2

Choose the correct word from the pair in parentheses.

1. Within a margin of error of three hundred pounds, Lester can guess almost anyone's (wait, weight).

2. The lucky lizard passed (its, it's) audition for the title role in *Godzilla*.

3. The (principal, principle) of our school moonlights as a mud wrestler.

4. "(There's, Theirs) a little bit of spittle on your lip," quipped Skip.

5. Morticia was (formally, formerly) a cosmetologist, but now she's a worm farmer.

6. To his credit, Langley doesn't try (to, too, two) change people; he just pretends (there, their, they're) someone else.

7. At Quentin's surprise party, people wore (there, their, they're) favorite vegetable costumes.

8. Has anyone ever (shone, shown) you how to make balloon bagworms?

9. Dr. Theet's orthodontist office uses (stationary, stationery) with a string of dental floss embossed at the top.

10. "The llama you (loaned, loned) me," claimed Kit, "spit."

11. After enjoying the party, Bea was embarrassed to see a (loan, lone) (peace, piece) of spinach hanging from her teeth.

12. To protect himself from the rainy (weather, whether), Dwayne wrapped himself in cellophane.

13. Nadine loves nothing more (than, then) startling strangers with her talking chicken.

14. "People with few (morales, morals) always try to (accede, exceed) the eight-item limit in the express checkout line," whined Tine.

15. Because they crave (peace, piece) and (quiet, quite), people who work in bell towers never sing in the shower.

16. "(Who's, Whose) marbles are these in the cream peas?" asked forgetful Aunt Louise.

17. "Because people shouldn't use (coarse, course) language," said Cedric, "I never discuss sandpaper in public."

18. "Sometimes I (loose, lose) my train of thought," sputtered Spacely, "and, uh, never mind."

19. The tourists on the first floor of the (capital, capitol) (passed, past) out when the hot air in the building (acceded, exceeded) government regulations.

20. After the new (principal, principle) (formally, formerly) introduced himself to the students, he explained that he had (formally, formerly) worked as a circus tightrope walker, but he had quit, even though the job (moral, morale) was (quiet, quite) high.

Exercise 3–Review Exercise

Once again, choose the correct word from those in parentheses.

1. Kelvin (complemented, complimented) Izzy on the way her fuzzy eyebrows (complemented, complimented) her frizzy hair.

2. Grace tripped on her shoelace, but she's (alright, all right) now.

3. Because Collin wore (all together, altogether) too much cologne, his friends (passed, past) out from holding (their, there, they're) (breathes, breaths) for (to, too) long.

4. The message in the fortune cookie (advice, advised) Addie not to chew with her mouth open.

5. Mr. Dunderwood was under the (allusion, illusion) that he had won lots of cash in the lottery, but he later discovered his prize was actually a (peace, piece) of pottery.

6. After his umbrella stand folded, Blain (immigrated, emigrated) from the (desert, dessert) to Spain where it always rains.

7. After tumbling from the top of the (capital, capitol), Grandpa landed on his (feat, feet), so, thank goodness, he's (all right, alright).

8. So that she never (accedes, exceeds) the speed limit, Carla always sets her cruise control at 6 m.p.h.

9. Though Ruford researched the (principals, principles) of hydraulics for (weaks, weeks), he was still unable to stop the faucet from leaking.

10. Tally lost all of her (capital, capitol) when she invested in a fitness farm for overweight snakes.

11. Iggy missed his chance to (farther, further) his education at Harvard because the pencil he used to take the entrance exam didn't have #2 (lead, led).

12. Boris enrolled in a fascinating (coarse, course) on the history of duct tape, but he didn't stick with it.

13. I always remember grandmother's best (advice, advise): never put a roast in a toaster.

14. My grandfather always (adviced, advised) me never to (loan, lone) snowshoes to a gnome.

15. Because he was experiencing chronic stomach (pains, panes), Pierce had to quit his swell job as a sword swallower.

16. In an amazing (feat, feet) of strength, Drew (through, threw) a caribou three (feat, feet) (farther, further) (than, then) Newt.

17. Laney likes to bowl, but his fingers won't fit in the (holes, wholes) of the ball because he's all thumbs.

18. After the (council, counsel, consul) from Tiberia had his tonsils removed, he couldn't eat (deserts, desserts) for a (weak, week) because he was (to, too) (weak, week) (to, too) chew.

19. (Weather, Whether) Dane plays the calliope or the kazoo, his cantankerous cockatoos squawk as though (their, there, they're) in (pain, pane).

20. Even though Uncle Drake put on the emergency (brake, break) so that his truck would remain (stationary, stationery), it still rolled into the lake.

21. The amount of beets Freda eats (affects, effects) how well she sleeps.

22. "(Hear, Here) is the xylophone you (loaned, loned) me, " returned Keyes.

23. Almost every single scientist (accedes, exceeds) that the (affect, effect) of artificial sweetener on lab rats is negligible, unless they're smothered by it.

24. When Joel fell into a mole (hole, whole), he (adapted, adopted) to the dark (quiet, quite) well.

25. Marion (formally, formerly) asked Mary to marry him on a merry-go-round in the (capital, capitol) city of Maryland.

26. The customers at the dollar store were annoyed because they had to (wait, weight) in line while the new employee kept asking for price checks.

27. When Aunt Leta (looses, loses) her mind, she usually finds it under the couch.

28. Whenever Tether wants to (affect, effect) a change in the (weather, whether), she washes the car and prepares for rain.

29. When bad (hair, hare) days drive Daisy (altogether, all together) crazy, she uses a mayonnaise glaze (to, too) mend her (loose, lose) split ends.

30. To lighten the mood of the trial, the judge, (formally, formerly) a ventriloquist, ordered all of the participants to wear (there, their, they're) favorite hand puppets.

Spelling Out Numbers

You would think that spelling out numbers would be a simple thing. Wrongo. The problem is that different sources give different rules. Some sources, for example say to spell out numbers one through ten, while other sources say to spell out one through ninety-nine. I've tried to pare down a vast number of sometimes differing rules on this weighty issue—I'm beginning to think I need to get a life—to a few that are fairly widely agreed upon.

1. As a general rule, write out numbers that require one or two words.

   *Waferly noted on his resume that he was **twenty-six** years old, and he had failed his bar exam with the relatively high score of **thirty-seven**.*

2. If the number requires more than two words, use the numeral.

   *In the next hour alone, **567,894** people will suffer from ingrown toenails.*

3. To reduce the length of numbers in the millions or billions, write out *millions* or *billions*.

   *Jillian made **327 million** frilly pillows to sell on the Home Shopping Network.*

4. Spell out a number if it begins a sentence.

   ***Sixty-five** spry butterflies flitted by.*

   If a sentence begins with a number that requires more than two or three words, try to reword the sentence.

   Wordy: *Three thousand three hundred twenty-six people protested in the year 2005 for the right to live openly as vampires.*
   Confusing: *In the year 2005, 3,326 people protested for the right to live openly as vampires.*
   Clear: *For the right to live openly as vampires, **3,326** people protested in the year 2005.*

5. It's okay to write time in numerals or words. Use AM and PM (or a.m. and p.m.) with numerals but not with words. Don't mix numbers and words.

   Note: AM and PM are usually printed in small capitals. If so, they don't need periods.

   Wrong: *4 in the morning   4 o'clock   four AM*
   Right: *four o'clock in the morning   4:00 PM*

Never use numerals to express noon or midnight.

6. Use the number or spell out the day when it follows the month.

   *Seventy-two of Santa's elves are sixty-five or older, and many of them have trouble staying up until **4:00 AM** on **December 25** (or **December twenty-fifth**).*

7. Use numerals or spell out years, but spell out decades, unless preceded by the numerals of the century.

   Right: *1888   eighteen eighty-eight   the sixties   the 1960s*

FYI The abbreviation *A.D.* precedes the year, and *B.C.* follows it.

A.D. 600   500 B.C.

8. Always spell out ordinal numbers (*first, second, third . . .*) in dates, or anywhere, for that matter.

   *On the **twenty-ninth** (not 29th) of every **July**, thousands of procrastinators arrive at the convention that's held on the **twenty-eighth** (not 28th) of the month.*

   *Conan won **third** (not 3rd) place in the olive-eating contest, but afterwards, he felt like the pits.*

9. If you have several numbers in a series, and some require only one or two words and some require more than two words, use numerals for all of them.

   *Harriette has been growing her hair for **twelve** years, **seven** months, **three** days, and **twenty-three** hours.*

   *In the election for mayor, **12** people voted for Mr. Bubba Duffleberry; **127** people voted for Viola Pimpleton; and **1,245** people voted for Skippy the Wonder Dog.*

10. Spell out and hyphenate simple fractions.

    "After doing research, I believe that over nine-tenths of the world's population populates," announced Bifford.

    Whole numbers plus simple fractions may be spelled out, but if several words are required, using numbers is better.

    For exercise, Cousin Coleman walks briskly around the flag pole two and one half (or 2 1/2) times every morning.

11. Here are some more categories at a glance.

Pages and chapters	*Chapter 9, page 23*
Bible verses:	*Ephesians 6:1*
Plays	*Act 3, scene 2 (or Act III, scene ii),*
	lines 36–40 of Macbeth
Addresses	*325 Pothole Road*
Percentages	*65% or 65 percent (always use*
	numerals)
Decimals	*55.7 0.67 0.85 (If a decimal num-*
	ber is less than one, include a
	zero before the decimal point.
Money (requiring more than two words)	*$77.50*
Money (round numbers)	*thirty-two dollars fifty cents*
Scores	*127-3*
Grade points	*4.00 3.50 .02*

Exercise 4

See how you do with these. If a number is written incorrectly, write it in its correct form. If a sentence is correct, write C.

1. Forty-two thousand cats auditioned for a cat food commercial last month, but all refused to follow stage directions.

2. "I may be only thirteen years old," announced highly intellectual Belinda, "but that's 91 in dog years."

3. In a survey of 200 doctors, six warned against eggs for breakfast, 2 warned against coffee, one warned against bacon, and one suggested eating everything because we're all going to die anyway.

4. On the 3rd day of December, Bartleby finally landed his 1st job as a flagpole.

5. Throughout the world, statistics show that three hundred twenty-seven million people will blow their noses at exactly the same time.

6. At 7:30 every evening, Cousin Jed reads little Howie six stories about trolls, 12 stories about fairies, and 127 stories about scary dairy cows.

7. After 27 years and 364 days of hard work, Uncle Ogden quit hog farming because he just couldn't bring home the bacon.

8. At four o'clock every morning, weird Mr. Fribbleday waters his driveway.

9. From the time he was 10 years old, Marvin has had trouble making friends because of the huge potato chip on his shoulder.

10. After getting up at midnight for the past thirty years to make the donuts, Fred the baker closed his shop because his wife complained that he always kneaded bread.

Some Commonly Misspelled Words

Beware of these sneaky spelling snares:

absence	calendar	forty	minute
access	chief	frequent	necessary
accidentally	conceded	friend	niece
ache	conceited	grammar	often
acquaintance	committee	gross	paid
again	congratulate	half	parallel
a lot (two words)	conscience	hour	possess
amateur	criticize	hungry	precede
analysis	definite	instead	privilege
analyze	disappoint	intelligence	proceed
answer	discipline	knowledge	psychology
arguing	doctor	lieutenant	recede
argument	does	literature	receipt
athlete	early	loneliness	receive
beggar	eighth	lovable	recommendation
believe	eligible	marriage	referral
benefit	exceed	meant	referring
business	February	medieval	restaurant

rhyme   separate   succeed   tragedy
rhythm   similar   successful   truly
said   since   surprise   vacuum
sergeant   sincerely   thief   Wednesday
scheme   sophomore   though   weird
scissors   subtle   tomorrow

Works Consulted

Bartleby.com. "English Usage, Style & Composition." 2005. 31 Jan. 2007 <http://www.bartleby.com/usage/>.

Boylan, Roger, et. al., ed. *Elements of Language: Third Course.* Austin: Holt, Rhinehart and Winston, 2001.

The Chicago Manual of Style. 15th ed. Chicago: University of Chicago Press, 2003.

"Colon FactMonster.com." *Fact Monster.* © 2000–2006 Pearson Education, publishing as Fact Monster. 31 Jan. 2007 <http://www.factmonster.com/ipka/A0771350.html>.

Fowler, H. Ramsey, and Jane E. Aarron. *The Little, Brown Handbook.* 5th ed. New York: Harper Collins, 1992.

Grammar and Composition Handbook. New York: Glencoe McGraw-Hill, 2000.

Hacker, Diana. *A Writer's Reference.* New York: St. Martin's Press, 1989.

Littell, Joy, ed. *Building English Skills.* Evanston: McDougal Littell, 1977.

The Purdue OWL Family of Sites. 26 Aug. 2005. The Writing Lab and OWL at Purdue, Purdue University. 31 Jan. 2007 <http://owl.english.purdue.edu/>.

Senn, J.A., and Carol Ann Skinner. *English Communication Skills in the New Millennium, Level 1.* Austin: Barrett Kendall, 2001.

Senn, J.A. and Carol Ann Skinner. *Heath English, Level 9.* Lexington: D.C. Heath, 1992.

Shertzer, Margaret. *The Elements of Grammar.* New York: Barnes and Noble, 2001.

Stilman, Anne. *Grammatically Correct.* Cincinnati: Writer's Digest, 1997.

Strumpf, Michael, and Auriel Douglas. *The Grammar Bible.* New York: Henry Holt, 2004.

Strunk, Jr. William, and E. B. White. *The Elements of Style.* 4th ed. New York: Longman, 2000.

Style Guide. 2002. University of Colorado at Boulder. 31 Jan. 2007 <http://www.colorado.edu/Publications/styleguide/index.html>.

Warriner's High School Handbook. Austin: Holt, Rinehart and Winston, 1992.

Warriner, John E. *English Composition and Grammar.* Orlando: Harcourt Brace Jovanovich, 1988.

Cathy Campbell grew up in Midland, Texas, and received a degree in English from the University of Texas at Austin. After a short stint working for a small ad agency in Austin, she moved to The Woodlands, Texas, where she has been delighting her high school English students with her hilarious, illustrated grammar lessons. *The Giggly Guide to Grammar* is her first book.

Discover Writing Press

www.discoverwriting.com

To view our other titles
and to order more copies of

The Giggly Guide to Grammar

visit our website at
www.discoverwriting.com

Phone: 1-800-613-8055 • Fax: 1-802-897-2084

Order with your check, credit card or purchase order

The Giggly Guide to Grammar
• Answer Key •

Chapter 1–Nouns and Pronouns

Exercise 1 (pp. 5-6)
Answers will vary

Exercise 2 (p. 9)
1. shelves
2. freshmen
3. elves
4. Chinese
5. oxen
6. heroes
7. trios
8. knives
9. sisters-in-law
10. babies
11. calves
12. potatoes
13. rodeos
14. pianos
15. editors-in-chief
16. commanders-in-chief
17. A's
18. spoonfuls
19. sopranos
20. deer
21. fish (or fishes)
22. libraries
23. passersby
24. 1980s (or 1980's)
25. octopi (or octopuses)

Exercise 3 (p. 9)
1. ladies
2. salmon
3. tomatoes
4. duos
5. oboes
6. lice
7. 13's
8. journeys
9. leaves
10. wolves
11. patios
12. selves
13. Americans
14. Japanese
15. teeth
16. halves
17. countries
18. fathers-in-law
19. delegates-at-large
20. sheep

Exercise 4 (p. 10)
1. sheep
2. lookers-on
3. lice / knives
4. mice / scarves (or scarfs) / radios
5. monkeys
6. oxen
7. Chinese / Japanese
8. (reindeers), chimneys
9. trout
10. runners-up

Exercise 5 (p. 11)
Answers will vary.

Exercise 6 (p. 15)
1. whose -- Aunt Zippy / she -- Aunt Zippy
2. he -- Uncle Cuthbert / his—Uncle Cuthbert
3. he -- Marvin / his—Marvin
4. who -- liars
5. her -- Jane
6. she -- princess / her -- princess
7. who -- no antecedent / her -- Aunt Britt
8. she -- Sarah
9. he -- Howie / himself -- Howie / she -- psychic / his -- Howie
10. who -- children

Exercise 7 (p. 16)
Possible response:
   Sally sells socks on the seashore. For each sock, she charges seven cents. As a bonus gift, she gives each customer a free sack of sand with every sock sold. One Saturday, Sally sold seventy thousand socks, and she retired. Now she lives with her sister, Sarah, in Seattle, and Sally and her sister sew socks for sumo wrestlers in Samoa. Sometimes the sisters still saunter by the sea, and they sing songs about seals, simians, and celery.

Exercise 8 (p. 19)
1. talent -- competition / Miss America -- contestant / four - ferrets / one—leg
2. irate -- shopkeeper / restless—class / missing—finger
3. new—boutique / electrolysis -- boutique / reduced—price / extra-thick—hair / back—hair / nose—hair
4. Thanksgiving—dessert / tasty—pudding / bologna – pudding / chocolate—sprinkles
5. every—night / extra—cash / speed -- bumps
6. tragic -- accident / freak -- accident / baking -- accident / oven -- door
7. friendlier -- image / police -- department / floral-scented -- mace / Velcro -- handcuffs
8. many -- issues / young -- patients / little—people / evil—people / spittle—people
9. wacky -- Uncle Wilbur / empty -- pods / alien -- people / pod -- people / attractive -- bins / sturdy – bins / storage -- bins / tool – shed
10. young – werewolves / coarse -- hair

Exercise 9 (pp. 22-23)
Answers will vary.

Chapter 2–Verbs and Adverbs

Exercise 1 (p. 27)
1. walked—intransitive / tripped – intransitive
2. hates -- transitive / loves -- transitive
3. unpacks -- transitive
4. buried -- transitive / croaked -- intransitive
5. tarries -- intransitive
6. writes -- transitive
7. made -- transitive
8. forgot -- transitive / covered—transitive
9. bought -- transitive
10. hates—transitive

Exercise 2 (p. 30)
1. is, Harry-bald
2. are, pants-torn
3. look, flip-flops-sloppy
4. look, toenails-pointy
5. smells, chicken-foul
6. is, gum-gooey
7. taste, crickets-delicious
8. sounds, *Snoologaloopy*-strange
9. is, cat-rat
10. feel, eels-slimy

Exercise 3 (pp. 30-31)
1. tripped – A
2. is – L
3. traded – A
4. change – A
5. catches – A
6. garbles – A / is – L
7. stubbed – A
8. looks – L / is – L
9. is – L / draws – A
10. are – L
11. causes – A
12. look – L
13. flicked – A / knocked – A
14. performed – A / landed – A
15. blabs – A / is - L

Exercise 4 (pp. 33-34)
1. give – A
2. live – A / should buy – A
3. decorated – A
4. should jog – A
5. should cry – A / are – L
6. become – L / does – A
7. rushed – A / suffered – A
8. seem – L / are – L
9. was – L
10. lifts – A / are - L
11. lost – A
12. passed – A
13. is drawing – A
14. dresses – A / dangles – A
15. grew – L / covered – A
16. think – A / is – L / is raising – A
17. is – L / collects – A / provides – A
18. dressed – A
19. mixes – A
20. perform – A / spend – A
21. shaved – A / replaced – A
22. can't hear – A / sticks – A
23. is – L / supplies – A
24. left – A / smelled – L
25. skates – A / juggles – A / twirls – A

Exercise 5 (p. 35) - Answers will vary.

Exercise 6 (p. 37)
1. slightly – loony / frequently – catches / lazily – swim / rather – deep
2. very – attentive / unbelievably – simple / extremely – tasty
3. never – wears
4. deeply – searched / eventually – decided
5. incredibly – useful / effectively – detects / potentially – dangerous
6. someday – will become
7. today -- sold / slightly – pudgy / too – much
8. recently – called / angrily – called / loudly – demanded
9. extremely –alarmed
10. too – much

Exercise 7 (p. 39) - Answers will vary.

Chapter 3–Prepositions, Conjunctions and Interjections

Exercise 1 (p. 44)
1. with tooth decay / at midnight / with skilled dentists / near graveyards / on the full moon / of each month
2. in dark and dirty kitchens / at their food
3. of three-headed eels / from the bottom / of a polluted lagoon / into the tires / of a stalled bus / to the International Florists' Convention
4. because of the large tattoo / of a rodent / beneath her left eye / as a receptionist / in a law office / in spite of the fact
5. inside of a giant toy store / for Etch-A-Sketches
6. with maple syrup / in the dirt / of bath soap / in addition to psychiatric treatment
7. according to the evening news / around tropical regions / from hearing loss / for some unknown reason / of wax/ inside of their ear canals
8. beneath baseboards / at night / with small potatoes
9. on Tuesdays and Thursdays / to her advanced underwater opera singing classes
10. to the amazement / of passersby / into crowds / of people / during rush hour / on their feet

Exercise 2 (p. 45)
1. adverb
2. preposition
3. preposition / adverb
4. adverb / preposition
5. preposition
6. adverb
7. preposition / adverb
8. preposition
9. preposition
10. preposition / adverb

Exercise 3 (p. 47)
1. Where did you leave your muskrat?
2. Why did you pluck all of the ducks?
3. I wonder to whom I should give this stray cockatoo.
4. Where is my imaginary friend sitting?
5. With what do you sharpen your toenails?
6. Where do vampire bats live?
7. With what should Biff eat his sliver of liver?
8. Where have all of the emus gone?
9. Grandpa never remembers where he parks his Harley.
10. What time do we get out of this class?

Exercise 4 (p. 49)
Some answers may vary.
1. On drizzly days, Lizzy's hissing lizard hides in her frizzy hair.
2. At the county fair in February, Cherrie won the big-hair contest.
   In February, Cherrie won the big-hair contest at the county fair.
3. In a freak accident, Uncle Flake was flattened by a giant falling finch.
4. In a large vat of ginger ale, Little Whitney keeps the whale that she ordered through the mail.
5. At posh parties, Tasha always wears her favorite squash-flavored lip gloss.
6. After years of trying, Brice finally finished a jigsaw puzzle of a piece of rice in an ice storm
7. With his mail order bobby pin business, Dobs hopes to make gobs of money.
8. With his jumbo leaf blower, Moe accidentally sucked up the skinny mailman.
9. Before his next movie role, Pinocchio knows he needs a nose job.
10. In Cousin Gomer's goatee, thirty flouncing fleas flourish.

Exercise 5 (pp. 51-52)
1. whether, or
2. either, or
3. and / but
4. so
5. for
6. not only, but also / and
7. either, or
8. neither, nor
9. and / but / for
10. so / and
11. both, and / and
12. yet
13. but / and
14. neither, nor
15. so

Exercise 6 (p. 54)
Answers will vary.

Chapter 4—Subject, Predicate, and Complements

Exercise 1 (p. 57)
1. Jake
2. Drakleberry's overweight snake
3. Bucky, an alert security guard
4. Ludwick, the unlucky Leprechaun
5. Wilameena
6. sequined-covered fish sticks
7. the company president
8. Derwood
9. Manfred
10. Perketta

Exercise 2 (p. 61)
Sample answer:
   Some strange people who actually enjoy camping in the woods probably also get a kick out of root canals. These people live in some alternate reality. Based on my last (and only) family camping "vacation," I avoid communing with nature for several reasons. First of all, vicious insects—ants, ticks, and mosquitoes, to name just a few—thrive in woods. I had to drench myself in gallons of bug spray for protection; mosquitoes would stick to me and drown. During the day, Mom, Dad, Sis and I watched trees and squirrels to pass the time, and at night we would simply sit around the campfire. Whoopee. (Actually, this ranks as the highpoint of the trip. I told my little sister that story about a guy with a hook who terrorizes kids left home alone. It made her cry.)
   Most importantly, though, the woods conceal dangers. Snakes and bears and even crazy squirrels lie just waiting to attack. Take my advice. Spend your time in a safer and more exciting way, counting floor tiles, for example. At least it beats providing the main course in a mosquito buffet.

Exercise 3 (p. 63)
1. (you)
2. Cyclops
3. Herby, Howie
4. Uncle Arnie
5. jelly
6. cats
7. Cousin Elmo
8. this
9. people
10. reasons
11. sharks, snails
12. blueprint
13. salesman
14. mosquitoes
15. unicorn

Exercise 4 (p. 65)
1. contact lenses / are
2. Tilly, Liv / shiver, quiver
3. Venus flytrap or flytrap / swallowed, spat
4. Newton / watches
5. Tye / found
6. Mrs. Granberry / delighted
7. you / did buy
8. people / should pluck, dye
9. Skippy / does keep
10. Kippy / played

Exercise 5 (pp. 72-73)
1. Bertha (S), bought (V), (bug) zapper (DO), boyfriend (IO)
2. stalkers (S), eat (V), quantities (DO)
3. people (S), are (V), flat (PA)
4. Professor Englebert (S), gives (V), lectures (DO)
5. vegetarians (S), are (V), green (PA), they (S), lean (V)
6. Mr. Potato Head (S), picks (V), nose (DO)
7. teacher (S), praised (V), Billy (DO)
8. Calhoun (S), turned (V), pruny (PA)
9. Ms. Perkinsky (S), showed (V), movie (DO), class (IO)
10. Harpo (S), told (V), story (DO), mother (IO),
11. Fillmore (S), invented (V), opener (DO), became (V), billionaire (PN)
12. Mr. Potato Head (S), finds (V), tuber (DO)
13. you (S), should check (V), catfish (DO)
14. Tod (S), taught (V), game (DO), toad (IO)
15. Carlos (S), gave (V), corsage (DO), Darcia (IO)
16. hair (S), is (V)
17. Ripley (S), gave (V), bag (DO), mother (IO)
18. Beatrice (S), was (V)
19. roaches (S), do die (V)
20. Marwood (S), molded (V), hair (DO)
21. cow (S), jumped(V)
22. man (S), mistook (V), child (DO)
23. squirrels (S), annoy (V), parents (DO), hang (V)
24. Fruitsy (S), sticks (V), gummy bears (DO)
25. cooks (S), mistake (V), bugs (DO)
26. babies (S), drool (V), spit (V)
27. rats (S), feed (V)
28. Uncle Hermie (S), came (V)
29. you (S), tiptoe (V)
30. Matilda (S), Manfred (S), have become (V), millionaires (PN)
31. something (S), is hanging (V)
32. possum (S), is (V)
33. you (S), walk (V)
34. you (S), don't make (V), volcanoes (DO)
35. Unger (S), gave (V), pat (DO), himself (IO), injured (V), lung (DO)

Chapter 5—Dazed by Phrases?

Exercise 1 (pp. 78-79)
1. like a dork (adv) / at dinner (adv) / with his fingers (adv)
2. because of some unknown cause (adv) / on Monday (adv) / at midnight (adv) / into a mole (adv)
3. from spiders (adj) / in Spain and Japan (adj)
4. after only two months (adv) / in business (adj) / for wimps and wannabe winners (adj)
5. because of the windy weather (adv) / with feathers (adv)
6. at midnight (adv) / on December 31 (adv) / in colorful party hats (adj) / around a campfire (adv) / until dawn (adv) / to their comfy coffins (adv)
7. in a terrible freak accident (adv) / during a normal day (adv) / at the office (adv) / to a document (adv) / about the number (adj) / of careless workplace mishaps (adj)
8. after his birthday party (adv) / into the night (adv) / instead of a beautiful white mare (adv) / of underwear (adj)
9. by Bork (adv) / during funny movies (adv) / like a porker (adv)
10. into lovely holiday ornaments (adv) / inside of boxes (adv) / with pictures (adj) / of tiny teeth (adj) / to his patients (adv) / with braces (adj)

Exercise 2 (p. 86)
1. prep
2. p
3. i
4. a , p
5. i , prep
6. g
7. i
8. g
9. g
10. p
11. i
12. g
13. a, i
14. a, i
15. a
16. prep
17. a, prep
18. g
19. p
20. i
21. i
22. i, g
23. g
24. i
25. g

Exercise 3 (p. 88)
1. g
2. prep
3. prep
4. p
5. p
6. i
7. prep
8. p
9. p
10. p
11. p
12. prep
13. prep
14. prep
15. i

Chapter 6—Eliminating Clause-trophobia

Exercise 1 (p. 91)
1. I
2. I
3. D
4. D
5. P
6. I
7. I
8. P
9. I
10. D

Exercise 2 (pp. 95-96)
1. who had no cavities in their teeth—people
2. that Adam swallowed whole—apple
3. , whose lung capacity is quite amazing, —Hazel
4. , which have no knees,—fleas
5. that's wrapped in bubble wrap—styrofoam
6. that prance around too fleetingly—sheep
7. who pay him large amounts of cash in small bills —students

8. that get too hot—otters
9. , who lifts weights to build strong arms, —Armstrong
10. that occur in this country—accidents
11. , who is in a constant state of denial, —Aunt Shashon
12. where Spot dug up Aunt Dot's ashes—spot
13. , whose face is covered with freckles, —Tamina
14. who sweats on a table setting at a banquet — guest
15. that Congress orders too many costly investigations—reason

Exercise 3 (p. 99)
1. because Fireman Myron tried to put out a fire with a hair dryer—was fired
2. when Tom kept thumping on his tom-toms— stomped
3. because she's always eating peanut butter— mumbles, mutters
4. as soon as he saw the hockey puck—ducked
5. before he made a mountain out of a molehill —filled
6. whenever she sees her daisies dancing like crazy—is dazed
7. because he's a swindler—wins
8. because Bob can't swim—bobs
9. because she grows her roses in circles, not rows —uses
10. when Stan is actually dancing—think
11. whenever Muffy muffs the muffins—have
12. as long as Pen has a penchant for chewing on pens—will be
13. when they should be buzzing—are beeeping
14. because of Cy's size—looks
15. when libations were served to librarians— ad-libbed

Exercise 4 (p. 101)
1. that Ben has been eating beans again, DO
2. why I got an F on my history report about the 1588 English defeat of the giant Spanish Armadillo, DO
3. whoever attended his birthday party , IO
4. whoever is competing in the district carp toss, S
5. what he learned when he worked as a human cannonball, DO
6. that people in glass houses should wear at least a twenty-five SPF sunscreen , PN
7. that his assailant was a tubby dachshund, DO
8. whoever walks by, S
9. whatever it takes to become a licensed phrenologist, DO
10. that cannibals in isolated jungle areas feast on finger food, DO
11. that finger puppetry is a very difficult occupation, DO
12. that she wants to grow up to be a potted plant, DO
13. that his tadpole had grown a tad moldy, DO
14. whoever will listen, IO
15. that she would quit licking gummy envelopes, DO

Exercise 5 (p. 102)
1. after he found his contact on the floor, adv.
2. who cover him in bubble wrap, adj. / whenever he goes out to play, adj.
3. when his mother told him to quit being a quitter, adv.
4. when it gagged on a feather ball, adv.
5. if dogs could dress their owners up, adv.
6. that he plans to give as gifts in tiny boxes made of sticks, adj.
7. before you eat, adv.
8. after his stress-ball factory failed, adv.

9. who sell plastic food containers, adj.
10. if a woodchuck were a duck?, adv.

Exercise 6 (p. 106)
1. s   3. cx   5. c-cx   7. c   9. cx
2. cx   4. cx   6. c-cx   8. cx   10. cx

Exercise 7 (p. 107)
1. cx (Miles-smiles / limes-slime)
2. cx (rats-star)
3. cx (pan-nap)
4. c-cx (goats, togas / Norma-Roman)
5. cx (Elvis-lives-Levis)
6. c-cx (spit-pits-tips)
7. s (ruled-lured / mites-times)
8. cx (capes-space / South-shout)
9. s (ticks-stick)
10. cx (steps-pests / pot-top)

Exercise 8 (p. 114)
Example response:
   When Squiggy was walking in the forest one evening, he stumbled upon a strange black lamp hidden beneath some fallen leaves. It looked like one he had seen in a storybook, so he rubbed the side of it. Lo and behold, a genie appeared before his very eyes. In a booming voice, the genie said that he would grant Squiggy one wish. Squiggy thought about asking for world peace, but he decided, instead, to wish for lots of cash. Unfortunately, the genie was slightly hard of hearing. He thought Squiggy had asked for a huge mustache. Suddenly and miraculously, hair sprouted from above the shocked boy's upper lip and streamed down to his feet. Needless to say, Squiggy was very disappointed, so he walked home. Because he tripped along as the hair wrapped around his legs and ankles, Squiggy felt hogtied, and the journey was difficult.
   Finally, he arrived home in his very hairy condition while his mother was cooking dinner. Irritated that he was late, she told him to bathe, shave, and go to his room and stay. In his room that night, Squiggy thought about the valuable lesson his adventure had taught him. As he rubbed a soothing gel on the bumps on his razor-burned face he muttered to himself, "Life isn't always predictable. You can ask for cash, but instead you might get a rash."
                                                    The End

Chapter 7—Fragments and Run-Ons

Exercise 1 (pp. 118-119)
Possible answers.
1. Hawks squawk.
2. Large-boned toads don't float.
3. Children chew food with their mouths open.
4. Cooter wears a shrimp suit.
5. Soggy dogs frolic in bogs.
6. Sidney, please stop twiddling your thumbs.
7. Abby spends too much time gabbing about flabby baboons.
8. Lizards hiss.
9. Mortimer eats more lumpy porridge.
10. Some hobbies, like snorkeling in Jello, are dangerous.
11. Delighted by a bright firefly, little Finnegan grinned.
12. Buzzy's sweater is covered with fuzz.
13. Snails see salt shakers.
14. Rodeo clowns frown.
15. Abby wears ear plugs around babbling babies.

Exercise 2 (p. 120)
Possible answers.
1. Cecil amused the class when he put breath mints up his nose.
2. My bus driver, who acts like she's crazy, playfully

drives toward pedestrians.
3. Trace thinks that space aliens hide in many places, such as inside of the small intestines of hamsters.
4. Darlene needs dental work because she eats ice and chews on broomsticks and marbles.
5. Elvira has many talents, such as yodeling and finger painting with vegetable extracts.
6. Fat cats eat chocolate rats.
7. Corintha, who is slightly clumsy, always trips over air.
8. Some self-conscious warthogs get nose jobs because they think that good looks will gain them more friends.
9. It's dangerous to drive on the freeway, especially when you're blindfolded.
10. Aunt Tallulah talks to her tulips and puts party hats on her petunias.

Exercise 3 (p. 121)
Answers and suggestions.
1. Doritha, who has many beauty secrets, bathes in mayonnaise for softer skin and scrubs her hair with sandpaper to remove the oily build up.
2. Uncle Herbert is famous for many things. For example, he invented the plastic tips on shoelaces.
3. Otis always smells good because of the odor eaters beneath his armpits.
4. C
5. Because Freda won the porcupine-riding contest, she received a trophy of a golden quill, along with a box of bandages.
6. After he ate a pound of licorice, Larry dreamed that he was attacked by the Tooth Fairy.
7. If you swallow an apple seed, a tree will grow in your stomach; if you swallow a piece of gum, it will stick to your ribs or lodge in your pancreas.
8. My English teacher, who is a genius, has a brain the size of a cantaloupe.
9. Vinnie has strong lips because he plays musical instruments such as the tuba.
10. C

Chapter 8—Subject-Verb Agreement

Exercise 1 (p. 130)
1. are-is   8. is-are
2. understand-   9. say-says
understands   10. C
3. C   11. have-has
4. C   12. C
5. have-has,   13. C
6. has-have   14. want-wants
7. get-gets   15. appreciates-appreciate

Exercise 2 (pp. 131-132)
1. count
2. does
3. uses   9. feeds   17. there are
4. plan   10. marches   18. is
5. adds   11. wear, their   19. are
6. wears   12. loves, she,   20. are
7. orders   wears   21. there are
8. attack   13. use   22. here are
                  14. uses   23.do
                  15. wants   24. is
                  16. is   25. refuse

Chapter 9—Pronoun-Antecedent Agreement

Exercise 1 (p. 138)
1. their—his or her   6. C
2. C   7. they—he
3. his   8. C
4. their—her   9. their—his
5. C   10. C

Exercise 2 (pp. 139-140)
1. C
2. his or her porch—their porches / works in their garden—work in their gardens
3. every townsperson comes—the towns people come)
4. C
5. their—his or her
6. C
7. their—his or her
8. their—his or her
9. C
10. C
11. their—his
12. C
13. C
14. C
15. their—his
16. their—the
17. their—the
18. their lives were—his life was
19. C
20. their—his or her
21. their suits—his suit
22. C
23. each person—the people / voice—voices
24. their—his / kazoos—kazoo / them—him
25. C
26. C
27. their—his
28. C
29. every citizen—the citizens
30. their—her

Chapter 10—Some Special Pronoun Predicaments

Exercise 1 (p. 148)
1. us
2. him and me
3. he and I
4. we, he
5. she, him and me
6. me
7. he
8. I
9. who
10. Homer and she

Exercise 2 (p. 149)
1. me
2. I
3. he and I
4. my best friend and I
5. she and I
6. he
7. you and me
8. him
9. my friend Darlene and I
10. Darlene and I
11. him
12. we
13. he
14. he
15. He and I
16. he
17. he and I
18. Darlene and I
19. he
20. he and I

Exercise 3 (p. 151)
1. her
2. me
3. I
4. us
5. us
6. he
7. who
8. whom
9. he
10. he

Exercise 4 (pp. 155-156)
Possible responses:
1. "I like going to English class because there I can catch up on my sleep," said Harley. (author's note: Harley, no doubt, will someday fall into a life of crime.)
2. Cindy Lou's little brother always makes her cry when he borrows her Barbie dolls and uses them for slingshot practice.
3. When a person has a job as an elevator operator, he or she has to be ready for the ups and downs.
4. For job security, the tooth fairy placed a bag of jawbreakers and a piece of taffy under little Wilbur's pillow, and he found the candy there in the morning.
5. After work, Mrs. Doobledorfer let the cat in, put

up the groceries, boiled the water, chopped up the chicken, and dropped it in the pot to simmer for several hours.
6. I was queasy during dinner because Uncle Beamer kept coughing on the roast beef and sneezing in his tea.
7. Nadine hates waking up at 2:30 every morning to do her hair and nails so that she can be at work by eight.
8. Marguerite and her girlfriends always swim around man-eating sharks because they know that the sharks won't eat them.
9. In school, the teachers and principal always tell students to wear clothes.
10. After Milly and her old boyfriend began dating again, she called Molly to tell her.; Milly called Molly to announce that she was dating Molly's old boyfriend again.

Chapter 11—Tense About Verbs?

Exercise 1 (pp.161-162)
1. swam
2. sung
3. C (or dreamed)
4. drank
5. fallen
6. sunk
7. C
8. broken
9. written
10. come

Exercise 2 (p. 167)
1. d
2. a
3. e
4. d
5. e
6. b
7. f
8. c
9. a
10. d
11. c
12. d
13. b
14. d
15. a

Exercise 3 (p. 168)
1. none
2. none
3. had had
4. had started; had begun; had minded
5. had shouted; had been

Exercise 4 (p. 170)
1. is picking
2. was haranguing
3. had been hoping
4. will be writing
5. will have been hiding
6. has been trying
7. was hoping
8. had been playing
9. will be making
10. is knitting

Exercise 5 (p. 171)
1. was doing
2. was jumping; was making; was explaining; was jumping; was answering
3. was grumbling; was saying; were calling

Exercise 6 (pp.172)
1. past perfect
2. past
3. past perfect
4. past
5. present
6. past
7. past progressive
8. past
9. present progressive
10. past
11. present
12. present perfect
13. past
14. past
15. past

Exercise 7 (p. 174)
Example: 1. wants—wanted
2. lives—lived / tend—tended
3. believe—believed / is—was
4. goes—went
5. C
6. rushes—rushed
7. C
8. C
9. jump—jumped / run—ran
10. run—ran
11. C
12. C
13. says—said / shoots—shot / crushes—crushed / can—could

Exercise 8 (pp. 176-177)
1. P
2. A
3. A
4. P
5. A
6. trick question— *were* is a linking verb and neither active or passive
7. P
8. P
9. P
10. A

Exercise 9 (p. 177)
1. Several guests suffered indigestion after someone found a mildewed shoe in the fondue.
2. At the party, Quirky the clown made balloon rutabagas for the children.
3. Sue sued a seamstress for mending her bathing suit with glue.
4. Billy's parents gave Billy an air guitar for his birthday, but he cried because the box was empty.
5. Stylish vultures carry carrion in carry-on luggage.
6. Because of a typo, the governor signed a proposal creating a twenty-thousand-acre skate park.
7. In a tragic accident, Fifi suffered a concussion when her doggy door stuck shut.
8. Uncle Howard thickened the clam chowder with foot powder.
9. Scientists announced that fireflies cause global warming.
10. Oberone the gnome suffered a backache when he tried to play the trombone.

Exercise 10 (pp. 179-180)
1. a
2. b
3. a
4. a
5. a
6. b
7. c
8. a
9. c
10. a

Exercise 11 (pp. 182-183)
1. lie
2. set
3. lying
4. sits
5. lies
6. sets
7. had laid
8. lay
9. sat
10. sat
11. is lying
12. lay
13. sits
14. laid
15. laying
16. sits
17. laid
18. sitting
19. setting
20. lay

Chapter 12—More Adverb and Adjective Tips and Tidbits

Exercise 1 (p. 189)
1. more—most
2. C
3. more—most
4. C
5. most—more
6. more sly—most sly or slyest
7. C
8. more—most
9. C
10. intelligenter—more intelligent

Exercise 2 (pp. 195-196)
1. further—farther / further—farther
2. good—well
3. no—any / nobody—anybody
4. anyone—anyone else
5. further—farther
6. most dumbest—dumbest
7. hairiest—hairier
8. C
9. C
10. good—well
11. most stickiest—stickiest / no—any
12. inexpensive—expensive
13. C
14. C
15. most loveliest—loveliest

Chapter 13—Capitalization Consternation

Exercise 1 (p. 204)
1. Coach, math teacher
2. Filmore High School Chess Club
3. Earth (or earth)
4. English, geography, History II, Plastic Surgery III
5. President, States, Congress, American, Olympics
6. Mother, Uncle

7. C
8. Track, Field Tournament
9. Mom, Hawaiian, Acme Cleaners
10. Industrial Revolution, South

Exercise 2 (pp. 205-206)
1. Caribbean Islands, aunt
2. Bridge, *Princess*
3. Professor Plimp, University, Jupiter's
4. Saint Patrick's Day, Nobel Peace Prize
5. C
6. Christmas
7. Museum Natural History
8. president, Students Against Students Who Are Always Against Stuff
9. High School
10. *The Attack Alien Gophers*, Twenty, Street, Avenue, New Yorkers
11. C
12. Houston Bar Association
13. C
14. Dad
15. C

Exercise 3 (pp. 206-207)
1. English
2. history
3. President, Civil War
4. C
5. England, Bridge
6. Greek
7. Health, Glamour
8. C
9. C
10. dad, congressman, Purple Heart, Medal, Grammy
11. High School, Forty, Street
12. mom, Parents, Children , Challenging Teens
13. C
14. birthday
15. Mom
16. Friday
17. Mother's Day, Godiva
18. C
19. algebra
20. C
21. of
22. English
23. biology
24. President
25. friend

Chapter 14—A Few Comma, Semicolon, and Colon Rules to Know and Love

Exercise 1 (pp. 213-214)
1. Driller, dentist, taffy, brittle
2. buildings,
3. C
4. Hippity-Hoppity, bunny, tacos,
5. kindergarten,
6. winters,
7. clips, opinion,
8. company,
9. C
10. Wednesday, March 10,
11. Maybelle, genius, kazoo, tuba,
12. No, dentist,
13. Goober,
14. dancing,
15. bikers, believe,
16. Mrs. Dweeble, neighbor,
17. Men, Box 456, Seattle, 90543,
18. doodlebugs, example,

19. Snodgrass, Jr., producing, marketing
20. year,

Exercise 2 (pp. 216-217)
1. February 3, 1992; November 18, 1993; June 1,
2. Thistledown, Jr., children; however, Skippy,
3. Baboons, earlobes, legs,
4. No, Semore,
5. plague; consequently,
6. should, opinion, face,
7. Quack, Box 231, Hollywood, 90211,
8. restaurant-mortuary;
9. football; nevertheless,
10. C
11. strange;
12. sister; example,
13. Horatio, brother,
14. January 8, 1962; October 9, 1968; March 12, 2008,
15. season, exhaustion, pain,
16. March 15, 2008,
17. rashes; therefore,
18. Doughboy, believe,
19. Hotline,
20. fries,

Exercise 3 (pp. 218-220)
1. houses, termites, speaking
2. 1996 (Note: Spelling out 1996 or 345 would eliminate any confusion. *In nineteen ninety-six, 345 million teachers...*), breakdowns,
3. tape, tweezers,
4. address: America, Box 123, Hollywood, 90210,
5. Saturday, March 8, 1997,
6. acne,
7. boils,
8. identity, Mr. Twipple, substitute,
9. Pageant,
10. Bumgarten, Jr., Foundation; furthermore, paper, pencils,
11. opinion, president,
12. C
13. wax,
14. flowers:
15. following:
16. C
17. No, Tell,
18. caps;
19. Monday, December 10, 2007; Wednesday, December 19, 2007; and Tuesday, January 29,
20. basketball; however,

Exercise 4 (pp. 221-222)
1. young, playful, chatting, chortling,
2. C
3. C
4. following: poles, ducks,
5. biceps,
6. Matilda, dishes, trash,
7. showers, parties,
8. surgery,
9. treating, gum, bars, jaw breakers,
10. platters,
11. Tremble, M.D.,
12. Company, Drive, Seattle, 77003,
13. Marx,
14. sing, toes, teeth,
15. surgeon,
16. speaking, intelligent,
17. Frederick,
18. Bittleman, Sr.,
19. C
20. Juneau, Alaska, Ernie,

Chapter 15—Those Crazy Little Apostrophes

Exercise 1 (pp. 227-228)
1. his
2. fleas
3. Everyone's
4. flea's
5. you're
6. grandmother's
7. tick's
8. its
9. flea's
10. It's

Exercise 2 (p. 228)
1. Head's
2. ducks'
3. Tod's
4. *i*'s, *t*'s
5. Irma's, it's
6. fleas', people's
7. person's
8. guppy's
9. Norman
10. C

Exercise 3 (p. 229)
1. Marvin's, Vinney's
2. squid's, vampire's, pigs'
3. mother's
4. weasels
5. D's (or Ds), parents
6. his
7. uncle's
8. armpits
9. students
10. Rudolph's, aerobics

Exercise 4 (p. 230)
1. C
2. tofu's
3. C
4. tourists', turkeys', birds'
5. turkeys'
6. ticks'
7. C
8. C
9. turkeys'
10. parents'

Chapter 16—Quotation Marks

Exercise 1 (pp. 235-236)
Rewrite the following sentences using correct punctuation.
1. "I collect jellyfish on the beach," said Ralph, "because they make excellent erasers."
2. " How did pioneer women fix their hair?" asked Dody. "I don't think they had blow dryers."
3. "My favorite song is 'Tomorrow,'" said Opie. "I wish I could play it on the xylophone."
4. "I prefer to play jumbo golf," said Durwin, "not miniature."
5. "I got a part in the school play!" exclaimed Bula. "I'm going to be a pitted olive!"
6. Horace exclaimed, "I can't believe those mutant gnats actually attacked a rhino!"
7. "I think the reason Maude is a starving artist," remarked Dodson, "is because she only paints pictures of cephalopods."
8. "As a member of the Ferret Preservation Society," remarked Waldo, "I've learned to appreciate rodents."
9. "Doctor," said Donald to his psychiatrist, "sometimes I think I'm a turnip."
10. "A pushy officer pulled me over," blurted Prissy, "and I was only going ninety-five in a school zone!"
11. "I've noticed," observed Egbert, "that clocks always run clockwise."
12. "I just heard a cow bark," remarked Opal. "It sounded like a Chihuahua!"
13. Wilamena excitedly told her mother, "For Halloween, I'm going to be a grilled cheese sandwich!"
14. "I bought a new mouse for my computer," muttered Mortimer Duncely, "but it crawls all over my monitor."
15. C

Exercise 2 (pp. 236-237)
1. " Large roaches," Hubert noted, "sometimes feed on cattle."
2. Timmy cried, "I want a pony for my birthday!" However, his parents gave him a pack of gum instead.

3. "I have insomnia," yawned Ronald, "but it doesn't keep me up at night."
4. "Ostriches with fleas," remarked Louise, "are often ostracized by their peers."
5. "I have a pet turtle," announced Roland, "and he looks just like my grandfather."
6. "I wish Christmas would come in July," whined Lizzy, "so the shops wouldn't be so busy."
7. "The reason my bulldog's face is flat," admitted Barker, "is because he chases parked cars."
8. "Sometimes I wish I were the windshield, not the bug," moaned Dudley.
9. "Instead of wearing a hat with my outfit," said Rhoda, "sometimes I prefer to wear a matching toad."
10. C
11. "I was shocked," said Holly, "when the principal shouted, 'We're having a meteorite storm! Take cover!'"
12. "For my poetry presentation," said Scuzzy, "I would like to read a selection entitled 'Dustmites.'"
13. Vinnie inquired, "Why is it impossible to tickle yourself?"
14. "I was so excited when Arnold looked into my eyes!" Zoey recalled. "I was crushed, though, when he told me that I had a piece of spinach between my teeth."
15. The guide shouted, "Watch out for the killer chiggers!"

Exercise 3 (p. 237)
At the County Fair, Senator Sham was campaigning furiously for his shaky reelection bid.
"Senator," asked one reporter, "will you raise taxes if you're reelected?"
"That's a good question," the senator replied, trying to look thoughtful. "So let me give you a straight answer. I don't intend to raise taxes unless, of course, in case of a serious situation like war or rain or something. However, even then I won't, unless I do."
The reporter looked puzzled but continued. "Will you support education?"
"Of course, I think that every young person should be illiterate enough to read and write."
"Also, Senator, how do you intend to handle the budget?"
"Simple. Let me give you some concrete ways. I'll make a detailed budget that's within budget. First, I'll clean out the attic and sweep out the dust. Then I'll budget for the budget with funds from various funds."
"And one last question, Senator. How do you explain your recent criminal conviction?"
The senator's tanned face turned slightly pale. "I'm sorry. I couldn't hear that last question," he finally stammered, and in a flash he was off to kiss a nearby baby and hug a retired person.

Exercise 4 (p. 238)
"Good evening. Welcome to the Jay O'Casey Show. Our guest this evening is Mr. Noah Life who has spent the last several years reading the complete fifty-volume set of the *Oxford English Dictionary*. Welcome, Mr. Life."
"Thank you, Mr. OKC."
"Call me Jay. Now tell me, what motivated you to read the entire dictionary?"
"Well, Mr. OKC, I mean J, because it was there."
"I see."
"J, those happen to be two of my favorite letters."
"Okay."
"Those, too, J."
"Let's move on. Let me ask you this. In addition to I, C, and O, K, what are some of your other favorite letters of the dictionary?"
"Well, I'd have to say P because it has *plot*, but the A section was pretty good too because it has *action*."
"I see. Do you like T?"
"No, I prefer coffee, thank you, J."
"You know, Mr. Life, some people say that you're quite a shallow person. How do you respond to these critics?"
"I enjoy deep sea diving, J."
"I see. Well, unfortunately we're out of time. Thank you for joining me."
"Uh, J, before I go, I'd just like to say hello to my kids, Dee, Bea, and Kay."
"Join me tomorrow night when our guest will be the great-great grandson of the inventor of the paper clip. Good night for now, America."

Exercise 5 (p. 239)
"Over
"I
"The
"I
life."

Exercise 6 (p. 241-242)
1. "Mossy Artichokes on a Psychedelic Tundra," *The Poetry of the Insane*
2. *The Revenge of the Killer Roly-Poly Bugs*, *Field and Stream*
3. *National Enquirer*, "Customer Spontaneously Combusts in Mexican Food Restaurant"
4. *Wheel of Stuff*
5. *The Flight of Sniffing Ferrets*
6. *Mona Lisa*
7. "Fear the Dark," *Vampires, Goblins, and Mutant Lice*
8. *The Unsinkable*
9. *Great Expectations, The Ultimate Guide to Eyebrow Waxing*
10. "The Bells," "The Raven"
11. *aardvark, a*'s
12. *Denver Post*, "Aliens Found in Frito Bags"
13. *tu madre esta loca, your mother is crazy*
14. *Pollen and Mold Spores*
15. "Pain in the Night," *Vampires with Cavities and Gum Disease*
16. *Hangnails, Cuticles, and Toe Hair*
17. *Donde esta el bano*
18. *Big Bird and the Existential Truth*
19. *Julius Caesar*
20. *bon voyage*

Chapter 17–Hyphens, Dashes, Parentheses, and Ellipses

Exercise 1 (pp. 246-247)
1. mayor-elect
2. forty-seven
3. self-improvement / one-half
4. ex-neighbors / spaceship-like
5. well-waxed
6. C
7. C
8. mid-life / mid-European
9. best-dressed
10. C
11. self-motivated
12. self-employed / rinky-dink
13. C
14. nine-to-midnight
15. crude-mannered / just-polished

Exercise 2 (p. 250)
1. C	3. I	5. I	7. I	9. I
2. I	4. I	6. C	8. C	10. C

Chapter 18–A Little Help with Spelling

Exercise 1 (p. 259-260)
1. advice / breathe
2. bear
3. council / dye / complement
4. brakes
5. bored
6. courses
7. councilman
8. immigrate
9. deserted / adapting / bare / except
10. accede
11. counselor / accepted
12. all right
13. allusion
14. alter
15. chose
16. illusion
17. bores / except
18. further / council
19. already
20. effects

Exercise 2 (pp. 268-269)
1. weight
2. its
3. principal
4. There's
5. formerly
6. to / they're
7. their
8. shown
9. stationery
10. loaned
11. lone / piece
12. weather
13. than
14. morals / exceed
15. peace /quiet
16. Whose
17. coarse
18. lose
19. capitol / passed / exceeded
20. principal / formally/ formerly / morale / quite

Exercise 3 — Review Exercise (pp. 269-271)
1. complimented / complemented
2. all right
3. altogether / passed / their / breaths / too
4. advised
5. illusion / piece
6. emigrated / desert
7. capitol / feet / all right
8. exceeds
9. principles / weeks
10. capital
11. further / lead
12. course
13. advice
14. advised / loan
15. pains
16. feat / threw / feet / farther / than
17. holes
18. consul / desserts / week / too / weak / to
19. Whether / they're / pain
20. brake / stationary
21. affects
22. Here / loaned
23. accedes / effect
24. hole / adapted / quite
25. formally / capital
26. wait
27. loses
28. effect / weather
29. hair / altogether / to / loose
30. formerly / their

Exercise 4 (pp. 274-275)
1. C
2. ninety-one
3. two hundred / two
4. third / first
5. 327 million
6. 7:30 PM (omit *every evening*), or seven-thirty every evening / 6
7. C
8. C
9. ten
10. C